Essential
Ethics
for Psychologists

Essential

Ethics

for Psychologists

A Primer for Understanding
and Mastering Core Issues

Thomas F. Nagy

American Psychological Association • Washington, DC

First printing June 2010
Second printing January 2014

Published by
American Psychological Association
750 First Street, NE
Washington, DC 20002
www.apa.org

To order
APA Order Department
P.O. Box 92984
Washington, DC 20090-2984
Tel: (800) 374-2721; Direct: (202) 336-5510
Fax: (202) 336-5502; TDD/TTY: (202) 336-6123
Online: www.apa.org/pubs/books/
E-mail: order@apa.org

In the U.K., Europe, Africa, and the Middle East, copies may be ordered from
American Psychological Association
3 Henrietta Street
Covent Garden, London
WC2E 8LU England

Typeset in Meridien by Circle Graphics, Inc., Columbia, MD

Printer: United Book Press, Baltimore, MD
Cover Designer: Naylor Design, Washington, DC

The opinions and statements published are the responsibility of the authors, and such opinions and statements do not necessarily represent the policies of the American Psychological Association.

Library of Congress Cataloging-in-Publication Data

Nagy, Thomas F.
  Essential ethics for psychologists : a primer for understanding and mastering core issues / Thomas F. Nagy.
       p. cm.
  Includes bibliographical references and index.
  ISBN-13: 978-1-4338-0863-0
  ISBN-10: 1-4338-0863-3
  ISBN-13: 978-1-4338-0864-7 (e-book)
  ISBN-10: 1-4338-0864-1 (e-book)
  1. Psychologists—Professional ethics. 2. Psychology—Moral and ethical aspects. 3. Professional ethics. I. Title.

  BF76.4.N338 2011
  174'.915—dc22
                                        2010005235

British Library Cataloguing-in-Publication Data
A CIP record is available from the British Library.

Printed in the United States of America
First Edition

This book is dedicated to the memory of my dear friend Richard Berenberg, a gifted neurologist and cherished father and husband whose ethical sense, honesty, fairness, and warmth have been important factors in shaping my professional work for many years, and to my granddaughter Elise Juliet, a bright sparkle whose energy, appetite for learning, and developing sense of humor are as joyful and contagious as her emerging ethical awareness, even at the tender age of 2.

Contents

Acknowledgments

Many have been helpful to me over the years, contributing to my knowledge of ethics and legal issues, and some have specifically assisted in the creation of this book as well. I'd like to first thank my wife, Kären, for her encouragement, good spirits, and endless resourcefulness; for spending countless hours reading drafts; for being ruthless but savvy in her recommendations for changes; and for cheerfully making the sacrifices that a family must make in order to complete a project of this scope. Also, I am grateful to Janet Thomas, who recently completed her own book, *The Ethics of Supervision and Consultation*, for taking the time to review excerpts of chapters. I would like to thank Gary Schoener not only for his tangible contributions to the book but for his encouragement as well. Also, I am appreciative of Margaret Lee's additions to the book based on her vast experience in forensic work. I am grateful to Steve Frankel, a practicing psychologist and attorney, for his prompt and comprehensive replies to various queries. I'm also indebted to Arreed Barabasz, an experienced clinician and ethicist, for his clear thinking on research and publication matters. Also, I'd like to thank Steve Behnke, the director of the APA Ethics Office, for being willing to respond to inquiries of all kinds as they surfaced over the years. I'd also like to express my gratitude to David Mills, who helped stimulate my original interest in ethics decades ago as director of the APA Ethics Office when I served on the Ethics Committee then and chaired the task force that revised the Ethics Code in 1992.

I'm also grateful to some older friends and colleagues who always seem to be available when I am writing a book and who have served to broaden my awareness of the intertwining of ethical, legal, and clinical matters. This includes Bill Carroll, a practicing attorney who is also a psychologist, who has contributed greatly to assisting, teaching, and defending psychologists for decades. I'd also like to thank Jose Maldonado for his unflagging willingness to be available for ethical and clinical consultation. And finally, I want to acknowledge the valuable input of David Spiegel, Bob Harris, Gerry Niewoehner, Robert Matano, Lisa Butler, Hugh Baras, James Moses, and countless others who have over the years contributed to my knowledge and understanding of ethical and professional matters in various areas. This list would certainly include my psychology post-doctoral students at Stanford University Medical Center, my clinical supervisees, and the clients and patients of all ages and all walks of life whom I have had the privilege to serve over the past 40 years.

Essential
Ethics
for Psychologists

Introduction

Regardless of what role psychologists may choose to play—that of researcher, practitioner, or teacher—they must understand and adhere to ethical principles. In general, their professional conduct is governed by the American Psychological Association's (APA's) "Ethical Principles of Psychologists and Code of Conduct" (Ethics Code; APA, 2010) and/or ethics codes of state psychological associations to which they belong, the regulations of state licensing boards, institutional policies, and state and federal law. However, there are certain underlying concepts that, once mastered, can help psychologists gain an understanding of their ethical obligations. This book presents those concepts, taken from the APA Ethics Code, and helps the reader learn how to apply them in a variety of settings.

Although the book is based on the APA Ethics Code, it will be useful to APA members and nonmembers alike because it provides an overall understanding of ethics in psychology. The reader will learn of common ethical issues in both fictional vignettes and true accounts of actual transgressions. Four ethical concepts applicable to all psychologists are explored: (a) competence, (b) informed consent, (c) privacy and confidentiality, and (d) avoiding harm and exploitation. The reader will also learn what happens when someone initiates a complaint against a psychologist in the role of therapist, supervisor, or some other capacity and the range of sanctions that could be imposed for the psychologist's ethical lapse. In addition, the book shows how the key ethical concepts apply to four broad areas of psychological work: (a) psychological assessment and test construction; (b) therapy (individual, marital, family, and group); (c) research and publication; and (d) teaching, training, and supervision.

Ethical rules evolved because psychologists appeared to need guidance in maintaining their objectivity and competence and avoiding harming others while carrying out their unusual work of studying and helping human beings. In my view, the two concepts that account for the vast majority of the ethical standards in the APA Ethics Code are *informed consent* and *avoiding harm and exploitation*. Each of these concepts has a dedicated chapter in this book. Sometimes ethical rules conflict with each other, and one needs a procedure for deciding which course of action to take. At times laws take over and address specific situations that are never mentioned in the APA Ethics Code. At times ethical rules and state and federal laws intermingle, requiring psychologists to act or prohibiting them from behaving in certain ways. And sometimes there are conflicts between ethical rules and laws. Psychologists must learn how to navigate through these occasionally turbulent waters while keeping their internal "moral GPS" switched on and updated.

This book is intended for students who have had minimal preparation in ethics, codes of professional conduct, or practice guidelines in health care as well as for psychologists who wish to review how fundamental ethical concepts apply to psychological practice, research, and teaching. I have attempted to present the actual issues, dilemmas, and surprises that confront psychologists in every role—as researcher, clinician, teacher, supervisor, and management consultant—with all the richness and diversity that is a part of their daily work. I hope that this book provides solid preparation in recognizing subtle ethical issues when they occur and experience in developing strategies for dealing with them. The vignettes and examples are fictional, but they are drawn from real life experiences and then altered and disguised to preserve confidentiality.

My objective is to provide a basis for comprehending the need for ethical rules that guide psychologists in carrying out their work as well as the origins of these rules and how they have evolved over time. The reader will develop an understanding of ethical concepts as distinct from legal issues—such as mandated reporting when a patient reveals that he may be a harm to himself or that he intends to injure or kill a third party. The reader will also learn of ways to identify an ethical dilemma when it presents itself and how to approach decision making to resolve the confusion. A variety of ethical decision-making models are presented to help the psychologist weigh situational and personal factors in a variety of professional roles and settings. An example is how to determine whether a therapist should begin a multiple-role relationship, such as befriending a patient who has just ended treatment, when there is always the possibility that he or she may wish to begin therapy again in the future (thereby creating the secondary role of friend in addition to the therapist role).

When approaching various topics in this book, I consistently faced a tension between providing a broad overview and providing an in-depth, detailed portrayal. It is my hope that a balance has been struck that does not bog the reader down with too much specific information yet provides enough detail to yield an accurate three-dimensional look at the work of psychologists. For specific areas of interest, the reader can consult the reading list that appears in this book's supplemental website (http://pubs.apa.org/books/supp/essentialethics/).

The book is divided into three parts and consists of 12 chapters. Each chapter has an introductory vignette that illustrates one or more of the ethical concepts discussed in the chapter and may pose questions for the reader for further exploration. Part I, which consists of three chapters, provides background in the development and evolution of the APA Ethics Code, aspirational and mandatory ethical concepts, and the variety of ethical questions that confront psychologists. In Chapter 1, I provide a brief overview of the kinds of ethical problems that can develop and describe the basis for formulating ethics codes deontologically and teleologically.

In Chapter 2, I discuss the historical evolution of the Ethics Code, emerging areas of interest, and an overview of the 2002 Code (amended 2010). In Chapter 3, I address the five general ethical principles of psychologists that form the skeleton of the Ethics Code.

Part II, which consists of four chapters, provides an examination of the four problematical areas for psychologists that are frequently the subject of ethics complaints, licensing board investigations, and malpractice allegations. In Chapter 4, I discuss the concept of competence, the bedrock of the science and practice of psychology. In Chapter 5, I discuss informed consent, which must be provided at the beginning of contact with clients, patients, research participants, supervisees, students, and others. In Chapter 6, I address privacy, confidentiality, and privileged communication with both ethical and legal ramifications. In Chapter 7, I address harm and exploitation, whether intentional or due to some combination of ignorance and incompetence.

Part III, which consists of five chapters, presents ethical-decision-making models and explores the ethical matters relevant to clinical practice, research, and teaching settings. In Chapter 8, the longest chapter, I present useful approaches to ethical decision making with an emphasis on multiple-role relationships because these constitute the most serious risks of harm to others. In Chapter 9, I focus on psychological assessment and ethical guidance for those who develop tests, provide assessments, write reports, and appear in court. In Chapter 10, I discuss psychotherapy and the ethical dilemmas of therapists working in hospitals, clinics, independent practice, and other settings. In Chapter 11, I address research and publication matters, the very heart of the science of psychology because they allow for evidence-based practice. In Chapter 12, I present the ethical and legal issues in teaching, training, and supervision from high school settings through postgraduate internship and beyond.

This book is designed to be used in conjunction with the Internet. By accessing the book's website (http://pubs.apa.org/books/supp/essentialethics/), the reader can view discussion questions for each chapter, a reading list, and selective supplemental material that would be overly detailed for inclusion in the book. The discussion questions provide a basis for in-class discussion, projects, or assignments and closely follow the content presented in each chapter. Other supplementary materials include the introduction and summary of the original 1953 APA Ethics Code, informed consent documents, an in-depth application of a decision-making model to an ethical dilemma, and other materials.

A companion piece to this book is my earlier work, *Ethics in Plain English: An Illustrative Casebook for Psychologists* (Nagy, 2005), which presents a simple English version of each ethical standard of the APA Ethics Code along with a detailed vignette and discussion questions. It may be useful to refer to this book for an interpretation of a particular ethical standard or topical area of the APA Ethics Code that is presented in these chapters. As with the current book, *Ethics in Plain English* contains vignettes portraying ethical issues in psychology. The vignettes describe conduct by psychologists in a variety of professional roles that is in compliance or in flagrant violation of a standard or sometimes a combination of the two. The discussion questions in *Ethics in Plain English* probe for deeper meanings of each ethical standard and prompt the reader to consider how psychologists might run afoul of the ethical standard even when no harm is meant. After reading the current book to obtain a big-picture understanding of ethical concepts in psychology, the reader may want to consult *Ethics in Plain English* for a detailed explanation of the 89 standards of the APA Ethics Code.

The current book represents my experience as a practicing psychologist for nearly 40 years in academic, medical, and independent practice settings. It also reflects nearly 30 years of working in the field of ethics, including chairing ethics committees, chairing the APA Task Force that revised the "Ethical Principles of Psychologists and Code of Conduct" (APA, 1992), serving as an expert witness in court cases concerning ethical misconduct, and countless hours consulting with mental health professionals who were either the subject of complaints themselves or were attempting to avoid becoming the subject of one. It is my hope that by reading this book the reader's interest will be piqued and his or her curiosity stimulated to further explore this fascinating and gratifying area of human endeavor.

INTRODUCTION TO ETHICS IN PSYCHOLOGY AND THE AMERICAN PSYCHOLOGICAL ASSOCIATION ETHICS CODE

T his section presents the two basic justifications for constructing ethics codes, the range of complaints that are brought
against psychologists, and the interface of ethics and laws. It
also provides a brief history of the 2002 American Psychological Association Ethics Code (amended 2010) and describes
the five general principles of the Code.

Thinking Critically About Ethics 1

The psychologist believes in the dignity and worth of the individual human being. He is committed to increasing man's understanding of himself and others. While pursuing this endeavor, he protects the welfare of any person who may seek his service or of any subject, human or animal, that may be the object of his study. He does not use his professional position or relationships, nor does he knowingly permit his own services to be used by others, for purposes inconsistent with these values. While demanding for himself freedom of inquiry and communication, he accepts the responsibility this freedom confers: for competence where he claims it, for objectivity in the report of his findings, and for consideration of these interests of his colleagues and of society. (American Psychological Association [APA], 1967)

Ethical awareness in psychological practice and research has long been in the consciousness of practitioners and researchers, even predating the publication of the first APA Ethics Code in 1953. However, formal education in ethics as a part of psychologists' formal training and supervision has evolved only relatively recently, with most graduate and professional schools of psychology currently requiring at least a fundamental knowledge of the subject.

When attempting to exercise good judgment in the course of carrying out professional work, a psychologist is generally confronted with a range of choices. The psychologist is guided by a variety of factors, such as (a) formal education and training, (b) life experience, (c) previous experience with the situation at hand, (d) ethical rules, (e) relevant state and federal laws, and (f) other conscious or unconscious factors that make his or her own unique contributions to the decision-making process. This book focuses on the assistance provided by ethical rules in resolving these dilemmas, fundamentally, how to avoid harming others and facilitate helping them by meeting stated goals while in the role of psychologist.

The challenge of an ethics code is to be instructive and provide guidance to psychologists in whatever setting they may work or professional responsibilities they may assume. However, an ethics code is also a dynamic document; it is constantly evolving, reflecting continual changes in the nature of psychological work concerning technology (e.g., computers, videoconferencing), the emergence of new human problems, (e.g., compulsive behavior involving the Internet), new areas of specialization (e.g., lesbian and gay lifestyles), legal requirements (e.g., state and federal laws), and changes in the culture (e.g., increase in racial/ethnic diversity, changing religious orientation and lifestyles). In view of the diversity of roles played by psychologists today—therapist, researcher, supervisor, professor, and management consultant, to name a few—it is unlikely that a single set of decision rules could provide guidance in sufficient detail to be practical. On the other hand, a document that would anticipate each and every scenario likely to be encountered by psychologists would be hopelessly long and legalistic in nature, allowing for the exercise of little independent judgment on the part of professionals. It would be more akin to a "paint-by-numbers" compendium of hypothetical scenarios that would spell out various courses of action for each situation.

As a result, the various revisions of the Ethics Code governing the conduct of psychologists for over half a century have attempted to strike a balance between being overly general, resulting in language that would be too be too vague and lacking in operational definitions, and overly explicit, resulting in such a narrow a focus that psychologists would likely miss the forest for the trees—obscuring the general ethical principle and providing mainly individual solutions. Although this type of vignette-driven document may indeed be useful, it is not sufficiently broad to teach ethics to those specializing in a variety of different areas (e.g., therapist, researcher, supervisor).

This chapter introduces the reader to various ethical concepts and issues. The remaining sections discuss the following: ethical problems that can be encountered by psychologists in different settings, intentionality in ethical conduct, ethics codes as a compendium of "musts" and "must nots," attributes of ethical actions, deontology and teleology as bases for developing codes of ethics, aspirational and mandatory sections of the APA Ethics Code, the relationship between ethics codes and laws, and complaints against psychologists.

A Sampling of Ethical Violations

The following scenarios describe four different ethical issues that can challenge a psychotherapist, researcher, and professor. The subject areas are (a) multiple-role relationship, (b) competence, (c) informed consent, and (d) privacy.

MULTIPLE-ROLE RELATIONSHIP

The following vignette describes the development of a multiple-role relationship in which a competent psychologist feels a sexual attraction to his patient.

> A therapist experienced a physical attraction to his new patient—a female high school teacher seeking treatment for obsessive–compulsive disorder. Nevertheless, he provided competent treatment for her disorder, ultimately concluding her treatment in 5 months. One year later, he encountered the woman at a workshop on attention-deficit disorder in children and adolescents. They were pleased to see each other again in this new setting, acknowledged their mutual attraction for one another, and tentatively began to explore a romantic relationship. As their personal relationship became stronger, the teacher experienced a relapse of her obsessive–compulsive symptoms but was confused about whether to discuss this with her former therapist now that their affection for one another had begun to include a physical component. The therapist also recognized the return of her compulsions, noticing that she was spending much time checking up on herself and having increased periods of anxiety and worry. He attempted to help by reviewing his original therapy interventions with her but found that he had much less patience now and began to be irritable with her and even sarcastic at times. He realized, belatedly, that the relationship had not turned out the way he thought it might and that he had harmed his former patient by beginning a romantic relationship with her.

COMPETENCE

In this vignette a psychologist experiences the conflict between his motivation to rapidly build his practice yet provide competent treatment to a needy patient.

> A therapist who had recently moved to a metropolitan area was treating a young woman for substance abuse and depression. After several weeks of therapy the patient informed her that there were really "four of her" living in the same body and that "the others" would like to talk with the therapist as well. The therapist hypothesized that this patient might meet the diagnostic

criteria for dissociative identity disorder. She had never encountered a patient with this degree of severe psychopathology. However, because she had recently opened her independent practice and did not want to turn away new patients, she arrived at the rationalization that she had the competence to continue treating this woman. Unfortunately, because of her busy schedule, she failed to augment her competence by consulting those who were knowledgeable about this disorder, attending workshops, or sufficiently researching the literature on dissociative disorder. After several weeks of treatment, one of the violent alternate personalities of this patient made a suicide attempt by driving her car into a tree, and the patient was hospitalized in critical condition. This was enough of a warning to the therapist about her inadequate skills in offering therapy to a patient with this diagnosis, and she promptly contacted a colleague who was experienced in the treatment of dissociative disorders for consultation.

INFORMED CONSENT

This vignette presents an inexperienced researcher who has not paid attention to important elements of informed consent before proceeding with her study.

A researcher was conducting an investigation on the effects on adults' mood and behavior from playing computer games that have violent graphic imagery. He was not affiliated with an institution and therefore was not required to submit his research protocol to an institutional review board for evaluation. Unfortunately, he failed to accurately describe the amount of time that would be required as a participant in the study, and he failed to fully disclose that the images viewed by participants would actually include excerpts from movies depicting acts of torture and brutality. After the study began, four participants decided to drop out when they realized that they would be spending hours more in the study than they had originally planned. Several other participants became panicky or physically ill during the exposure to the imagery and decided to withdraw from the study at that point. Another participant, a veteran of the Iraq war, experienced a flashback during one of the screenings and needed emergency therapeutic intervention with medication to treat his psychotic symptoms. It was apparent to the researcher that he had failed to provide adequate informed consent at the outset about the intended experiences of the participants and that he had also failed to adequately screen for evidence of posttraumatic stress disorder or other diagnoses among them.

PRIVACY

This vignette demonstrates how easy it is for a well-meaning psychologist to breach a patient's privacy when playing the role of both therapist and professor.

A psychologist was teaching a course on marital therapy to graduate students and used examples from her clinical practice to illustrate various theoretical approaches. To protect their anonymity, she changed the names and ages of the husbands and wives in her examples. Unfortunately, in describing one of the husbands as "a well-known lawyer" and in accidentally revealing his specialty area, intellectual property, she divulged too much information to protect the husband's anonymity. Furthermore, it so happened that one of the graduate students in the class was acquainted with this particular man because her husband had graduated from the same law school. Some others in the class simply knew the man by his local reputation because there was only one lawyer in town who specialized in intellectual property matters.

Intentionality in Ethical Conduct

As can be seen in each of these ethical lapses, the psychologist made a decision or a series of decisions that might be conceived of as unethical based on the psychologist's ignorance or lack of experience—an "accidental" unethical act. A decision was made in the course of carrying out professional work that resulted in harm or potential harm to another person. None of the psychologists intended to be exploitative of others at the outset; in fact, each might have considered his or her professional conduct to be above reproach, and each might have thought of him- or herself as having the highest regard for ethical conduct in the role of therapist, researcher, or instructor. However, in each case the psychologist made a decision that ultimately led to an ethical infraction. How could this happen, and how does an ethics code anticipate these situations? Before directly addressing this question, I briefly examine the nature of ethics codes and two fundamental models—deontology and teleology—that determine the bases of ethical decision making.

Ethics Codes: Musts and Must Nots

One might consider a code of professional conduct as a list of rules that both mandates and prohibits certain behavior while one is functioning in the role of psychologist. This is fundamentally a way of assisting in decision making about day-to-day behavior that will presumably prevent harming others and ideally also serve to further the task at hand, whether it is carrying out psychotherapy, clinical supervision, research, management consulting, or teaching. Referring to any code of professional conduct as a list of "shoulds" and "should nots" would mitigate the mandatory nature of the code to that of guidelines or recommendations. It would be more accurate to conceive of the code as a list of "musts" and "must nots," that is, absolute rules that leave little to the imagination yet still are sufficiently generic to address a broad range of situations and variables.

A rule involving informed consent for treatment, for example, must be able to address the specific problems of providing adequate consent for the psychologist who is about to offer psychotherapy to an outpatient, treatment for bipolar disorder to an inpatient, therapy to a committed couple living together, biofeedback to a patient with chronic back pain, hypnosis for a patient who wants to stop smoking, or any other type of intervention. The language of the rule must strike a balance between being sufficiently precise and detailed to be useful in providing informed consent in a specific situation while at the same time sufficiently broad to generally address a variety of different situations.

For example, a rule of conduct must apply with equal relevance and clarity for each of the following groups:

- psychologists who have different theoretical orientations (a cognitive–behavioral therapist, a psychoanalyst, a therapist carrying out in vivo desensitization),
- psychologists who work in various settings (e.g., outpatient clinic, hospital, independent practice, high school or college counseling center, the military, forensic setting, industrial and organizational setting, university—teaching or doing research),
- psychologists who provide a broad variety of interventions (e.g., neuropsychological assessment, individual psychotherapy, family and marital therapy, group therapy, hypnosis, biofeedback, behavioral interventions, business consultation),
- psychologists who intervene and specialize with various populations (e.g., men or women and their special issues, lesbian and gay clients, those of particular developmental ages ranging from childhood to the elderly, battered women, divorcing couples, patients with chronic illness, those seeking midlife vocational changes), and
- psychologists who intervene with clients and patients of certain diagnostic categories (e.g., anxiety disorders such as phobias, obsessive–compulsive disorder, posttraumatic stress disorder; depression including bipolar disorder, major depression; eating disorders such as anorexia or bulimia; schizophrenia and other psychotic disorders; substance-related disorders for alcohol, cannabis; personality disorders including paranoid, borderline, narcissistic; sexual and gender identity disorders).

What is the rationale for creating these rules, and what is the basis on which the actual rules themselves are founded? To answer these questions I turn briefly to the nature of ethical acts themselves and then to two concepts that underlie the evolution of ethical standards as they are today.

Attributes of Ethical Actions

Actions are generally held to be ethical if they possess the following three attributes: (a) They must be principled; (b) they must result from the reasoned outcome of applying the principles; and (c) they must be generalizable (Hass & Malouf, 1995). An action is said to be principled when the actor bases his or her actions on some specific and generally acceptable moral principle (e.g., avoiding harming others or protecting patient autonomy). The reasoned outcome consists of the actor executing the logical implementation of the principle, such as telling the truth to a patient about the impending treatment, as based on the principle honesty, instead of misrepresenting what the treatment will consist of. And, this course of action must be generalizable; it must be able to be recommended to others in comparable situations, such as requiring every researcher to debrief research participants after their participation has ended as part of an ethical principle of avoiding harming others.

These three attributes form the basis of ethical standards in the health care professions currently, as they did with the first ethics code written by the physician Hippocrates approximately 2,500 years ago. Over the centuries, as the practice of medicine evolved, and much later, as the practice of psychology emerged as a separate and distinct discipline, ethics codes have also been able to address specific topics of concern. For example, issues as diverse as sexual harassment, bartering with patients and clients, and media presentations are included in the most recent APA Ethics Code; these were certainly not in evidence in the first edition of the *Ethical Standards of Psychologists: A Summary of Ethical Principles* (APA, 1953b). Conversely, topics have been removed from ethics codes over the years, as committees performing revisions saw that a particular topic was overly narrow, too general in nature, or otherwise inappropriate (such as the requirement that psychologist "show sensible regard for the social codes and moral expectations of the community in which he [sic] works" in the 1953 code or a prohibition against teaching hypnosis to laypeople in the 1992 revision).

Over the years, the Ethics Code became a more useful and richer document by including a broad array of topics that had surfaced as problem areas in the course of psychologists' work. It became increasingly clear as complaints against psychologists surfaced which areas needed to be addressed and what kinds of guidance psychologists needed to avoid the pitfalls of inflicting harm in the course of carrying out their work—harm to others (clients, patients, colleagues), harm to the psychological knowledge base (shoddy or fraudulent research), or harm to the profession of psychology itself (eroding confidence and the public perception of psychologists by their public actions). How this diversity and how these rules evolved is the focus of the next section through the examination of the concepts of deontology and teleology as two fundamental ways of conceptualizing ethical standards.

Deontology and Teleology: Two Bases for Ethical Decision Making

Deontology is defined as "ethics based on the notion of a duty, or what is right" (Blackburn, 2008). This important concept was first articulated by Immanuel Kant (1724–1804), whose "categorical imperative" required that individuals should act only according to that maxim whereby they can at the same time will that it should become a universal law (Schneewind, 1993). Hence, a deontological means of justifying the ethical quality of one's actions focuses on a small or narrow set of moral values or characteristics. It does not consider specific exceptions or outcomes, mitigating circumstances, or the subjective judgment of the individual pondering which course of action to take. Rather, it is rigidly dichotomous in nature—engage in this behavior always, in every situation, regardless of factors or variables that might cause one to consider a different course of action.

An example of a deontologically justified ethical principle might be "Always be honest." Incorporating such a rule into one's professional conduct could be interpreted as "Always tell the truth" or never deliberately make factual misrepresentations or "spin" the facts in oral or written communications. Another example, in the case of medical ethics, might focus on valuing life. This might be manifested in medical practice as "Always preserve life under any circumstances," such as always choosing to engage in medical interventions that would support prolonging the patient's life, regardless of its quality or the patient's wishes.

Unfortunately, ethical rules can come into conflict with each other when an ethics code is based solely on a deontological foundation. It is useful to consider the dilemma of a medical doctor who believes that he or she (a) must always state the literal truth and (b) must always preserve life whenever possible. How would this individual resolve the dilemma posed by the following scenario? The setting is a German hospital in World War II, and a Nazi soldier inquires of a physician who is the chief administrator of the hospital if there are any Jewish patients inside. Such a question immediately places the physician in conflict because he cannot simultaneously comply with both ethical rules; he cannot tell the truth and preserve life if, in fact, there is a Jewish patient inside.

Similarly, there could be conflicting rules for the psychologist who is committed to (a) always telling the truth and (b) always protecting the welfare of patients and clients. It is useful to consider the following scenario.

> A marital therapist met with a high-conflict couple one time and observed during the session that the husband was intoxicated and loudly castigated his wife for her "shortcomings." The next day, the therapist received an urgent telephone call from the wife, who told him that she had fled her home in the middle of the night for the safety of a women's shelter because her husband had started beating her with his fists. Several hours later the repentant husband also telephoned the marital therapist inquiring if she knew where his wife had gone, that he was concerned about her and about to file a missing persons report with the police.

Again, it is impossible to simultaneously comply with both mandates—providing an honest reply to the violent husband's question concerning his wife's whereabouts and protecting the wife's welfare. Disclosing information about the wife's location could jeopardize her safety; however, preserving her safety and welfare by telling a lie or refusing to answer would violate the requirement to honestly respond to all questions. There is no clear way for the psychologist to honor both mandates in an ethics code that is wholly deontologically based—to always preserve the welfare of all clients and patients and to always tell the absolute truth.[1] The gray areas present problems that intuitive reasoning alone cannot always solve. This brings psychologists to another model for constructing ethical standards and helps resolve these intrinsic contradictions.

Teleology is defined as "the study of the ends or purposes of things" (Blackburn, 2008). This utilitarian philosophy on which to base ethical decision making was developed by the British philosopher Jeremy Bentham (1748–1832), also a legal scholar and linguist, and elaborated

---

[1]In point of fact, the APA Ethics Code does not require absolute honesty in every situation, and the standard addressing public statements is defined by the code in such a way as to allow for a variety of situations in which absolute truth telling would not necessarily always be in the best interest of the patient (e.g., providing a diagnostic assessment of a paranoid patient prematurely before the therapy relationship has had a chance to develop or refusing to release the patient's clinical record to the patient because it could ultimately result in harm to the patient).

on later by John Stuart Mill (1806–1873), also an economist and political theorist (Callan & Callan, 2005). Bentham promulgated the philosophical concept that ethical decision making should rest on the concept of aspiring toward realizing the greatest good and happiness for the greatest number of people. Hence, a teleological or utilitarian justification for an ethical rule focuses on the results or endpoints (greatest good and happiness) as a consequence of the action completed; it attempts to link cause and effect by creating a rule that would facilitate or prevent certain outcomes.

How did the framers of the first APA Ethics Code ascertain whether a certain behavior of a psychologist would hurt or harm another person? Absent any database, a code of ethics would necessarily be founded on broad philosophical concepts such as beneficence and maleficence, autonomy, and social justice, but they would not necessarily be closely linked to the actual work that psychologists perform in their various roles. It was necessary to develop an ethics code that closely tracked the day-to-day activities of psychologists and provided needed guidance in a variety of situations.

As is discussed in more detail in Chapter 2, the first APA Ethics Code was based on a scientific method of systematically gathering data from 1,000 psychologists concerning ethical dilemmas that they had experienced in the course of their work (Canter, Bennett, Jones, & Nagy, 1994). Such a database allowed for a distillation of topical areas—competence, confidentiality, client welfare, and informed consent, to name a few. Each of these topical areas contained specific rules that informed the choices of an ethically compliant psychologist. An example is Principle 8, Client Relationship, Paragraph c: "Psychologists do not normally enter into a clinical relationship with members of their own family, intimate friends, close associates, or others whose welfare might be jeopardized by such a dual relationship" (APA, 1953a). Another example is Principle 6, Confidentiality, Paragraph a: "Information received in confidence is revealed only after most careful deliberation and when there is clear and imminent danger to an individual or to society, and then only to appropriate professional workers or public authorities." In these rules there are specific musts and must nots. The first rule forbids entering into a dual-role relationship and then proceeds to define how one would identify such a situation. The second rule states that information obtained in confidence must remain so, except under a very specific circumstance, in which case psychologists must break confidentiality and even then in a narrowly defined way.

These rules evolved because of negative consequences that resulted from engaging in prohibited activities. For example, the practice of attempting to provide individual psychotherapy to a family member or close friend would have resulted in possibly harming that person because the psychologist's objectivity would have been impaired, calling into question his or her competence and customary good judgment in providing treatment. Or, revealing a client's disclosures in therapy to friends, associates, or family members might irrevocably damage trust in the therapeutic relationship, likely inhibiting the honest exchange that is so essential to the process or simply bringing an end to treatment. Hence "operating rules" evolved to avoid such harmful consequences to those who interacted with psychologists. There was a close connection between the rule and the outcome, cause and effect; this is the very nature of a teleologically based code of ethics.

Evolution of the APA Ethics Code

As the Ethics Code evolved, additional standards were added. Some of these were driven by technology. As electronic recording of therapy patients or research participants became possible, a standard was developed requiring that formal consent by the individual be acquired before recording. Some additions were driven by questionable practices of psychologists, such as soliciting testimonials from their current clients to be used in advertisements. This capitalized on the undue influence held by the therapist over the client and was exploitative; hence a rule was developed to prohibit this practice. And some additions were driven by changes in the culture of patient care, including, among other things, managed health care and litigiousness on the part of patients who felt wronged by their health care providers.

The requirement for psychologists to document their clinical work with patients was considered to possibly enhance treatment on a week-to-week basis (charting the patient's history, diagnosis, goals, progress, setbacks, and plans) and provide better continuity of care if there was an interruption to treatment, such as the patient or therapist leaving the area or the therapist becoming ill. Case managers for health insurance companies came to rely on therapists' clinical records to document progress in treatment or to substantiate requests for allocating additional sessions above and beyond those originally allowed. Good record keeping was also considered an invaluable resource in the event of patient dissatisfaction or failure by the therapist to meet the standard of care as prescribed by ethics codes, laws, professional guidelines, and professional standards published by the APA or other professional associations of which the therapist might be a member. In these cases, a psychologist's clinical record would ideally provide a chronology of treatment events, sometimes over a period of many years (far longer than memory would adequately serve) that would best be relied on in the case of an ethics complaint or lawsuit by a patient. Such a record increased accountability and responsibility of the therapist by documenting important interventions, significant changes in the patient, and milestones and benchmarks that otherwise would be lost as the years progressed. It would also serve as a primary means by which psychologists could defend themselves against charges of incompetent practice, negligence, abuse, or other forms of malpractice.

Educational settings also offered a similar opportunity for documentation that was omitted in the earlier editions of the Ethics Code. Those who provided individual supervision of psychology trainees were now required to provide informed consent at the outset as well as document the course of supervision in some way (APA, 2002, 2010). This was felt to improve the quality of supervision by (a) letting trainees know in advance exactly what they were to expect in the course of supervision and (b) putting supervisors on notice that they should carry out their work according to some theoretical model that included didactic and experiential elements considered to be relevant, useful, and ultimately evidence based. Indeed, some state licensing boards required that psychologists functioning as supervisors must take continuing education in clinical supervision at regular intervals if their supervision was to be considered legally valid.

Aspirational and Mandatory

The APA Ethics Code underwent a major change in 1992, resulting not only in revising the mandatory ethical standards (i.e., the actual nuts and bolts of the document) but also adding another section at the beginning of the code titled General Principles (Nagy, 1992). They were (a) Competence, (b) Integrity, (c) Professional and Scientific Responsibility, (d) Respect for People's Rights and Dignity, (e) Concern for Others' Welfare, and (f) Social Responsibility. The general principles were reduced to five in number in the 2002 revision and contain a descriptive paragraph for each. These general principles, some of which have long been held as important values in health care work, are couched in language that is broad ranging in nature, yet lofty in aspiration; their purpose is to inspire, not to set minimal standards of compliance. The general principles are discussed more fully in Chapter 3.

The opening sentence of the first principle of the 2002 Ethics Code, Beneficence and Nonmaleficence, states: "Psychologists strive to benefit those with whom they work and take care to do no harm." Although lofty in its objective, this statement is so general in concept and lacking in an operational definition that it offers little guidance about how to actually execute it. The remainder of the paragraph is similarly wide-ranging in scope, as it should be. The specific musts and most nots occur later in the document, in the form of the actual ethical standards. These are essentially a list of specific behavioral rules about a broad array of topics, such as competence, record keeping, advertising, providing informed consent for research, and maintaining patient privacy.

Clearly, these two sections of the Ethics Code—general principles and ethical standards—although all part of the same document, are fundamentally different in nature. The general principles may be seen as largely deontologically based, as described in the previous section. They focus mainly on a narrow set of moral values or characteristics, such as integrity, justice, or respect for people's rights and dignity, helping psychologists set their sights high while in their professional role. However, the ethical standards themselves are more teleologically based. They clearly link actions and outcomes. By providing good informed consent at the outset of therapy or research, a psychologist has prepared a particular client, patient, or research participant for the experience that lies ahead. Such actions directly contribute to the person's autonomous decision making and could be said to potentially add to their own good or happiness in some way. On the contrary, foisting an experience on an unprepared recipient of psychological services (e.g., aversive experiences in treatment, unusually high fees) would likely be perceived as diminishing the individual's good or happiness and contributing to feelings of being harmed or exploited.

The natural outcome of diminishing the welfare of others might include complaints to a licensing board or ethics committee or attempts to gain compensation from the offending psychologist.

A teleologically based code of ethics, then, offers protection to both psychologist and recipients of their services. By complying with each ethical standard, the psychologist not only contributes to the welfare of those with whom the psychologist works but also, ultimately, protects him- or herself from costly repercussions that can result from a consumer who feels hurt, angry, or exploited in some way.

Options available to consumers for dealing with offending psychologists are discussed in the last section of this chapter. I turn now to another utilitarian means of limiting and mandating how psychologists behave when interacting with others.

Ethics Codes and Laws

In addition to observing ethical standards, psychologists who render services to consumers (e.g., psychological assessment, psychotherapy, management consulting) must also observe the laws of the land. Why do we need both, and is there not a risk of redundancy or confusion by conflicting rules? To answer these questions I first examine the nature of laws and ethics and the purpose and jurisdiction of each.

Law may be defined as "a rule or system of rules recognized by a country or community as regulating the actions of its members and enforced by the imposition of penalties" (Compact Oxford English Dictionary, 2009). Every psychologist who holds a license to practice is required to comply with relevant state and federal laws as well as state psychology licensing regulations. Compliance with laws such as reporting child or elder abuse, taking appropriate action when there is a serious threat that a patient will harm himself or others, abstaining from sexual relations with patients, or permitting clients to view their own clinical record forms the legal skeleton of professional conduct on which all psychologists base their decision making in addition to complying with codes of ethics. The configuration of this skeleton varies from state to state because psychologists are licensed by the state in which they practice, and some states may not address such practices as informed consent or record keeping as fully as others.

Conflicts between the Ethics Code and state law have been treated differently by the APA over the years. In the 1992 edition of the APA Ethics Code, psychologists were obliged to follow the "higher standard" of the two rules, ethical and legal (APA, 1992). If the ethical standard actually conflicted with a requirement of law, then psychologists were obliged to "make known their commitment to the Ethics Code and take steps to resolve the conflict in a responsible manner" (APA, 1992). An example is breaking confidentiality in response to receiving a subpoena ordering the release of a patient's clinical record, although the Ethics Code specifically states that psychologists must only do so with client authorization. This is addressed more fully in Chapter 7. If psychologists' attempts to resolve the conflict were unsuccessful, then they were supposed to consider other professional materials (e.g., published practice guidelines, official white papers of the ethics committee, or other documents), the dictates of their own conscience as well as consultation with other psychologists.

The 2002 revision of the code took quite a different approach to conflicts by allowing psychologists to "adhere to the requirements of the law, regulations, or other governing legal authority" if the conflict was found to be unresolvable, as stated in Standards 1.02 and 1.03 (APA, 2002, 2010). This change was criticized by some as being a woefully inadequate solution to the problem of conflicting mandates, essentially allowing psychologists to engage in ethically questionable practices and justifying their conduct by claiming that they are merely following the Ethics Code, as delineated in the previously quoted sentence (Olson, Soldz, & Davis, 2008;

Pope & Gutheil, 2009).[2] Dissenting psychologists were passionate about this matter, with some acting on their objection by withdrawing their membership from the APA.

In response to the persistent outcry about these standards, 8 years after the revision of the Ethics Code, the APA took the rare action of amending the two standards, the amendments taking effect in June 2010 (APA, in press). The APA adopted new wording that required psychologists to *"clarify the nature of the conflict,* make known their commitment to the Ethics Code, and take *reasonable* steps to resolve the conflict *consistent with the General Principles and Ethical Standards of the Ethics Code"* (italics indicate amended wording; APA, in press). A final sentence stated unambiguously that *"under no circumstances may this standard be used to justify or defend violating human rights."* This new rule applied to any situation in which ethical standards conflict with law, regulations, or other governing legal authority (Standard 1.02), or any situation in which ethical standards conflict with organizational demands (Standard 1.03). This was a momentous change that now clearly prohibited psychologists from using their own discretion to comply with an employer who expected them to violate human rights in the course of their work. It is possible that these new standards could lead to some confusion, as they are the only standards in the Ethical Standards section of the Ethics Code that cite or even mention the general principles and require psychologists to act in accordance with them while resolving an ethical dilemma.[3] However, the introductory paragraph that precedes the general principles in the code clearly states that "General Principles, in contrast to Ethical Standards, do not represent obligations and should not form the basis for imposing sanctions. Relying upon General Principles for either or these reasons distorts their meaning and purpose." To their credit, these changes firmly established the concepts articulated by the

---

[2]Following the publication of the 2002 revision of the APA Ethics Code and the series of events following the September 11, 2001, terrorist attacks, a question was raised about the participation of psychologists in possibly unethical acts, primarily in military settings. This included such behaviors as allegedly participating in some aspects of interrogation and/or torture of prisoners who were held in the Guantanamo Bay prison or other prisons where inmates were allegedly exploited with the knowledge (and some would say with the assistance) of psychologists on site.

[3]As mentioned previously, the general principles are considered to be aspirational in nature, and the ethical standards are mandatory. However, this new standard now could be interpreted by some as making the general principles "mandatory," possibly eroding the distinction between the two sections of the code. Requiring psychologists to comply with the general principles may cause some uncertainty about possible exposure of psychologists to increased liability as well because the "minimal standards" implicit in the ethical standards are now being raised considerably to a much higher level—to that of the general principles.

general principles as relevant to the daily work of psychologists, and they placed the responsibility squarely on the shoulders of psychologists to be aware of human rights and not just "follow orders" when carrying out their work if discharging their professional responsibilities could abrogate others' human rights and be harmful to them.

Infractions of laws pertaining to psychological practice may range from a misdemeanor to a felony. Penalties could include a monetary fine, a temporary suspension of license with certain requirements (e.g., taking training in ethics, consulting with a supervisor, undergoing psychological treatment), permanent loss of license to practice, and even prison for the most egregious offenses.

Of course, federal laws pertaining to both therapists and researchers have uniform application across states. One example is the Health Insurance Portability and Accountability Act of 1996, which requires that therapists comply with certain rules involving clinical practices, such as informed consent, confidentiality, record keeping, and grievance procedures. Researchers are also governed by the principles of the Health Insurance Portability and Accountability Act as they bear on the recruitment of research participants and documentation. The National Institute of Mental Health also has policies regulating the conduct of researchers, concerning informed consent, voluntariness, and other matters. If a researcher has received funding from the National Institute of Mental Health (or any other government agency), the researcher must comply with all of the regulations, including such fundamental protections of participants' welfare as informed consent, avoiding harm, maintaining privacy, and debriefing.

As mentioned previously, ethical standards (or codes of conduct) are fundamentally a list of rules, as are laws—the musts and must nots that control what psychologists do. However, they do not have uniform applicability. Only those psychologists who belong to a professional association must comply with its ethics code or code of conduct. For example, the jurisdiction of the APA or the Association for Applied Psychophysiology and Biofeedback consists of the association's members only. If one does not belong, one need not comply with the rules of that association. Although it may appear to be a simple dichotomy that laws regulate the actions of every licensed psychologist and ethical standards of professional associations regulate the behavior of their members, it is not quite that simple.

Even codes of conduct have found a way into state laws. Well over half of the states in this country have chosen to incorporate the APA Ethics Code into their laws, thereby effectively endowing each of its regulatory standards with the force of law. It is likely that as the Ethics Code continues to undergo further revisions that will better address the welfare of both individuals and society, these revisions will also be incorporated into the laws of additional states.

Complaints Against Psychologists

It is a serious matter when psychologists violate an ethical standard or a state or federal law, and their actions have a variety of consequences. Patients, clients, supervisees, and others who interact with psychologists generally have at least three standard ways of complaining against a psychologist who they think has broken a regulation or harmed them in some way in addition to or instead of directly confronting the psychologist. Psychologists may choose to use the services of an attorney in their own defense in responding to the complaint. The three ways in which a complainant might seek redress are (a) initiating a complaint with the APA or state psychological association ethics committee,[4] (b) initiating a complaint with the state licensing authority (also called *board of psychology* or *licensing board*), or (c) initiating a lawsuit against the psychologist. In some cases there would be a fourth option to initiate an in-house process if the hospital, clinic, university, or institution has a patient advocate office, grievance committee, ombudsman, department chair, institutional review board, or some other entity that is known to receive and adjudicate complaints against psychologists. This method may be the most accessible option for the complainant and has the possibility of providing excellent outcomes unless the problem behavior is pervasive within the system, spawning conflicts of interest for those attending to the complaint or the problem behavior is egregious, necessitating a legalistic remedy. I examine the other three methods in the sections that follow.

INITIATING A COMPLAINT WITH THE APA OR STATE ETHICS COMMITTEE

This choice would only be available to a complainant if the psychologist were a member of APA or the adjudicating state association.[5] Even if a potentially offending psychologist belongs, he or she is given the choice of withdrawing membership when contacted by the ethics office to begin a preliminary investigation to determine whether an ethics case should be formally initiated. The APA Ethics Office has full clerical and legal support and depends on a panel of psychologists and one public member who volunteer their time to participate in adjudication of complaints.

---

[4] It should be noted that the ethics committees of the APA and state psychological associations have no connection whatever with each other; they have different rules and procedures, different jurisdictions, and a different range of sanctions that are imposed on offenders.

[5] Very few state associations continue to adjudicate complaints.

It has well-established rules and procedures governing such things as statute of limitations on complaints, time limits on responding to complaints, failure to cooperate, appealing a decision, and the range of available directives and sanctions (APA, Ethics Committee, 2001). A complaint brought to the Ethics Office may take many months to resolve, and it is not uncommon for some complaints to go on for a year or more, allowing for the careful gathering of data from multiple parties. Due process in adjudicating ethics complaints always involves informing the psychologist of the issue that has been raised and providing him or her an opportunity to respond.

The committee ultimately makes a decision whether to impose a sanction (punitive order) on the psychologist. Possible sanctions are

- reprimand, issued when there clearly has been a violation of a particular ethical standard but no harm came to an individual or the profession of psychology (e.g., making a false statement on one's résumé);
- censure, administered when an ethics violation has resulted in harm to someone, but not in a substantial way (e.g., deliberately providing erroneous informed consent about the nature, course, and duration of treatment to engage the patient in psychotherapy);
- expulsion, administered for egregious acts resulting in harm to another or to the profession (e.g., having sex with a patient, fabricating data on a major research project, committing a felony); and
- stipulated resignation, also for serious violations but allowing the psychologist to resign from the APA for a period of time, comply with certain stipulations or directives (listed previously), and then reapply for membership following full compliance (e.g., engaging a patient in a multiple-role relationship resulting in harm or failing to comply with directives that had been issued previously). It should be noted that even if one is expelled from the APA, one may continue to practice, because one's license remains intact unless the state licensing authority chooses to investigate and decides to suspend or permanently revoke a license.

The APA ethics committee has the option of imposing a directive as well, if warranted. They are as follows, from least to most serious:

- cease and desist order requiring the psychologist to immediately stop the unethical conduct (e.g., advertising that guarantees results of treatment, or violating the code in some other way);
- other corrective actions;
- supervision requirement mandating that the psychologist submit to a period of supervision in ethics, clinical work, or some other area;
- education, training, or tutorial requirement requiring a range of didactic experiences;

- evaluation and/or treatment requiring a formal psychological evaluation and, if warranted, treatment for a mental disorder; and
- probation mandating a period of monitoring by the ethics committee to ensure that the psychologist is complying with the directives that were mandated.

INITIATING A COMPLAINT WITH THE STATE LICENSING AUTHORITY

The state licensing authority or board of psychology is a consumer agency that regulates the practice of psychology and offers useful information to the public, such as a patient's "bill of rights," licensure status of particular individuals, recent board actions, or the status of a particular complaint, among other things. If an individual thinks that a psychologist has broken a state law pertaining to psychological practice or an important ethical rule (e.g., failure to remain within the standard of care by using an inappropriate therapeutic technique that harmed a patient, having a sexual relationship with a supervisee), that individual may initiate a formal complaint. The complaint is filed with the state licensing department whose disciplinary supervision of psychologists is handled by its psychology board. States vary with regard to the range of disciplinary actions they may take when warranted, but the major categories of sanctions are letter of warning, probation, suspension, and revocation of license.

LAWSUITS, CIVIL CHARGES, AND CRIMINAL CHARGES

Clients, patients, trainees, or anyone else who feels that they have a serious cause of action against a psychologist for the harm they believe the psychologist has caused them (e.g., sexual relationship with the patient or a close family member, gross incompetence) after consultation with an attorney may bring an action for damages (lawsuit) against a psychologist. Another reason for initiating a lawsuit could be a dispute about fees, such as obtaining money from a patient by misrepresentation. This might include billing the patient for services that the psychologist knew or should have known had no therapeutic value for the patient. A patient may sue the psychologist in addition to bringing an ethics complaint and/or notifying the licensing board of any concerns. Suing a psychologist may initially exert a significant financial toll on the complainant, and it could have serious financial repercussions for the therapist too.

Sometimes, unethical, harmful behavior that provides grounds for a civil suit may rise to the level of criminal conduct under the criminal statutes of the state. If so, the state might independently bring criminal charges against the offending psychologist.

Psychologists commonly defend themselves by notifying their malpractice insurance carrier, and they are then assigned an attorney who participates in their defense in the pending suit. This is generally a lengthy procedure and could easily last several years until it is settled, either in court or out of court.

It is true that clients and patients may feel harmed or disappointed at times and occasionally bring ethics complaints even when the psychologist has done nothing wrong. Under these circumstances, after close scrutiny by an ethics committee or licensing board, the psychologist is usually exonerated and accepts this as a learning experience. By understanding aspirational and mandatory ethical concepts, as described in the chapters ahead, psychologists reduce the likelihood of ever receiving an ethics complaint of any kind, unfounded or not.

A Brief History and Overview of the APA Ethics Code

2

Dr. Burgess offered biofeedback training and psychotherapy to her clients for pain management and psychological symptoms associated with chronic illness. She also maintained an interest in nutrition and was self-taught in the areas of vitamins, herbal supplements, and weight loss. She had recently created a website on which she claimed results for products that were not always evidence based. There was little quality control, and the research was scanty for some products' safety and effectiveness.

She began suggesting that her clients access the website to purchase unique combinations of supplements that she thought would be beneficial for both physical and mental health. Her clients liked her and regarded her as the "local guru" for health and nutritional supplements. Dr. Burgess was unprepared for a late-night urgent phone call from a client with bipolar disorder who was having an apparent allergic reaction to a particular supplement. Little did she suspect that patients taking other medications might be susceptible to an adverse drug interaction caused by one of her "special combinations" of supplements. The patient recovered from this crisis but ended treatment shortly thereafter and eventually complained to the state licensing board about Dr. Burgess's lack of competence in treating her.

Introduction

The American Psychological Association (APA) was incorporated in 1925, and by 1930 it had a total of 1,101 members and associates (Fernberger, 1932). Before a formal ethics code was developed, the APA created the temporary Committee on Scientific and Professional Ethics in 1938. This committee began to receive complaints of unethical conduct and handled them "privately and informally, with apparently good results" (W. C. Olson, 1940). The committee recommended that it continue adjudicating complaints of an ethical nature and defer work on the development of a formal ethics code.

In 1940, the committee was charged with not only continuing to investigate complaints but also with formulating over time a set of rules or principles that would be adopted by the association (W. C. Olson, 1940). The APA Council of Representatives reached a consensus that it would "never be practical or desirable to devise a 'complete' or a 'rigid' code" (APA, Committee on Scientific and Professional Ethics, 1947). One member of this committee, Ernest R. Hilgard of Stanford University, revealed in a letter that although the committee had no formal ethics code to use as a standard for judging ethical compliance of APA members, the committee members had a well-developed sense of professional and ethical conduct and "knew" what was ethically acceptable and what crossed the line (E. Hilgard, personal communication, August 16, 1998). However, as psychologists became more professionally active in such areas as industrial consulting and diagnosis and treatment of mental disorders, the need for an ethics code increased (Hobbs, 1948). In this chapter, I describe the development and evolution of this code.

Developing the First Ethics Code

At the end of World War II psychologists were in great demand. Much of the burgeoning of psychological services was driven by the immediate need for treatment of returning troops by the Veterans Administration, the U.S. Public Health Service, and state hospitals (Albee, 1991). More psychologists than ever were joining the APA, and the need for ethical guidance became increasingly apparent.

In 1947, the first Committee on Ethical Standards for Psychologists was formed as a separate committee from the ongoing Committee on Scientific and Professional Ethics. It was chaired by Edward C. Tolman, the well-known behaviorist from the University of California, Berkeley

(Canter, Bennett, Jones, & Nagy, 1994).[1] The new committee began its work by developing a process for this ambitious undertaking. It was determined that a critical-incident method would be used, whereby each of the APA's 7,500 members would be invited to "describe a situation they knew of first-hand, in which a psychologist made a decision having ethical implications, and to indicate . . . the ethical issues involved" (APA, 1953a, p. v). Ultimately, over 2,000 members contributed substantially to formulating the document (APA, 1953a).

This empirical approach was innovative and ultimately became a prototype for developing codes of many other associations later on (Holtzman, 1979). Engaging APA members in this process resulted in the submission of more than 1,000 vignettes that determined the content, structure, and format of the first Ethics Code. Draft versions of this Code were printed in the *American Psychologist* for review by the membership, and the final edition was published in 1953. It was a lengthy document— 171 pages—by far the longest of any subsequent revision of the Code. It contained six sections, 310 rule elements, 162 principles, and 148 subprinciples (Canter et al., 1994). The sections were (a) Public Responsibility, (b) Client Relationships, (c) Teaching of Psychology, (d) Research, (e) Writing and Publishing, and (f) Professional Relationships (APA, 1953a; the introduction and summary of the 1953 Ethics Code are available on this book's supplemental website, http://pubs.apa.org/books/supp/ essentialethics/). A shorter version was also printed; it omitted all of the incidents and detailed elaboration and was known as *A Summary of Ethical Principles* (APA, 1953b). This summary version, intended for distribution to other professional workers, legislators, and the public, was further revised, modifying some of the principles, omitting some others, and included a number of subprinciples (Adkins, 1952).

Revisions to the Ethics Code

The Ethics Code was intended to be used for a period of 3 years and then revised, with additional incidents involving ethical issues to be solicited from the membership. The goal of this planned revision was to address criticisms of the original edition—its length, codifying etiquette (i.e., matters of courtesy or professionalism but not necessarily ethics), and redundant principles—as well as revising the overall structure.

[1]Although Edward Tolman was the first chairperson of this new committee, Nicholas Hobbs chaired it from 1948 until completion of the Ethics Code and authored the article describing the process of creating the Code, which was published in 1948.

The committee wished to preserve "the major strengths of the present Code while changing its form to a more useful, readable one" (APA, Committee on Ethical Standards of Psychologists, 1958, p. 266). As it turned out, the next edition was available for review in 1958 and accepted in 1959. It consisted of 19 principles, compared with 162 in the first edition. The first six principles broadly addressed the concerns of all psychologists; three more addressed the concerns of every psychologist except those engaged in research; two more focused on industrial, clinical, and counseling psychology; and the last two dealt with research and publication. Teaching was addressed in a limited way, and there was no mention of the ethical issues involved in the supervision of psychologists in training.

The structure of the 1959 edition was simple. It began with a four-sentence preamble and then listed and described the numbered principles. Each principle had a brief title, generally one or two words long, and was followed by one or two sentences describing the general nature of the principle. These descriptions were at times lofty and somewhat vague, but they provided a clear and helpful context for the principle being addressed. Following each principle were two to eight paragraphs of specifics stating the expected behavior, beliefs, and prohibitions for the ethical psychologist These paragraphs constituted the substance of the Code—what was mandated and what was forbidden. They had no titles but were set off by letters of the alphabet. The titles and general themes of these principles were as follows:

- Principle 1: General (assumptions and goals of researchers, teachers, and practitioners)
- Principle 2: Competence (boundaries of competence, personal impairment, reporting unethical psychologists)
- Principle 3: Moral and Legal Standards (one sentence about community standards, social codes, and moral and legal standards)
- Principle 4: Misrepresentation (accuracy when promoting one's own services)
- Principle 5: Public Statements (accuracy when interpreting psychological findings or techniques to the public)
- Principle 6: Confidentiality (informing patients about the limits of confidentiality, danger to self or society, informed consent for disclosures, use of clinical data for teaching and publishing)
- Principle 7: Client Welfare (the longest standard by far, it included conflict of interest, termination of services, informed consent, referring patients, assessment, teaching, and professionalism in the clinical setting)
- Principle 8: Client Relationship (providing informed consent about therapy, avoiding multiple-role relationships—family, friends, or close associates)

- Principle 9: Impersonal Services (providing diagnosis or treatment only in the context of a professional relationship, not in public presentations, such as on radio or television)
- Principle 10: Advertising (accuracy, "modest" listings prohibiting "display" advertising of psychological services)
- Principle 11: Interprofessional Relationship (prohibiting offering psychological services to someone already receiving them)
- Principle 12: Remuneration (fees, prohibiting rebates for referrals and exploitation of clients)
- Principle 13: Test Security (prohibiting revealing test items to the general public)
- Principle 14: Test Interpretation (revealing test results only to those who are qualified to interpret and use them properly)
- Principle 15: Test Publication (selecting test publishers who promote tests accurately and professionally, preparing a comprehensive test manual; also refers readers to *"Technical Recommendations for Psychological Tests and Diagnostic Techniques,"* APA, 1954)
- Principle 16: Harmful Aftereffects (debriefing research subjects about deception; also refers reader to *Rules Regarding Animals*, drawn up by the Committee on Precautions in Animal Experimentation)[2]
- Principle 17: Publication Credit (accuracy in claims for authorship credit)
- Principle 18: Organizational Material (ownership of professional work products when working within an institution—clinical work, research, authorship, etc.; APA, 1959)

In 1964, a 19th principle was added by the Ad Hoc Committee on Ethical Practices in Industrial Psychology; this committee concluded that the major ethical consideration involved in the practice of industrial psychology was protecting the public and created an ethical standard to address this issue (APA, 1964).

Around this time, the Committee on Ethical Standards of Psychologists suggested that a casebook be written that would contain disguised material drawn from actual deliberations of the Committee on Scientific and Professional Ethics from 1959 to 1962 (APA, 1967). It was first published in 1963 and then updated in 1967 and consisted of 46 actual cases, along with details of the adjudication process and the final opinions of the Ethics Committee. It was a valuable resource in educating psychologists in general, of course, but it was also useful in providing training for those charged with adjudicating ethics complaints—the APA Ethics Committee

---

[2]In 1924 the APA president was asked to appoint a three-person committee to focus on animal experimentation as a result of unfavorable publicity about certain surgical procedures that were used. This committee developed the document in 1927 and distributed it to various laboratories conducting research on animals (Fernberger, 1932).

as well as ethics committees at the state and local level. In the words of the Committee,

> A code has both a judicial and an educational function. It represents the set of "laws" on the basis of which decisions are made; it also constitutes a guide to ethical practice. The *Casebook* and the Code, taken together, are designed to clarify the judicial function and to serve an educational purpose at the same time. (APA, 1967, p. viii)

The number of violations of critical standards in the code was relatively low for the 25-year period between 1956 and 1981. Only 12 psychologists received the most punitive sanction, expulsion or dropped membership; about one individual lost membership every other year (Nagy, 1989). However, between 1981 and 1989 the rate increased by an extraordinary amount, approximately 2,200%, to about 11 lost memberships per year. Serious violations that warranted expulsions included having sexual relationships with a patient, being convicted of a felony, or being expelled from a state psychological association for some other reason. It was unclear whether such an increase in serious infractions reflected a general falling away from high standards by psychologists, revisions of ethics codes resulting in loftier standards that were slow to be absorbed by psychologists, a higher awareness by consumers leading to more frequent reporting of questionable conduct, a change in how the APA Ethics Office processed complaints, or some other factor. But it is safe to say that changes in society, emerging awareness by psychologists of ethically complex areas, and the frequency and type of complaints against psychologists all contributed to the need for ongoing revisions of the Ethics Code.

There have been 10 revisions since the publication of the original Ethics Code in 1953, and each revision has been based on the 1959 Code's structure and format, including principles, but no incidents (vignettes).[3] Some of these revisions have been minor tune-ups, and some have been major overhauls. The minor tune-ups focused on change in the code's content by adding or deleting rules or concepts or modifying nuances in the text that reflected changes in psychological research, teaching, or practice. The major overhauls consisted of deeper changes, including the structure and format of the Ethics Code. An example of this was the 1992 revision in which an entirely new section of aspirational ethical principles was added and the general principles and introductory paragraphs of each section were deleted or revised to be incorporated within those aspirational principles.

---

[3] The revisions were adopted in 1958 (APA, 1959), 1962 (APA 1963), 1965 (APA, 1968), 1972 (APA, 1972), January 1977 ("Ethical Standards of Psychologists," 1977), August 1977 (Conger, 1978), 1979 (APA, 1979) 1981 (APA, 1981), 1989 (APA, 1990), 1992 (APA 1992), and 2002 (APA, 2002), and there was a change in two standards only, in 2010 (APA, in press).

Research

The APA demonstrated an interest in research with animal subjects as early as 1925 by adopting animal use guidelines, developed by the Animal Experimentation Committee (Canter et al., 1994). Nearly 30 years later, with the advent of the first Ethics Code, APA members were required to abide by the *Rules Regarding Animals,* a document developed by the Committee on Precautions in Animal Experimentation in 1949. The Ethics Code itself, however, did not contain specific rules or guidance about the treatment of animals used for research (APA, 1953b). This did not occur until the 1963 revision with the insertion of one small sentence in the introduction to a section titled Research Precautions: "The psychologist assumes obligations for the welfare of his research subjects, both animal and human" (APA, 1963).

In addition to the APA's interest in guiding researchers toward ethical practices in general, another incentive to expand the ethical rules for research with human participants was new regulations by the U.S. Department of Health, Education, and Welfare stating that "no grant involving human subjects at risk will be made to an individual unless he is affiliated with or sponsored by an institution which can and does assume responsibility for the protection of the subjects involved" (APA, Ad Hoc Committee on Ethical Standards in Psychological Research, 1973, p. 3). This policy placed the onus squarely on the shoulders of the APA to further study the topic and establish ethical rules for those doing research that would hopefully define and protect the rights of research participants and reduce the risk of harm as well.

The Ad Hoc Committee on Ethical Standards in Psychological Research undertook the task of creating such a document following essentially the same empirical procedure developed 20 years previously in developing the original Ethics Code. This consisted of the two-step process of (a) inviting APA members to supply ethical problems related to research as the raw materials for the synthesis of ethical principles and (b) revising these principles and eventually adapting them as formal rules that reflected the Association's input (APA, Ad Hoc Committee on Ethical Standards in Psychological Research, 1973). This approached yielded 5,000 descriptions of research cases, including a broad array of conduct and issues on such topics as informed consent, confidentiality, investigator bias, deception, avoiding exploitation, declining participating in research, and many of the other concepts that psychologists currently consider to be fundamental considerations in planning and carrying out research.

This was a major undertaking and resulted in the publication of the *Ethical Principles in the Conduct of Research With Human Participants* (APA,

Ad Hoc Committee on Ethical Standards in Psychological Research, 1973). This 100-page booklet provided specific guidance to investigators who were members of the APA carrying out research in any setting, such as hospitals and clinics, universities, primary and secondary schools, industrial settings, and prisons. It consisted of 10 ethical concepts (principles), accompanying vignettes (incidents) and a discussion section for each of the principles. The 10 principles were promptly incorporated into the 1972 edition of the *Ethical Standards of Psychologists* (Canter et al., 1994). The pioneering work carried out by this committee formed the basis of ethical practice for researchers and has been included, often with verbatim excerpts, in every subsequent revision of the Ethics Code after 1972.

The 1977 revision of the Ethics Code resulted in a major reorganization of the document, although there were few changes in the area of research (Canter et al., 1994). In 1981, a new principle emerged, titled The Care and Use of Animals. It specifically listed many topics concerning animal research, including acquisition and disposing of animals, minimizing pain and discomfort, proper supervision of assistants, and related matters (APA, 1981). This principle survives in an updated and shortened version in the 2002 Ethics Code.

Emerging Ethical Issues

The Ethics Code continued to evolve as a living document, reflecting both cultural and societal changes as well as changes in the field of psychology itself. The very mutations that were observed often paralleled changes in the American way of life. As LSD, marijuana, and other drugs became popular for recreational use in the 1960s, the 1965 Ethics Code added two principles addressing the "use of accepted drugs for therapeutic purposes" and research "using experimental drugs (for example, hallucinogenic . . . or similar substances)" (Newman, 1965). In addition to the changes in ethical standards involving research, several other specific areas of focus have emerged over the years that have resulted in new ethical standards. These relate to multiple-role relationships, sexual misconduct, advertising and other business aspects of clinical practice, and information technology.

MULTIPLE-ROLE RELATIONSHIPS

The term *multiple-role relationships,* first addressed as *dual relationships,* refers to a secondary social role that a psychologist plays with a recipient of his or her services in addition to the primary professional role, such as psychotherapist, researcher, clinical supervisor, or teacher. Certainly psychologists have long engaged in multiple roles. Professors have coauthored articles and books with their own graduate students, teachers have entered business relationships with their students, and researchers have befriended and mentored their research assistants and research participants. It is not that a multiple-role relationship per se is the problem; rather, it is that the psychologist may hold authority or power in the primary role that trumps the secondary role and that participating in two roles simultaneously may interfere with the psychologist's objectivity and competence, ultimately resulting in harm to the other person.

> A clinical supervisor who specializes in eating disorders is supervising a bright, ambitious graduate student who is completing her required postdoctoral supervised experience as a prerequisite for licensure. The supervisor has the creative idea of developing a website on anorexia as an additional resource for patients but lacks the technical competence to execute his idea. The graduate student is very literate in the use of computers and willing to spend extra time creating a website for her supervisor. She ultimately creates an elegant, interactive website, and soon it is besieged with many hits as the general public discovers this informative resource.
>
> Gradually it consumes an increasing amount of her time to keep it current and accurate and to respond to questions and comments from those who access the website. Much of her weekly supervisory hour is now taken up with the clinical and business aspects of keeping the website up and running. Furthermore, some differences of opinion emerge about the business aspects, such as whether to charge a fee for website visitors as a professional consultation and whether to encourage visitors to contact the clinic for further information. The supervisor comes to expect that the website will be his trainee's first priority and voices his disapproval when she complains that it is taking up too much of her time. Unrelenting, he disapproves of her failing to be "on call" whenever he needs her advice about a problem, and his resentment begins to contaminate the clinical supervision, what little is left of it.
>
> The supervisee is no longer receiving adequate supervision for her difficult anorectic patients, and several suicidal patients are showing signs of deteriorating. The stage is now set for a tragic event that could have been avoided if only the supervisor had recognized the dangers of entering into a multiple-role relationship at the outset—that of supervisor and business partner.

Not every multiple-role relationship is unethical, but when a psychologist's objectivity and competence are compromised, the psychologist may find that personal needs and ambitions surface, diminishing the quality of his or her work. The framers of the first Ethics Code were aware of this in 1953 in prohibiting a psychologist from having "clinical relationships with members of his own family, with intimate friends, or with persons so close that their welfare might be jeopardized by the dual relationship" (APA, 1953a, p. 4). In 1963 the ethical standard was broadened to include any professional relationship; this change of one word from *clinical* to *professional* immediately invoked all the nonclinical roles played psychologists—those of professor, supervisor, consultant, and researcher, to name a few.

By 1977, the Ethics Code had addressed the issue of social power intrinsic to many multiple-role relationships by citing psychologists' "inherently powerful position vis-à-vis clients" and adding further prohibitions against "treating employees, supervisees, close friends or relatives" (Canter et al., 1994). Changes in the 1981 revision further broadened the concepts of power, making the prohibitions more general in nature and specifically adding students and subordinates to the list. Also, the inventory of prohibitions was increased to include multiple-role relationships in research or treatment of students to employees, supervisees, close friends and relatives (APA, 1981).

With the major revision in 1992, *dual relationships* became *multiple relationships*, now addressing the reality that sometimes psychologists would simultaneously play any number of roles, not just two—that of clinical supervisor, psychotherapist, and friend, for example. The new standard clearly prohibited psychologists from "entering into or promising another personal, scientific, professional, financial or other relationship with such persons" if it might "impair the psychologist's objectivity or otherwise interfere with . . . effectively performing his or her functions . . . or might harm or exploit the other party" (APA, 1992, Standard 1.17, Multiple Relationships). Further, as of this revision, psychologists had to resolve a harmful multiple-role relationship that developed, with "due regard for the best interests" of the other person. And finally, in 2002, the list was expanded further to include a second-order closeness so that a multiple relationship was now defined as being in a relationship with a person who is "closely associated" with or "related to" the person with whom the psychologist has the professional relationship (APA, 2010). However, no prohibitions were placed on relationships that were not reasonably expected to result in impairment, exploitation, or harm.

SEXUAL MISCONDUCT

Sexual misconduct by psychologists may be seen as a subset of multiple-role relationships (Borys & Pope, 1989). It has a high risk of harming others and is always prohibited within professional relationships. It consists of explicitly adding a sexual component to the professional relationship, regardless of who might have initiated it, with the key factor being the psychologist's motive of deliberate sexual arousal and gratification. The devastating effects to therapy patients are well documented, with a significant increase in depression, mistrust, rage, psychosomatic disorders, suicidality, and other psychological symptoms (Bouhoutsos, Holyroyd, Lerman, Forer, & Greenberg, 1983; Pope & Vetter, 1991). Multiple-role relationships are explored more fully in Chapter 7, "Avoiding Harm and Exploitation."

The earliest codes did not mention sexual intimacies but instead asked psychologists to show "sensible regard for the social codes and moral expectations of the community," thereby avoiding "damaging personal conflicts" that would "impugn his [sic] own name and the reputation of his profession" (APA, 1959, p. 279). It was not until 1977 that sex with the recipients of psychological services was first addressed directly with the addition of the simple statement, "Sexual intimacies with clients are unethical" ("Ethical Standards of Psychologists," 1977, p. 4). This curt, straightforward prohibition only seemed to address current clients, not those who recently terminated treatment, and it was the only standard in the entire Code that directly addressed the topic of sexuality in any professional role played by psychologists. However, it said nothing about banning sex with students, supervisees, research participants, or anyone else with whom psychologists form professional relationships. Nevertheless, it was the first step in tackling this problematical area, and the language remained unchanged for the next 15 years.

With the 1992 revision of the Ethics Code, no fewer than six standards specifically addressed the sexualizing of a professional relationship. They prohibited the following behaviors: (a) sexual harassment; (b) sexual exploitation of students, supervisees, employees, research participants, and clients or patients; (c) sex with students and supervisees in training, even at the student's initiative; (d) sex with current patients or clients under any circumstances; (e) psychotherapy with former sexual partners; and (f) sex with former patients under any circumstances within a 2-year period following the formal termination of psychological treatment. This novel standard further stated,

> Because sexual intimacies with a former therapy patient or client are so frequently harmful to the patient or client, . . . psychologists do not engage in sexual intimacies with former therapy patients and clients *even after a two-year* [emphasis added] interval except in the most unusual circumstances. (APA, 1992, Standard 4.07, Sexual Intimacies With Former Therapy Patients)

This seemed to effectively raise the standard from a 2-year posttermination rule for sexual relationships to almost never because some members on the task force that revised the Ethics Code thought that it would be nearly impossible to satisfy all the stated conditions before initiating a sexual relationship with a former patient. These specific conditions are discussed in Chapter 10, "Ethics in Psychotherapy."

ADVERTISING AND OTHER BUSINESS ASPECTS OF CLINICAL PRACTICE

Ethical rules limiting the advertising and promoting of psychological services have resulted in some of the more interesting and controversial evolutionary changes in the Code over time. Advertising was addressed in the very first Ethics Code, which required psychologists to describe public announcement of their services with "accuracy and dignity, adhering to professional rather than to commercial standards" (APA, 1953a, p. 9). Even the details of what could be printed on a business card were limited, and listings in the telephone directory were restricted to name, highest relevant degree, certification status, address, and telephone number. Furthermore, "display advertising of psychological services" was outlawed altogether. This was a far cry from today's advertisements in the yellow pages, in newspapers, and on the Internet, where one can find psychologists' photos, detailed descriptions of services, and even claims for therapeutic interventions and outcomes.

Relatively major changes occurred in the 1963 revision with the addition of a new principle titled Promotional Activities, which focused on the "promotion of psychological devices, books, or other products" (APA, 1963). With the 1977 revision the "professional rather than commercial" phrase was deleted. This eliminated a gray area and represented a liberalizing of the standards because psychologists were no longer required to make such fine distinctions ("Ethical Standards of Psychologists," 1977). Two years later, there was a further relaxing of these rules, by stating that "psychologists *may* list the following information" instead of *must*, as in the previous editions (APA, 1979). A major concession to further permitting advertising messages was made by stating that psychologists could add other "relevant or important consumer information" as long as it was not prohibited by other sections of the ethical standards.

The 1981 revision introduced major changes by addressing topics that were previously ignored. Required conduct included the following: (a) maintaining accuracy in advertising statements, (b) providing a clear statement of purpose of "personal growth groups" (i.e., providing accurate descriptions in course catalogs, presenting the science of psychology fairly and accurately), and (c) correcting others who do not comply with the guidelines. Prohibited conduct included (a) exaggeration in advertising messages, (b) using a current patient's testimonial endorsing the psychologist for advertising purposes, (c) using language that is likely to appeal to a client's fears if he or she failed to begin treatment with the psychologist, (d) offering services to patients already in treatment with someone else, (e) in-person solicitation of prospective patients (i.e., face-to-face), (f) giving any remuneration to another for referral of a client or patient for professional services, (g) compensating a journalist for an interview or professional publicity in a news item, and (h) participating for personal gain in commercials for products or services (i.e., a psychologist endorsing Corona beer or the Google search engine).

Despite the general liberalization of restrictions concerning advertising, in 1986 the Federal Trade Commission's (FTC's) Bureau of Competition set its sights on the APA Ethics Code concerning what it considered to overly restrictive standards.[4] The FTC required the APA to formally rescind the following prohibitions: (a) using patient testimonials regarding the quality of services, (b) making statements implying one-of-a-kind abilities, (c) making statements likely to appeal to a client's fears concerning the possible results of failure to obtain the offered services, (d) making statements concerning the comparative desirability of offered services, (e) making statements of direct solicitations of individual clients, (f) giving or receiving remuneration for referring clients for professional services, and (g) offering services directly to persons receiving the same services from another mental health professional (Canter et al., 1994). As a result of this ruling, the APA stopped accepting ethics complaints based on these seven criteria in 1986, and 3 years later they were formally rescinded, with the 1989 amended version of the Ethics Code (APA, 1990). However, after extensive negotiations between the APA and the FTC, a compromise was reached, and a consent agreement was issued in 1992 by the FTC that reversed some of the seven exceptions. This allowed the APA to create ethical standards prohibiting the following: (a) any false or deceptive representations by psychologists, (b) uninvited in-person solicitation of business from persons who, because of their particular circumstances, would be vulnerable to undue influence (such as approaching a mourning widow at her husband's funeral), and (c) solicitation of testimonial endorsements from current psychotherapy patients or from other persons who, because of their particular circumstances, are vulnerable to undue influence ("FTC Consent Order," 1993). To this day these ethical standards are present in the Ethics Code.

COMPUTERS

The blossoming of information technology brought many innovative applications to those doing psychological work. Mainframe computers had offered researchers computing power for data gathering and statistical analysis that was unparalleled for many years. But it was not until the availability of the personal computer for small business and home use and of the portable laptop computer in the early 1980s that psychologists

---

[4]The FTC had previously initiated investigations with other groups prior to the investigation of APA, including what it considered to be overly restrictive requirements by the American Medical Association and the American Dental Association.

began to fully appreciate their benefits.[5] Using the Internet and communicating by e-mail eventually became common practices in American society, and psychologists and the institutions in which they worked naturally incorporated technology into everyday practice. This included (a) business aspects, such as appointments, billing patients for services, and managing health insurance; (b) clinical aspects, such as administering psychological tests by computer and maintaining treatment records; (c) communicating via e-mail (i.e., clients, patients, students, supervisees, research participants); (d) websites for providing psychological information to the public as well as promoting and advertising psychological services and products; and (e) the use of videoconferencing for real-time interaction with recipients of psychological services, such as for those living in rural areas or those who were incarcerated.

This proliferation of computers brought unique ethical and legal issues to the everyday work of psychologists involving competence, confidentiality, informed consent, and public statements, to name a few (Nagy, 2001). Some therapists developed websites displaying their résumés and offering psychoeducational materials for general consumption (e.g., information about anxiety disorders or weight loss, career counseling, or resolving marital problems). Some websites purported to offer psychological assessment and career counseling, such as taking and scoring the Myers-Briggs Type Inventory or Strong Internet Inventory online and obtaining an interpretation. Some revealed actual test items of the Minnesota Multiphasic Personality Inventory, boasting that those facing a psychological evaluation could learn how to select responses so as to bias the results in their favor (e.g., for a child custody assessment in which divorcing parents were in litigation against each other). And some therapists were attempting to offer counseling and psychotherapy by e-mail, even though they had never been trained to do this and little empirical basis existed for such a practice. Unique problems began to surface, such as dealing with a suicidal emergency by a therapist in one state who was doing e-mail therapy with a patient in another. The psychologist would not be able to necessarily respond adequately to a crisis situation because he or she would not be familiar with the local resources (e.g., hospital, emergency psychiatric team).

Although the Ethics Codes rarely addressed computers directly (never even using the word *computer*), in 1987 the APA as a professional organization began formally addressing the issue of computer-assisted assessment by publishing *Guidelines for Computer-Based Tests and Interpretations* (APA, 1987). Practice guidelines were not considered to be the equivalent of ethical standards—they were recommended practices, but they were not compulsory or sanctionable, as are ethical standards. A

---

[5]The first laptop computer, the Osborn 1, was created in 1981, and the first Macintosh in 1984.

psychologist could depart from a particular guideline if he or she could provide a suitable rationale. They were created for the purpose of providing professional guidance to psychologists in relation to the following topics: (a) development of new technology (e.g., using computers for maintaining or transmitting clinical records); (b) new, expanded, or complex multidisciplinary roles (e.g., collaborative roles in genetic counseling commensurate with scientific advances in genetic testing); (c) advances in theory and science (e.g., new data concerning sexual orientation and gender issues); and (d) professional risk management issues (e.g., guidelines on record keeping that helped protect psychologists from complaints or lawsuits from consumers when state or federal regulations were insufficient; APA, Board of Professional Affairs, Committee on Professional Practice and Standards, 2005).

The first mention of *electronic,* implying computer usage, or *Internet* appeared in the 2002 edition of the Ethics Code. It states: "This Ethics Code applies . . . across a variety of contexts, such as in person, postal, telephone, Internet, and other electronic transmissions" (APA, 2002, Introduction and Applicability). And only four standards specifically mention *electronic* in their paragraphs—Standards 3.10, Informed Consent; 4.02, Discussing the Limits of Confidentiality; 5.01, Avoidance of False or Deceptive Statements; and 5.04, Media Presentations. The impact of technology on these four areas along with benefits and risks is discussed more fully in later chapters.

A Major Overhaul: The 1992 Revision

When the Ethics Committee Task Force began the process of revising the Ethics Code in 1986, it had little awareness that it would turn into a 6-year project, resulting in major changes in both structure and content (Nagy, 1989). The three major structural changes were (a) adding a seven-paragraph Introduction to the entire document describing aspirational versus enforceable rules of conduct and other general matters about application and the history of the Code, (b) labeling each and every ethical standard with its own title, and (c) adding a section in the beginning titled General Principles. Previously, only the sections of the Ethics Code had titles, such as Confidentiality or Responsibility, and the various paragraphs were simply set off by sequential letters of the alphabet (a, b, c, etc.). The task force thought it would be a more useful document in general and easier to comprehend if each standard had its own title, thereby helping psychologists to thread their way through the verbiage (e.g., Describing the Nature and Results of Psychological Services, Fees and Financial Arrangements, or Deception in Research).

The general principles were derived in part from the introductory paragraphs to each of the 10 sections of the 1981 edition. These introductory paragraphs were titled Preambles and were occasionally cited by ethics committees in adjudicating ethics complaints. However, sometimes technical questions were raised by psychologists against whom complaints were lodged, or their defending attorneys, about whether a preamble should be considered to be the equivalent of an actual ethical standard and whether a psychologist should be held to both the preamble and the ethical standard. The language of the preamble was more general in nature and the tone more aspirational than the ethical standards, and in some cases, the behavioral objectives of the preambles appeared to be far too lofty. The Task Force solved this problem by deleting all the preambles and creating six general principles that more or less served the same purpose. They were Competence, Integrity, Professional and Scientific Responsibility, Respect for People's Rights and Dignity, Concern for Others' Welfare, and Social Responsibility. Further, the general principles were clearly described as being aspirational and not enforceable (APA, 1992). They would constitute the highest ethical targets on which all psychologists might set their sights but would not be sanctioned for failure to achieve (Nagy, 1989).

In addition to changes in structure, the 1992 Code also included some needed innovations by addressing areas that had been vague or ignored in prior editions. These included the following five areas (Nagy, 1990).

FORENSIC MATTERS

Psychologists became increasingly drawn into litigation, such as in child custody assessments and evaluation of defendants in criminal cases and other settings. Also, there was a sharp increase in the number of attorneys in the United States in the 1970s and a tripling of the number of attorneys in the last quarter century. In 1961, there were 1.25 lawyers per 1,000 people, and within 15 years, in 1986, the ratio had more than doubled, with 2.76 lawyers per 1,000 people, that is, about one lawyer for every 362 persons (Hagan & Kay, 1995).

Psychologists were being subpoenaed to appear in legal proceedings, they were sought as expert witnesses for the defense or prosecution, and they were being hired by attorneys as consultants in cases involving psychological malpractice, workers' compensation, long-term disability, and the like. Although some of the ethical standards present in the forensics section were redundant with others in the Ethics Code, they focused on important areas, such as avoiding conflicts of interest and making unfounded statements. Some titles of standards in this section were Clarification of Role, Truthfulness and Candor, and Compliance With Law and Rules.

SEXUAL RELATIONSHIPS

No area generated more feedback and created more dissent among APA members than multiple-role relationships with clients and patients that involved sex (Nagy, 1989). There was a general consensus that sex with current clients and patients was taboo; however, there was much disagreement about the status of former recipients of psychological services. If the therapist terminated treatment on Friday, could the therapist invite his "former" patient out on a date Saturday night? What if the termination of therapy had been hastened in the service of developing a romantic relationship? What if a patient who had naturally terminated treatment might want to begin again 6 months later?

The true question that emerged was, "When is a patient no longer a patient?" The task force, with a consensus of feedback from the membership, eventually answered this question by ultimately implying that "once a therapist, always a potential therapist," resolving that once a psychologist has treated someone, he or she should not engage in a posttermination sexual relationship for a period of 2 years. Complaints and lawsuits about sexual relationships after therapy had ended generally focused on abuses that occurred within that 2-year period; therefore, it was judged by the task force to be an adequate time frame.

Other new regulations included prohibiting offering treatment to former sexual partners and prohibiting sex with students or supervisees in training "over whom the psychologist has evaluative or direct authority." In previous editions, the rule relating to students had required that psychologists must not "exploit their relationships with clients, supervisees, students, employees, or research participants sexually or otherwise." This seemed to allow a "true love" exception—that sex would be permissible with a current student as long as it was not exploitative (the therapist truly loved the patient). By having a flat rule banning all sex with current students, supervisees, or others engaged in professional relationships, the new rule simultaneously raised the bar considerably and simplified decision making by psychologists, in hopes of protecting the public against exploitative or predatory professionals.

TEACHING SETTINGS

For the first time, ethical standards were developed that applied to academic settings specifically requiring or limiting the professional conduct of professors and instructors. Teachers were now obliged to provide accurate descriptions of education and training programs in advance, whether in academic settings or workshops that included course outlines and the nature of course experiences. They also had to establish objective means of providing student feedback and evaluations and state these in advance as well.

RESEARCH

New rules for researchers included more detailed elaboration of informed consent (e.g., understandable language, informing of significant factors that would influence their willingness to participate), informing participants about any intention of sharing the research data with others in the future, and an obligation to provide research participants with conclusions of the research when the study has been completed. Furthermore, in the interest of maintaining accuracy and honesty in analyzing data and stating implications of the research, investigators were now required by a new rule to make their data available to other "competent professionals who seek to verify the substantive claims through reanalysis." This allowed other psychologists, for the first time ever, to have access to the raw data of a primary investigator to review his or her statistical analysis on which the resulting conclusions and implications were based (APA, 1992).

INFORMED CONSENT

An important change in all psychological settings was the new requirement to inform clients and patients in advance about the exceptions to confidentiality. This included such exceptions as a patient who was a danger to him- or herself (e.g., suicidal), a danger to others (e.g., threats to harm another), and revelations about ongoing child or elder abuse. Frequently confidentiality and privacy matters were addressed by state law also, and the psychologist was required to be aware of current regulations to adequately inform clients and patients.

Other areas of informed consent addressed interruptions in treatment and how psychologists would inform clients and patients at the outset about how these transitions would be managed (e.g., extended vacations, moving to a different geographic location, untimely death of the psychologist), including the transfer of records or referral to new therapists. Finally, there was a new rule about third-party requests for services. A psychologist providing service at the request of the court (e.g., assessment, expert witness testimony) must discuss the matter with his or her patient and the implications for confidentiality, conflicting roles, and possible complications of accepting the new role or refusing it. An example of such a complication would be the patient who discovers his or her therapist's diagnostic impression of him or reads his or her own clinical record for the very first time in preparation for a court appearance by his or her therapist. It could be disturbing to learn that one's therapist considered one to have a personality disorder (e.g., narcissistic or borderline) before adequate time had passed to fully understand and access this in the course of treatment.

Overview of the 2002 Ethics Code Revision

The 2002 revision maintained the general format and content changes of the 1992 edition, valuing brevity and clarity in formulating the standards (Knapp & VandeCreek, 2003). Both editions begin with an Introduction and Applicability section. In the 2002 revised Ethics Code this consists of one page describing the target audience of the Code (augmented to include students for the first time); the filing of complaints; how to deal with conflicts between ethics and laws; and specifically addressing a variety of professional roles and contexts, including personal interactions, correspondence, telephone conversations, the Internet, and other electronic transmissions. It also makes clear for the first time that "the Ethics Code is not intended to be a basis of civil liability"; that is, a finding that a psychologist violated a particular standard does not mean ipso facto that he or she has violated the law or is legally liable in a court action (APA, 2002). This needed clarification plainly separates the process and outcome of adjudicating an ethics complaint from the legal arena, reducing the likelihood that the Ethics Code could be used to discipline psychologists unfairly (Knapp & VandeCreek, 2003).

The next section, a three-paragraph Preamble, consists of broad general statements about the commitments, values, and goals of psychologists. The opening sentence concisely states the fundamental assumption of the APA currently by announcing that "psychologists work to develop a valid and reliable body of scientific knowledge based on research." It further lays out the goals as maintaining the welfare and protection of those with whom psychologists work and educating members and the public about psychologists' ethical standards.

The third section, the General Principles, was revised and shortened with the elimination of one principle, Competence, and addition of another principle, Justice. The five principles are Principle A: Beneficence and Nonmaleficence (formerly Concern for Others' Welfare), Principle B: Fidelity and Responsibility (formerly Professional and Scientific Responsibility), Principle C: Integrity, Principle D: Justice (a new principle emphasizing entitlement of everyone to access to and benefit from psychology and warning psychologists to be aware of their biases and boundaries of competence), and Principle E: Respect for People's Rights and Dignity. Each of these principles is fully explored in Chapter 3.[6]

---

[6]These five general principles reflect more closely the areas of focus that have emerged from the abuses in the name of medical research during World War II and the ethical rules that were developed to protect human participants in research settings in such documents as The Nuremberg Code (1947), the Declaration of Helsinki (1964), and The Belmont Report (1979).

The ethical standards themselves come next and were written in such a way that a majority of the standards potentially applied to every psychologist. This may seem obvious at first, but the 1992 revision had a slightly different approach. It contained eight sections, the first of which was titled General Standards. This was the longest section, 27 standards, that contained ethical standards applying to the professional and scientific activities of all psychologists.[7] It was followed by the remaining seven sections of the Code that presumably did not apply to all psychologists, such as Evaluation, Assessment or Intervention (containing standards only applying to those psychologists doing assessment), or Therapy (only applying to those doing therapy).

By contrast, the 2002 edition of the Ethical Standards is divided into 10 sections: (a) Resolving Ethical Issues, (b) Competence, (c) Human Relations, (d) Privacy and Confidentiality, (e) Advertising and Other Public Statements, (f) Record Keeping and Fees, (g) Education and Training, (h) Research and Publication, (i) Assessment, and (j) Therapy. The entire Forensic Activities section from the 1992 edition, consisting of six ethical standards, was deleted. However some of the substance from the standards was retained and moved to other parts of the Code. I examine the ethical standards in some detail, beginning in Chapter 4, but first I consider the five general principles, those broad concepts from which each of the 89 ethical standards are derived.

The APA Ethics Code continues to evolve as a living entity, growing more adaptive and relevant with each revision. These changes reflect legal actions and changes in the nature of complaints received by ethics committees and licensing boards as well as changes in culture, technology, and how psychological services are conceptualized and delivered. All of these changes help increase the safety and effectiveness of what psychologists have to offer, further benefitting clients and patients, students, research participants, and everyone who interacts with them.

---

[7] This lengthy standard was a catchall consisting of standards relating to competence, ethics and legal issues, informed consent, basis for scientific and professional judgments, nondiscrimination, avoiding harm, multiple roles, exploitation and sexual harassment, personal impairment, supervision, record keeping, and fees, The 2002 edition for the most part has retained these standards but has placed them under various sections in the document reflecting their content—such as Competence, Human Relations, or Record Keeping and Fees.

The General Ethical Principles of Psychologists 3

Dr. Johnson was invited by a television journalist to participate in a documentary on eating disorders in women, an area in which he had recently published a book for the general public. The journalist also requested that he bring one of his current patients who was willing to describe the ups and downs of treatment and how she had improved over time. The journalist's motive was to dispel the stigma attached to eating disorders and provide hope to the thousands in the television audience with a similar problem.

Dr. Johnson was deliberate in his response. He considered the issues of patient privacy, exploitation, coercion (could she easily decline her therapist's request?), informed consent, and the ultimate impact on treatment. He then discussed the matter with a senior clinician, who advised against it, stating that inviting a patient to participate in a media event creates a multiple-role relationship: (a) current psychotherapy patient and (b) copresenter with Dr. Johnson describing treatment successes. Dr. Johnson decided to accept the journalist's invitation to discuss his treatment of eating disorders but declined, on ethical grounds, to bring a patient. The journalist was disappointed but understood his rationale and proceeded with the interview.

Introduction

This chapter focuses on the general principles of psychologists, ethical topics that have been a part of the Ethics Code in one form or another since it was first published in 1953. "The Ethical Principles of Psychologists and Code of Conduct" (American Psychological Association [APA], 2010) consists of two sections: General Principles and Ethical Standards. The general principles may be compared to the prologue of a play, reviewing the general themes, whereas the ethical standards constitute the play itself in all of its rich detail. They consist of five broad concepts, undergirding the ethical standards: (a) Beneficence and Nonmaleficence, (b) Fidelity and Responsibility, (c) Integrity, (d) Justice, and (e) Respect for People's Rights and Dignity. The selection of these five principles reflects in part the work of Karen Kitchener, who served on the original 1986 task force that produced the 1992 revision (Kitchener, 1984).[1]

As noted in Chapter 2 of this volume, the purpose of the general principles, as originally conceived by the Ethics Code Task Force in 1992, was twofold: (a) to identify the general ethical concepts that form the philosophical foundation of all the ethical standards, or rules, of the Ethics Code of psychologists; and (b) to physically separate them from the rest of the Code so that there would be no question about which sections were aspirational and which parts required mandatory compliance (Nagy, 1992).

The general principles are voluntary in nature; that is, psychologists should ideally set their sights on these as guidelines while serving in their professional roles, but they are far too general to require compliance. The ethical standards, on the other hand, constitute the specific rules of conduct for all psychologists who are functioning in a variety of professional roles. The general principles could be thought of as "what psychologists believe," whereas the ethical standards could be thought of as "what psychologists must do." It is important to note that understanding the values and goals outlined in the general principles provides the contextual keys to unlocking the meaning and rationale for each ethical standard.

In this chapter, I first discuss the importance of using general principles to resolve possible conflicts between ethical standards. Then, I describe each of the general principles in depth.

---

[1]Following the work of Beauchamp and Childress (1979), Kitchener suggested that autonomy, beneficence, nonmaleficence, fidelity, and justice constitute the general concepts on which psychologists should base ethical decision making at the evaluative level.

Using General Principles to Resolve Conflicting Ethical Standards

A common problem for psychologists attempting to comply with the many ethical standards is encountering rules that seem to contradict each other. Occasionally ethical rules do conflict, creating a dilemma for the psychologist attempting to apply them in real-life situations. For example, psychologists are obligated to respect the autonomy of clients and at the same time protect them from harm. In the following two scenarios this causes a dilemma for the therapist.

> A 56-year-old commercial airline pilot with chronic neck pain continues to fly even though his pain medication clouds his judgment and makes him sleepy. He has not informed his employer or copilots of his medical problem but has told his psychotherapist. He refuses to acknowledge that continuing to fly may well endanger the lives of others.

> A psychotherapist makes a decision to break confidentiality to preserve the safety of his patient. The psychotherapist contacts the police to hospitalize a physically healthy patient with major depression who has just revealed his serious intention and detailed plan to drive his car over a cliff at midnight tonight.

Are there potential conflicts among the ethical standards, and if so, how are psychologists to understand and balance the values and protections inherent in them? The suicidal patient may feel that his privacy is being violated by the disclosure of his intent to kill himself to the police or the psychiatric emergency team. He may also feel that he is being harmed by having his freedom restricted by involuntary hospitalization, even though the intent of the psychologist was to preserve his life. The resolution of conflicting ethical standards is not always as immediately apparent as in this example. However, conflicts can frequently be resolved by focusing on the concept of *the greater good,* either to the individual or to society.

In the case of the suicidal patient, it is clearly more urgent to take steps that would prevent an imminent suicide than it is to protect patient confidentiality in psychotherapy, despite the patient's right to privacy and autonomous decision making. The first case is more complex, however, because it involves a psychologist's duty or right to break confidentiality when his or her patient's conduct is likely to endanger others and involves legal statutes and contractual issues as well. This becomes more apparent in later chapters, as I focus on the specific ethical standards and how they complement or, at times, contradict each other.

Psychologists rely heavily on the Ethical Standards section of the APA Ethics Code because it articulates the actual rules that they must follow. These are divided into 10 sections: (a) Resolving Ethical Issues, (b) Competence, (c) Human Relations, (d) Privacy and Confidentiality, (e) Advertising and Other Public Statements, (f) Record Keeping and Fees, (g) Education and Training, (h) Research and Publication, (i) Assessment, and (j) Therapy. Each section consists of the specific "musts" and "must nots" that direct psychologists in carrying out their work. Although this section of the document is titled Ethical Standards, it is something of a misnomer, and it should be thought of instead as a *code of conduct.* The actual rules that make up this section are directives, such as documenting clinical work, cooperating with an ethics committee investigation, or maintaining patient confidentiality. They are not true ethical concepts as psychologists have come to think of them, however, such as integrity, justice, or respect for people's rights and dignity. Those are within the realm of the general principles and, as mentioned, provide the general context and guidance for the code of conduct. Thus, the general principles are a means of assisting in ethical decision making and serve as general guidelines in the face of conflicting ethical standards.

Although some psychologists may not be aware of this, when joining the APA they immediately become duty bound to comply with every ethical standard and are so notified on their annual billing statement. Furthermore, well over half of the states have incorporated the APA Ethics Code in the body of their mental health code or practice rules and regulations, requiring every licensed psychologist to abide by them, whether or not they are members of the APA. I now examine the general principles and how they orient psychologists to the overall topics that are so important in the profession of psychology.

General Ethical Principles of Psychologists

The ethical standards might be thought of as the "floor" in the house of ethics, stating the minimal standards of compliance, whereas the general principles can be seen as the "ceiling." In the general principles that follow, it is interesting to note the nature of the language used, which asks psychologists to "exercise reasonable judgment," "take care," be "concerned," and be "alert to," words and phrases that rarely appear in the ethical standards themselves.

PRINCIPLE A: BENEFICENCE AND NONMALEFICENCE

Psychologists strive to benefit those with whom they work and take care to do no harm. In their professional actions, psychologists seek to safeguard the welfare and rights of those with whom they interact professionally and other affected persons, and the welfare of animal subjects of research. When conflicts occur among psychologists' obligations or concerns, they attempt to resolve these conflicts in a responsible fashion that avoids or minimizes harm. Because psychologists' scientific and professional judgments and actions may affect the lives of others, they are alert to and guard against personal, financial, social, organizational, or political factors that might lead to misuse of their influence. Psychologists strive to be aware of the possible effect of their own physical and mental health on their ability to help those with whom they work. (APA, 2010)

The first general principle, Beneficence and Nonmaleficence, has long been a tenet of ethical codes in the helping professions. Loosely translated from Latin, *beneficence* means helping or assisting from the Latin *bene,* meaning well or favorably, and *facere,* to make or do—literally, to do good. *Nonmaleficence* means avoiding harming others in the course of carrying out one's professional work from the Latin *non,* meaning not, and *male,* meaning badly or ill. Beginning with the Hippocratic oath in the 4th century BCE, health care practitioners have been attempting to balance competing demands in helping their patients and clients and avoiding harming them.

An example is training a psychotherapist to competently establish a working alliance with a patient while at the same time prohibiting a friendship or romantic relationship from developing, lest the psychologist lose his or her objectivity and, ultimately, his or her competence. In this case, it is important for the therapist to always balance the personal relationship with the professional one. This is an ongoing part of clinical work that could be said to form the essence of the artistry and science of psychotherapy. Or consider the supervisor who must balance training his or her supervisee with the welfare of the client being treated in psychotherapy. In some cases the patient might be better served by consulting a more experienced therapist, but with competent supervision of the training therapist, the treatment will likely progress satisfactorily. However, if the supervisor is lax in his or her duties, then both the training therapist and the client could be harmed.

Psychologists are supposed to be aware of personal, financial, social, organizational, or political factors that might lead to misusing their power or influence. In most professional settings there is a power differential—those on the receiving end are clients, patients, supervisees, students, or research participants, to name a few. Psychologists may, at times, be tempted to use their power or authority unfairly under the guise of helping or training, for example.

Returning to the vignette at the start of this chapter, the inherent power differential in the therapist–patient relationship could result in the psychologist easily persuading a current patient with an eating disorder to appear on a television talk show. However, he may be unfairly leveraging his authority if he makes no attempt to disguise her identity or discuss the potential risks of such an appearance at the outset. These risks might include such things as feeling pressure to perform in front of the camera; losing her anonymity and exposing her private thoughts to family members, neighbors, friends, and coworkers who might be watching; and experiencing a change in the relationship with her therapist that lasts long after the on-camera interview, perhaps permanently changing the therapy dynamics. However, the patient may feel she has little choice in the matter if her therapist asks her to "volunteer" to participate in the broadcast. Although the apparent motive might be to educate the public about this difficult disorder, the psychologist's additional motive might also be to promote his own clinical practice, thereby obtaining free publicity for his eating disorders practice.

Psychologists are also supposed to be mindful of problems with their own physical and mental health and how their problems could impact others. It is useful to consider the therapist with chronic back pain necessitating medication that tends to dull the person's awareness. How effective will the therapist be in carrying out diagnostic testing or listening carefully to the more challenging therapy client, such as a divorced father with major depression who is having difficulty parenting his autistic child? Psychologists are subject to the same human frailties as anyone else. The competence of an otherwise excellent supervisor, teacher, or therapist could be significantly affected by a chronic medical condition, medication, sleep deprivation, or major life stress, such as the death of a family member, divorce, or financial adversity. Therapist competence and personal impairment are discussed more fully in Chapter 4 of this volume.

PRINCIPLE B: FIDELITY AND RESPONSIBILITY

> Psychologists establish relationships of trust with those with whom they work. They are aware of their professional and scientific responsibilities to society and to the specific communities in which they work. Psychologists uphold professional standards of conduct, clarify their professional roles and obligations, accept appropriate responsibility for their behavior, and seek to manage conflicts of interest that could lead to exploitation or harm. Psychologists consult with, refer to, or cooperate with other professionals and institutions to the extent needed to serve the best interests of those with whom they work. They are concerned about the ethical compliance of their colleagues' scientific and professional conduct. Psychologists strive to contribute a portion of their professional time for little or no compensation or personal advantage. (APA, 2010)

The second general principle, Fidelity and Responsibility, consists of two concepts. Fidelity, from the Latin *fidelis,* meaning faithful, refers to the trust and commitment that psychologists hold toward those with whom they work. It may also refer to how faithfully psychologists translate the ethical principles into their every day professional conduct as therapists, teachers, and researchers. The concept of responsibility, from the Latin *respondere,* meaning to answer, refers to individual accountability on the part of psychologists. Psychologists must ultimately answer for the consequences of their actions in the various roles they play with consumers, students, and supervisees.

Fidelity and responsibility may also include the notion of informed consent. This has long been an important concept for psychologists, requiring them to explain in advance to clients, patients, and other recipients of their services how they intend to intervene in their lives. Those who are about to consult a psychologist for the first time generally have a minimal concept of what to expect concerning such basics as fees, an approximate duration of treatment, and theoretical orientation, and they would welcome some clarification and information.

Psychologists consulting with school systems or business entities are also expected to provide some manner of informed consent about their intended services. They are responsible for making good on their word, that is, for carrying through on commitments, usually spelled out in a letter of agreement or contract, explaining the nature of the fiduciary relationship.

Also included in Fidelity and Responsibility is managing conflicts of interest, lest individuals, groups, or society be harmed by psychologists' actions or failure to act. It is useful to consider the situation in which a man experiencing depression and rage because he has recently lost his job confides to his therapist that he has an impulse to get revenge on his former boss by murdering him. Must the therapist protect the client in treatment and shield him from any consequences of revealing his disclosures to a third party such as the police or the intended victim? Or does the psychologist owe a duty to society when such destructive intentions are revealed, and should the psychologist take some action that would risk ending the therapeutic relationship and potentially harming the patient? This kind of conflict of interest is regulated by law in many states, and therapists have specific rules, which they must follow to resolve such a conflict. This is further examined in Chapter 6.

Other conflicts may be less clear. It is useful to consider the marital therapist who is treating a real estate agent and her husband and is also in the market for a new house. By relying on the wife's occasional input and assistance in the local realty market, the therapist may be tempted to form an alliance with her that might decrease his objectivity with this couple and make him less able to accept the husband's point of view in the therapy sessions. Clearly the husband could feel harmed in this instance by being in a "one-down" situation.

This general principle also advises therapists to serve the best interests of others and be ready to refer them to other professionals and institutions as needed. This includes other health care professionals (e.g., psychopharmacologist, neuropsychological examiner) or other resources (e.g., group therapy, Alcoholics Anonymous) as needed.

Part of serving the best interests of others involves monitoring one's professional colleagues' adherence to high ethical standards. In this sense, psychologists are "their brother's keepers" and should make an attempt to address ethical infractions by others, either by directly contacting the psychologist or possibly by some other means. Choosing the right intervention, particularly with a colleague who may be unapproachable, feel threatened, be self-righteous, or be adversarial, may be particularly challenging. Yet failing to take any action would likely not be in keeping with the spirit of this principle and might result in harm to patients and clients later on. If Dr. Green discovered that a colleague was going online to a social networking site and revealing some details of his successful therapy experiences with certain clients, then Dr. Green should tell him about the significance of these potential breaches in confidentiality and potential harm to those clients.

Finally, serving the best interests of clients might at times include offering services to consumers at no cost. Although this is not an absolute requirement (true of all these general principles), it is recommended that in certain situations psychologists offer their professional contribution without regard to fee or personal compensation. This is of great potential benefit to financially disadvantaged clients and patients, schools with less financial resources, nonprofit organizations, and other entities that could benefit from psychological services but do not have the ready means to pay for them.

PRINCIPLE C: INTEGRITY

> Psychologists seek to promote accuracy, honesty, and truthfulness in the science, teaching, and practice of psychology. In these activities psychologists do not steal, cheat, or engage in fraud, subterfuge, or intentional misrepresentation of fact. Psychologists strive to keep their promises and to avoid unwise or unclear commitments. In situations in which deception may be ethically justifiable to maximize benefits and minimize harm, psychologists have a serious obligation to consider the need for, the possible consequences of, and their responsibility to correct any resulting mistrust or other harmful effects that arise from the use of such techniques. (APA, 2010)

Integrity is defined as "the quality of being honest and morally upright" (Compact Oxford English Dictionary, 2009). It is derived from the Latin *integritas,* meaning soundness, purity, honesty, or innocence. The original *Ethical Standards of Psychologists* published in 1953 contained a standard that included some of these concepts; it was titled Moral and Legal Standards, and it emphasized psychologists' adherence to "the social codes and moral expectations of the community in which he works" (APA, 1953a). It warned psychologists that failure to do so could "involve his clients, students, or colleagues in damaging personal conflicts" that might "impugn his own name and the reputation of his profession." It is interesting that the word *moral* can no longer be found in the 2002 psychology Ethics Code.

As this principle elaborates, the concept of integrity includes promoting accuracy, honesty, and truthfulness in every psychological role, whether in the area of teaching, carrying out research, or applied psychology (e.g., assessment, psychotherapy, management consulting). Practicing with integrity means avoiding deceiving others or misrepresenting facts that psychologists are aware of or should be aware of in the course of carrying out their duties. This principle also prohibits subterfuge, such as deliberately using deception to achieve a private goal. It is useful to consider the psychologist who bills a patient's insurance company for a psychotherapy session that did not happen (the patient forgot), claiming that it occurred. He might feel entitled to extra payment because there had been many telephone calls from the patient between office visits that did not qualify for reimbursement. However, this general ethical principle would prohibit such a fraudulent practice because the psychologist deliberately misstates the facts, which is unethical to be sure, and this case also constitutes insurance fraud, which is illegal.

In some cases, a breach of the principle of integrity might result in harming others. An example is the researcher who at the outset withholds information from prospective participants in a research study. The protocol may involve experiences that could provoke feelings of anxiety or anger, such as viewing graphic or violent images, with a hypothesis regarding the impact of limbic system arousal on memory and cognitive functioning. However, the investigator might neglect to include a statement in the informed consent document describing the possible range of visual stimuli to which participants would be exposed or the possible emotional reactions that might be elicited, fearing that such information might discourage people from volunteering. The possibility of harm from this deliberate deception would increase if a participant happened to have a preexisting mood disorder, a history of childhood abuse, or some other traumatic experience (e.g., experience as a soldier who fought in a war) that could elicit panicky feelings or dissociative reactions during the exposure to such powerful visual stimuli. Investigators have an obligation to provide accurate informed consent at the outset of psychological research, and to deliberately omit or misrepresent facts that would make a difference to one's decision to participate is in violation of the spirit of this ethical principle. Research conducted in universities, hospitals, and other institutional settings usually afford protections against these abuses by requiring approval of research protocols by the institutional review board.

Psychologists must also keep their promises and avoid commitments that are unwise or vague in nature. If a psychotherapist working in a group practice agrees to be on call for a particular weekend, the psychologist has a fiduciary responsibility to both his or her colleagues in the practice and the needy clients and patients who might require services on that particular weekend. The psychologist must honor this obligation or delegate the responsibility to another once he or she has made the commitment. An example of an unclear commitment follows.

> A psychologist who also happens to be a Catholic priest has agreed to see a member of his congregation who has admitted to molesting a 9-year-old child over the past few years. He reassures the man that he will consult with him in confidence and that a religious approach to pederasty offers the highest chances of success.
>
> It is also clear, however, that as a licensed psychologist he is required by state law to notify the child protective services of the county in which he practices within 24 hr of learning that his patient has sexually molested a child.
>
> It may be unclear whether he is planning to work with the man as his priest, who has learned of the molestation in the confessional, or as his psychologist, who learned of it in the consulting office. In any case, vague or unclear reassurances at the outset, particularly if the man relapses into old patterns of child sexual assault, are not helpful to the client, his future victims, or ultimately, the priest-psychologist himself. Fully clarifying one's role at the beginning of treatment, including confidentiality and its exceptions, is essential in maintaining clear commitments.

The principle of integrity also addresses situations in which it is ethically justifiable to use deception to maximize benefits and minimize harm. For example, a psychologist may wish to preserve the naiveté of research participants to maximize the robustness of research findings. This is done by deceiving research participants about the research hypothesis being tested while providing informed consent, lest they consciously or unconsciously provide biased responses in their role as subjects. An example is informing participants that the purpose of an investigation is to measure the effects of fatigue on short-term memory and varying the amount of sleep they are allowed to have the night before. However, the research might actually be assessing how social pressure by an authority figure impacts on decision making. It could employ the services of a confederate research assistant (an actor) who administers the test items and then behaves differently with different subjects, according to the protocol, to influence their responses to test items. The research participants would thus remain naive until the end of the data gathering and be debriefed at that point.

Deception may be used under certain circumstances; however, the investigator must never deceive prospective participants about any experiences they are likely to have that would affect their willingness to volunteer for the project.

PRINCIPLE D: JUSTICE

> Psychologists recognize that fairness and justice entitle all persons
> to access to and benefit from the contributions of psychology and
> to equal quality in the processes, procedures, and services being
> conducted by psychologists. Psychologists exercise reasonable
> judgment and take precautions to ensure that their potential biases,
> the boundaries of their competence, and the limitations of their
> expertise do no lead to or condone unjust practices. (APA, 2010)

Unlike the other general principles, *justice* usually finds application
more generally in the legal arena than elsewhere. Taken from the Latin
justitia, meaning justice or equality, this concept has been defined as
follows in legal settings: "1) fairness. 2) moral rightness. 3) a scheme or
system of law in which every person receives his/her due from the system,
including all rights, both natural and legal" (from http://dictionary.law.
com/default2.asp?selected=1086&bold=lllll).

As applied to psychology, justice requires that everyone has the
same access to and is entitled to the same benefits from the contributions
that psychology has to offer our culture. Specifically, the burden is on
psychologists who teach, do research, and provide therapy and consultation to honor this principle by doing what they can to maximize their
accessibility to the general public. This might be accomplished by offering
a range of services, extending from individualized counseling and teaching to activities that might have a bearing on society at large, such as
working in the media or in administrative or governmental settings in
which decision making and policy development could have major implications for large numbers of people. It might also have a bearing on the
researcher to promulgate the results of his or her study that would be
helpful to disadvantaged groups. Such research might have application
to those who are economically or educationally underprivileged, such
as those living in public housing, who generally would not have access
to this information.

It is useful to consider the school psychologist working in an inner
city high school with a high percentage of ethnic minority students and
a high dropout rate. The psychologist would have a moral obligation to
attempt to provide psychological services—testing, counseling, developing individual education plans, and more—for all students, regardless
of ethnicity, gender, values, or socioeconomic status. Although the
psychologist might find that students who are more compliant, gifted,
or verbal may be easier to work with, he or she would be obliged to also
attempt to help those who have developmental disorders (e.g., Asperger's
syndrome), drug addiction, or mental illness. The Ethics Code does not
require a psychologist to take on overwhelming challenges, but it would
demand that the person at least make an attempt to offer his or her
services to every student equally, regardless of personal values, cultural
differences, or biases (within her area of competence, of course).

Also, this principle asks psychologists to consider a broad overview—organizational or political factors that may diminish the availability of psychological services to all. For example, if there were a systematic bias in the school administration against students who were Latino, the school psychologist should do what he or she can to raise awareness of this fact among the faculty and administration and to begin to encourage changes that would benefit Latino students, such as recruiting bilingual teachers or counselors.

The psychologist who also sits on a school board or plays an active role in state politics may have even a greater opportunity to effect policies that impact many people. Proposing initiatives that fund programs for disadvantaged students might constitute a way of actively applying the tenets of justice. Or more broadly, supporting political initiatives that would promote the psychological welfare of those in lower socioeconomic groups would also meet the spirit of this general principle (e.g., initiating and funding after-school programs for students in primary and middle school). In short, the concept of justice is not restricted to the individual conduct of a psychologist who is personally rendering psychological services to a consumer. The ramifications include the impact a psychologist can have on society at large as well.

PRINCIPLE E: RESPECT FOR PEOPLE'S RIGHTS AND DIGNITY

> Psychologists respect the dignity and worth of all people, and the rights of individuals to privacy, confidentiality, and self-determination. Psychologists are aware that special safeguards may be necessary to protect the rights and welfare of persons or communities whose vulnerabilities impair autonomous decision making. Psychologists are aware of and respect cultural, individual, and role differences, including those based on age, gender, gender identity, race, ethnicity, culture, national origin, religion, sexual orientation, disability, language, and socioeconomic status, and consider these factors when working with members of such groups. Psychologists try to eliminate the effect on their work of biases based on those factors, and they do not knowingly participate in or condone activities of others based upon such prejudices. (APA, 2010)

Respecting the rights and dignity of people might best be summarized by the concept of *autonomy*, defined as having "the quality or state of being self-governing" (from http://unabridged.merriam-webster.com/cgi-bin/collegiate?va=autonomy). And *dignity*, from the Latin *dignus*, meaning worthy, along with respecting others' rights, can best be understood as honoring others' right to self-determination.

One of the ways that psychologists facilitate self-determination rests in protecting others' privacy and confidentiality once they have begun a professional relationship. Privacy is a right of Americans that was alluded to in the U.S. Constitution since its adoption in 1787, and the concept has been refined and expanded by judicial decisions ever since. Confidentiality, on the other hand, pertains to the legal and ethical obligation by psychologists to refuse to promulgate or release any information about others acquired in the course of their work. This obligation also extends to judicial settings (e.g., court) in which psychologists must never reveal information about clients and patients unless compelled to do so by a valid subpoena, court order, or authorization by the patient him- or herself. This is particularly important in litigious situations, such as divorcing spouses engaged in the process of child custody evaluation or an employee injured at work who is suing his former employer. In each of these situations, the psychologist who has a litigant as a patient must be aware of the confidentiality obligation and prepared to encounter attempts by other parties involved in the litigation to obtain private information contained in the psychologist's clinical records (i.e., by means of a subpoena or a court order).

There are occasions when psychologists might have to initiate safeguards to help ensure the autonomy and safety of individuals or communities. This is reflected in cultural, individual, and role differences as well as a lengthy list of human attributes that describes the vulnerabilities in today's society in which one's personal rights and access to legal protections may be threatened. The list, as it appears in the principle, consists of the following 12 categories:

- age (e.g., children and adolescents below the age of majority, older people),
- gender (e.g., male or female),
- gender identity (e.g., how one views oneself—male or female—regardless of genotype),
- race (e.g., physical traits, skin or hair color),
- ethnicity (e.g., shared cultural traits, such as Asian or Hispanic, regardless of national origin),
- culture (e.g., shared beliefs, customs, arts, practices, achievements, and social behavior of a particular nation or people, such as Caribbean or Native American),
- national origin (e.g., Japan, Mexico),
- religion (e.g., Roman Catholic, Muslim, Buddhist, Jewish),
- sexual orientation (e.g., heterosexual, lesbian, gay, bisexual),
- disability (e.g., physical or psychological impairment such as being blind or deaf or having a mental disability),
- language (e.g., native language or sophistication in comprehension and use—education level), and
- socioeconomic status (e.g., income level, social class).

This general principle requires that psychologists examine their own prejudices and blind spots concerning each of these 12 areas and pursue ongoing education to broaden awareness as needed. Furthermore, they are required to take corrective action to eliminate or reduce possible negative effects on those with whom they work. In some cases, this might involve referring the client or patient to another psychologist who has more expertise in the area in question.

It is useful to consider the training supervisor of a lesbian psychology intern who has never worked closely in a professional relationship with a gay woman before. The supervisor may find in the course of the emerging supervisory relationship that he unconsciously attributes values and attitudes to the intern that reflect his own bias. He may assume that she holds a negative view toward men and therefore would be less likely to be successful with male clients or less able to maintain her objectivity in marriage counseling. He may also believe that she is prone to amorphous sexual boundaries that might result in seductive behavior toward female colleagues and patients, with or without her awareness. Obviously, either of these beliefs or assumptions could profoundly affect the quality of supervision and could result in depriving the trainee of her right to impartial and competent supervision of her professional work. These beliefs also may demean her as a person and detract from her worth as a clinician and a colleague. What sort of reference letter could this supervisor provide when his trainee is applying for work, given his stereotypical prejudices against her as a member of the lesbian community?

Or consider the psychologist who works in the inpatient unit of the state psychiatric facility where abuse of patients is a persistent problem. This could include any of the following: substandard mental health care, improper monitoring of medications, patient neglect, verbal abuse, physical abuse, improper health care (e.g., provision of dental care without proper analgesia), improper restraints (e.g., shackling or otherwise inappropriately restraining patients), sexual harassment and sexual assault, or other indignities. A pattern of neglect and abuse of inpatients could be seen by some as acceptable predicated on the assumption that inpatients are not entitled to the same competent and humane treatment that others would be, say, in an outpatient clinic. This is clearly a bias or belief that could lead to a variety of demeaning and inhumane practices. A psychologist working in such a setting has the obligation not only to eschew participation in abusive practices but also to avoid condoning such acts by others by turning a blind eye. The psychologist is expected to take steps, if possible, to call attention to any violations of the ethical standards and patients' rights as he or she learns of them in the hospital. To continue working in such a setting without taking some corrective action or attempting to publicize ethical, legal, and relevant institutional obligations is tantamount to condoning the abuses.

Psychologists commonly rely more on the ethical standards than the general principles in the course of their work because they are likely to have had more formal instruction about the former. Also, the ethical standards usually form the basis of the ruminations by ethics committees and courts when adjudicating complaints. However, psychologists should always strive to deepen their understanding of the broad values espoused by the five introductory concepts of the Ethics Code, the general principles. The remainder of the book examines how these values become transformed into rules of conduct that address all the roles played by psychologists.

GENERAL ETHICAL CONCEPTS APPLICABLE TO ALL PSYCHOLOGISTS

II

This section discusses the four general concepts of competence, informed consent, avoiding harm and exploitation, and confidentiality. In particular, chapters in this section explain how these concepts broadly apply to the work of psychologists who are engaged in almost any professional role, including therapist, researcher, supervisor, or professor. Although the relevant ethical standards may vary in application depending on the setting and the nature of the professional relationship, they have a direct bearing on mandating and prohibiting behavior by psychologists who carry out their professional responsibilities in a variety of situations.

Competence | 4

A recently licensed school psychologist opened a private office in the county adjacent to the primary and second schools in which she worked. In addition to providing services to children, she developed an interest in offering marital therapy to troubled couples, even though she had received no formal training. She had, however, consulted with many parents about their adolescent children in the course of her work in the schools and had taken an online seminar on marital therapy.

One day a woman telephoned her about her husband who had recently lost his job as an auto mechanic and had begun drinking heavily every night. She met with the couple for several weeks, attempting to treat the husband's alcohol dependency. She sided with his wife in lecturing him about the destructiveness of drinking and urged him to use "willpower" to stop his addictive behavior. In the middle of the third session the man suddenly stood up, declared that he was "tired of being ganged up on by two crazy women!" and walked out of the session, never to return.

The psychologist realized at that point that she did not have the skills to treat such a couple; she had never addressed the husband's depression about not working and had never considered the wife's contribution to the marital problems. She had also failed to consider options for treating his addiction, such as referral to an addictions counselor, a rehabilitation program, or Alcoholics Anonymous. She realized that to "retread" from school psychology to clinical work would require a substantial amount of academic training and supervision; instead, she decided to focus her energy on her work as a school psychologist, for which she was competently trained.

Introduction

Clinical competence has been defined as "the habitual and judicious use of communication, knowledge, technical skills, clinical reasoning, emotions, values, and reflection in daily practice for the benefit of the individual and community being served" (Epstein & Hundert, 2002, p. 226). By remaining within one's field of competence, psychologists maximize the odds of making positive changes in the lives of those with whom they interact in psychotherapy, supervision, research, and other settings. Conversely, going beyond one's area of competence increases the chance of harming others. Examples of the latter are failing to provide the kind of treatment that is needed, failing to recognize the urgency of a potentially dangerous situation (e.g., a patient disclosing his intent to harm a third party or a research participant who becomes suicidal), and providing substandard clinical supervision.

More recently, in applied psychology, there has been an emphasis on the concept of evidence-based approaches.[1] Even since the earliest days of psychology, with the establishment of the first psychological clinic in 1896, clinical competence has been linked to an evidence-based approach to patient care, requiring psychologists to base their interventions on relevant clinical experiences or research (American Psychological Association [APA] Presidential Task Force on Evidence-Based Practice, 2006). The intent was not to inhibit creative interventions with clients and patients but to reduce the likelihood of idiosyncratic or self-serving behavior that might possibly harm recipients of their services while maximizing interventions likely to be effective. A neophyte therapist might have confidence that his creative clinical strategy for a new patient with social phobia constitutes the best treatment because it helped him to get over his own social anxiety in past years. In a sense, this approach would be evidence based because the therapist has the evidence of his own experience to rely on. However, he is lacking clinical experience with other patients with the same diagnosis, and he is failing to rely on evidence-based interventions in diagnosing and treating this particular patient. His approach—relying on his own personal experience—may differ little from advice that one friend might give to another under similar circumstances.

Competence is one of the standards that is commonly cited when ethics complaints are brought against psychologists. There are many ways for a psychologist to demonstrate incompetence:

---

[1]Other names for evidence-based practice are *empirically supported treatments, empirically supported therapy,* and *empirically based interventions.*

- A chemical dependency counselor could improperly evaluate a depressed alcoholic male with a history of suicide attempts and fail to hospitalize him when needed (clinical incompetence).
- A therapist could misinterpret an Asian woman's avoidance of eye contact as a sign of deception or withholding and change the therapy strategy accordingly, thus alienating an already anxious client (incompetence in multicultural assessment).
- A marital therapist could befriend the wife in a couple he was treating as they move toward divorce and invite her to go for a walk with him on a Friday afternoon after work (incompetence in maintaining proper boundaries).
- A researcher may understate the risk of psychological distress on the consent form in hopes of obtaining a greater number of participants for his study (incompetence in providing adequate informed consent).
- A psychologist appearing on television may overstate the value of his innovative treatment for addiction to Internet pornography (incompetence in media presentations).

In each of these situations the psychologist has failed to meet the minimally acceptable standard to carry out psychological work with adequate skill, ability, or efficiency. And as a result, an individual—the patient, patient's spouse, research participant, or television viewer—could have been harmed.

How do psychologists cope with such an all-embracing standard as competence in the great diversity of professional roles that they play? Does a doctoral degree from a regionally accredited university or professional school of psychology necessarily confer competence on an individual aiming for a career in management consulting or carrying out research? And for psychotherapists who are just beginning their careers, how does the concept of evidence-based practice help define competence in the field of health care?

In answering these questions, one should consider the different roles played by psychologists—researcher, teacher, supervisor, therapist, evaluator, consultant, forensic specialist, case manager, and administrator, to name a few. In each role, maintaining competence is an ongoing process rather than a static goal based on knowledge learned during initial training. Maintaining competence is in a constant state of flux and renewal—to be created and recreated on a daily basis.

Furthermore, a psychologist's competence in any role is vulnerable to the effects of stress and life events (e.g., illness, changes in mental health, major life transitions such as divorce or deaths of loved ones) that can impair his or her ability to function adequately. It can be argued that psychologists have an ethical imperative to maintain both their professional competence and their personal mental health at all times or to take steps that would remedy the situation (Norcross & Guy, 2007). These steps might include participating in educational and growth-promoting activities such as reading books and professional journals, attending seminars and other educational activities (e.g., lectures, hospital grand rounds, online continuing education, psychological convention workshops and presentations) obtaining individual or group consultation, or seeking psychotherapy.

In the remainder of this chapter, I examine four areas of competence that psychologists must master: (a) achieving and maintaining their competence while in their professional role, (b) keeping within their boundaries of competence and limitations of their techniques, (c) maintaining competence in matters of human diversity in practice and research, and (d) protecting others' welfare when standards of competence are lacking.

Achieving and Maintaining Competence

Those aspiring to become psychotherapists commonly complete doctoral studies at a regionally accredited institution, follow their studies with a period of clinical supervision and/or internship, pass the examination for professional practice in psychology, and show evidence of a thorough working knowledge of the state laws affecting clinical practice.[2] After completing these steps one may then become licensed to publicly refer to oneself as a psychologist, to engage in activities that are commonly understood to be psychological in nature, and to offer professional services to the public for a fee. Such services include individual or group psychotherapy, marital therapy, assessment, forensic activities, clinical supervision of trainees, and management consulting.

Those working in academic or health care settings as teachers, researchers, administrators, or in some other nonclinical capacity would not normally need to obtain a psychology license. Although not directly offering clinical or consultation services to the public and billing for those services, they must still be mindful of maintaining competence in their chosen area.

---

[2]The APA allows its members to claim a doctoral degree from a nonregionally accredited institution only if it serves as the basis for licensure in the state. This means that a psychologist who wishes to move to a different state at some point may not use the title *Dr.* in the new state if his or her degree is from a nonregionally accredited institution of learning. It is possible for a professional school of psychology or university to be licensed by a particular state but at the same time fail to meet the standards of the regional accrediting body, such as the North Central Association of Schools and Colleges or the Western Association of Schools and Colleges.

EVIDENCE-BASED PRACTICE

Evidence-based practice in psychology is an integration of science and practice and has become an important goal in current health care systems and health care policy. It primarily pertains to clinical practice and was defined by the APA Presidential Task Force on Evidence-Based Practice (2006) as the integration of the best available research with clinical expertise within the context of patient characteristics, including culture, values, and preferences. This definition grew from a similar concept formulated by the Institute of Medicine (2001) and has as its purpose to "promote effective psychological practice and enhance public health by applying empirically supported principles of psychological assessment, case formulation, therapeutic relationship, and intervention" (APA Presidential Task Force on Evidence-Based Practice, 2006, p. 34).

The APA Presidential Task Force on Evidence-Based Practice considered "best available research" to include scientific results derived from intervention strategies, assessment, clinical problems, and patient populations in both laboratory and field settings as well as clinically relevant results of basic research in psychology and related fields. The report spells out eight components of clinical expertise:

- assessment, diagnostic judgment, systematic case formulation, and treatment planning (e.g., accurate diagnostic judgments, setting goals and tasks appropriate to the patient);
- clinical decision making, treatment implementation, and monitoring of patient progress (e.g., skill and flexibility, tact, timing, pacing, framing of interventions, balancing consistency of interventions with responsiveness to patient feedback, monitoring progress);
- interpersonal expertise (e.g., forming a therapeutic relationship, encoding and decoding verbal and nonverbal responses, creating realistic and positive expectations, empathy);
- continual self-reflection and acquisition of skills (e.g. capacity to reflect on one's own experience, knowledge, hypotheses, emotional reactions, and behaviors; awareness of limits of knowledge, skills, and biases affecting one's work);
- evaluation and use of research evidence in both basic and applied psychological science (e.g., having an understanding of research methodology, validity, and reliability; being open to data, clinical hypothesis generation; and having the capacity to use theory to guide interventions);
- understanding the influence of individual, cultural, and contextual differences on treatment (e.g., individual, social, and cultural variables, including age, development, ethnicity, culture, race, gender, sexual orientation, religious commitments, and socioeconomic status);

■ seeking available resources as needed (e.g., seeking consultation, recommending adjunctive or alternative services when needed, acquiring cultural sensitivity); and having a cogent rationale for clinical strategies (e.g., a planful approach to treatment of psychological problems, reliance on the therapist's well-articulated case formulation concerning the client or patient, reliance on relevant research supporting the effectiveness of a certain treatment if it exists).

To date, the majority of treatments that qualify as evidence-based practice in psychology are the cognitive–behavioral treatments, ranging from 60% to 90% of available interventions (Norcross, 2004).

PRACTICE GUIDELINES

Growing from the foundation of evidence-based practice, the APA has developed professional guidelines and statements, in addition to the Ethics Code, that apply to those offering direct services as well as those who teach or do research. These guidelines and statements are generally aspirational in nature. Unlike the ethical standards, with which psychologists must comply, these guidelines offer psychologists help and practical advice in competently carrying out their daily work in a variety of situations. They do not raise or lower the bar established by the Ethics Code; they simply flesh it out, going into far more detail than an ethics code ever could or should. Although there may be no penalty for a therapist's failing to comply with a specific guideline, the therapist may wish to carefully consider any deviation and have a well-developed rationale for doing so if ever questioned later, particularly in a forensic setting.

The practice guidelines are all published by the APA, APA divisions, or APA committees, and many are available online at http://www.apa.org/practice/guidelines/index.aspx. They are periodically revised and updated, reflecting changes in American culture, demographics, and laws, as well as the nature of psychological practice.[3]

■ *Guidelines for Child Custody Evaluations in Family Law Proceedings* (2009),
■ *Guidelines for the Evaluation of Dementia and Age-Related Cognitive Decline* (1998),
■ *Guidelines for Psychological Evaluations in Child Protection Matters* (1999),

---

[3]Additional resources for members at large are as follows: *APA Disaster Response Network Member Guidelines* (2005), *Criteria for Evaluating Treatment Guidelines* (2002), *Criteria for the Evaluation of Quality Improvement Programs and the Use of Quality Improvement Data* (2008), *Criteria for Practice Guideline Development and Evaluation* (2002), *Statement on the Disclosure of Test Data* (1996), and *Statement on Services by Telephone, Teleconferencing, and Internet* (1997).

- *Guidelines for Psychological Practice With Girls and Women* (2007),
- *Guidelines for Psychological Practice With Older Adults* (2004),
- *Guidelines for Psychotherapy With Lesbian, Gay, and Bisexual Clients* (2000),
- *Guidelines on Multicultural Education, Training, Research, Practice, and Organizational Change for Psychologists* (2003),
- *Guidelines Regarding the Use of Nondoctoral Personnel in Clinical Neuropsychological Assessment* (2006),
- *Record-Keeping Guidelines* (2007), *and*
- *Specialty Guidelines for Forensic Psychology* (2008).[4]

RESEARCH, PUBLICATION, AND INSTITUTIONAL REVIEW BOARDS

There are more ethical standards addressing research and publication activities and than in any other section of the APA Ethics Code. These standards provide rules and guidance in the areas of planning research, informed consent, inducements to research participants for volunteering, deception, debriefing, animal research, reporting results, publication credit, plagiarism, sharing research data, and reviewing grant proposals.

Researchers are obliged to comply with ethical standards in planning and carrying out investigations and also in the use of research assistants. In addition, the scientific aspects of the design and implementation of the study, investigators must be fastidious about how they interact with human participants, providing thorough informed consent at the outset, avoiding harming them, considering alternatives to deception, debriefing, providing results, and other matters (U.S. Department of Health and Human Services, National Institutes of Health, 1996). In addition to complying with ethical standards, investigators working in hospitals or universities must also submit their research proposals to their institutional review board before proceeding. These topics are addressed in Chapter 11.

An example of an ethical dilemma is the therapist who desires to do clinical research with patients currently in treatment. This poses a conflict of interest because the two roles have potentially opposing goals. As a scientist, the investigator's responsibility is to gather data and make new discoveries by carrying out research in accordance with the best possible protocol. However, as a therapist, the psychologist's primary role is to offer the best possible care to the participant (in this case, patients; Sales & Lavin, 2000). If therapist–researchers decide to recruit clients to become participants in research, they must exercise caution to avoid placing their roles as therapist and researcher in conflict out of

---

[4]This guideline was being revised when the current volume went to press.

their desire to achieve a research goal that might not be in the clients' best interests. The best way to avoid this potential conflict of interest is by recruiting clients and patients who have no direct relationship with the therapist–researcher; ideally, the therapist should not be conducting research with his or her own patients.

ACADEMIA AND TRAINING SETTINGS

Psychologists in teaching settings at the high school, undergraduate, and graduate school levels instruct, train, and supervise students as they progress through various developmental stages of their education. They may bring the first exposure to the formal study of human and animal behavior to students. The APA's (2005) *National Standards for High School Psychology Curricula* is a detailed compendium of suggested content areas to be covered in psychology courses at the secondary school level. With a focus on sound research methodology for generating a database, this document describes four principle topical areas: (a) cognitive (learning, memory, individual differences), (b) developmental (life span development, personality and assessment), (c) biopsychological (sensation and perception, motivation and emotion, stress, health), and (d) variations in individual and group behavior (diagnosis and treatment of psychological disorders, social and cultural issues).

At both the undergraduate and graduate levels, the teaching of psychology provides an academic foundation for pursuing most subspecialty areas in psychology. At the master's and doctoral levels, research, training, and supervision in school, clinical, and counseling psychology are generally carried out by those who are licensed to practice psychology. The Association of State and Provincial Psychology Boards (2003) promulgated guidelines for the supervision of doctoral, nondoctoral, and uncredentialed individuals who provide psychological services as well as other important information, such as guidelines for continuing education for licensed psychologists.

After successfully completing a doctoral degree, the neophyte psychologist may obtain additional training in the form of a postdoctoral internship. This process is facilitated by the Association of Psychology Postdoctoral and Internship Centers, which is responsible for matching individuals with internship settings for additional clinical experience and supervision at hospitals and clinics in the United States and Canada. Their website (http://www.appic.org/) is extremely useful for graduate students who wish to learn about opportunities for further supervised training in the field before they sit for the licensing examination.

As with every subspecialty area, those psychologists who teach have an ethical obligation to update their knowledge by familiarizing themselves with the current professional literature (e.g., journals, books) and participating in continuing education (e.g., seminars, workshops, online presentations). Although not required, becoming a member of profes-sional associations and reading their journals is an excellent way to remain well-informed about the latest research and professional matters affecting competence.

ETHICS CODES OF OTHER PROFESSIONAL ASSOCIATIONS

Psychologists who belong to professional associations other than the APA often encounter other ethics codes that require compliance. These codes are likely to be shorter and less comprehensive than the APA Ethics Code and to have a specific focus reflecting the goals and needs of the organi-zation. These organizations usually have their own means of adjudicat-ing complaints that are brought forward about their members, by means of their own ethics committees. A sampling of professional organizations with their own ethics codes includes the American Group Psychotherapy Association, the American Music Therapy Association, the American School Counselor Association, the Association for Applied Psycho-physiology and Biofeedback, the Society for Clinical and Experimental Hypnosis, the Feminist Therapy Institute, and the Society for Research in Child Development. Sometimes a particular ethical standard of an association will be more or less rigorous than a similar standard in the APA Ethics Code. In the case of conflicting rules, the psychologist belong-ing to both associations resolves the conflict by adhering to the standard that is more rigorous and provides greater protection to clients, patients, or other recipients of services. A complete list of ethics codes is available through Pope's website (http://kspope.com/ethcodes/index.php).

Keeping Within One's Boundaries of Competence and Limitations of Techniques

The Ethics Code requires psychologists to keep within their areas of competence as therapists, researchers, teachers, supervisors, or in any other professional role. Competence may be measured by one's formal education, training, supervision (unlicensed), consultation (for licensed practitioners), continuing education and independent study, and pro-fessional experience. As a part of this rule, psychologists must also refrain from using techniques or interventions that go beyond their intended use on the basis of the empirical data, hence, evidence-based techniques.

TREATMENT

An example of a situation that can suddenly emerge that might push a therapist to venture beyond his area of competence is illustrated in the following scenario.

> A psychologist in a metropolitan area receives an urgent phone call from the father of a 14-year-old boy who threatened him with a baseball bat just hours before. In addition, the boy smashed a table in the living room and bashed several holes in his bedroom wall, all the time cursing and yelling at his father. There were also other changes in his behavior over the past month, including being absent from home during the evening hours, and hanging out with a new group of older friends whom his father had never met. The psychologist did not treat adolescents but recognized that immediate intervention was important. He referred the father to another psychologist in town who specialized in adolescents and family therapy, rather than attempting to provide treatment himself.

Sometimes it is more difficult to remain entirely within one's area of competence when practicing in a part of the country that lacks broad mental health resources. If the therapist described in this scenario had recently moved to a small town in Oklahoma and opened the only psychology practice in town, he would be presented with many situations that might require that he go beyond his area of formal training and experience, particularly if he were recently licensed and lacked much clinical experience. In this setting, it would be essential for him to consult with experienced clinicians to provide the best care to his patients, including telephone consultation or videoconferencing, pursuing online training seminars ("webinars"), attending workshops whenever possible, and taking advantage of other opportunities to upgrade his skills.

In recognizing the limitations of one's expertise, a psychologist must be attuned to what can reasonably be expected and accomplished with certain strategies, interventions, or techniques. Those lacking evidence of effectiveness provide the most obvious examples of failure to recognize the limitations of their expertise, as mentioned earlier. But sometimes a patient can be unwittingly complicit in tempting a therapist to exceed his or her boundaries of competence.

> A therapist who has been treating a young man for depression for 3 months and has a good working relationship with him is now asked by the patient if she could use hypnosis with him for treating his symptoms of irritable bowel syndrome. He has read about this intervention online, and one of his friends in another state had consulted a hypnotist with excellent results for the same disorder. The young man has faith in his therapist, likes her, and hopes that she will be willing to do hypnosis with him.

The therapist had attended an introductory workshop in hypnosis the previous year but has no specific training in the protocol for treating irritable bowel syndrome, though she is aware that such a protocol exists. She wisely declined his request for hypnosis on the grounds that she was not sufficiently trained to treat irritable bowel syndrome at the present time but stated that she would attempt to locate a health care provider who was trained in the hypnotic protocol for irritable bowel syndrome or obtain the necessary training herself.

A patient with panic disorder who is having nightmares about childhood sexual abuse approaches her therapist with a request for hypnosis to treat her panic and also "learn about her abusive past." Although she may have confidence in this therapist's ability and the use of hypnosis as a tool for uncovering the past, she may not understand that if hypnosis were improperly used it could help "create" memories of childhood sexual abuse that may not be entirely accurate (Brown, Scheflin, & Hammond, 1998; Nagy, 1995; Nash, 1994).

It is important to note that although others may have confidence in the psychologist's abilities to carry out certain interventions, it is the therapist's obligation alone to determine his or her own level of competence and when to refuse and refer the patient to a more competent clinician. Sometimes peer consultation is helpful for a therapist in determining whether he or she has the requisite competence in a given situation.

An example of limitations of a technique is illustrated by the psychologist who is competent to use biofeedback training for pain management but also believes, absent any supporting research, that biofeedback alone can reverse the course of metastatic pancreatic cancer. In promoting this intervention to a depressed cancer patient, he is engaging in professional activities that are misleading, fraudulent, and potentially abusive because there is no empirical basis for his claims. On the other hand, if there were preliminary research showing that certain cancer patients had more frequent remissions and a better quality of life as a result of biofeedback training, then such claims by a therapist could be supported, at least in a tentative fashion, with appropriate disclaimers and informed consent. The ethically cautious therapist would never let his enthusiasm be a substitute for scientific rigor, resulting in false guarantees or assurances to the patient.

TECHNOLOGY

The use of technology can sometimes lure psychologists to exceed the boundaries of their competence or limitations of techniques. An example is the therapist who attempts to provide long-term psychotherapy over the telephone or via e-mail to individuals who have never been evaluated in a face-to-face setting and who have serious psychopathology, such as a personality disorder. The therapist may be competent but is attempting to use his or her skill in a setting or milieu for which effectiveness may never been established. Attempting treatment exclusively over the telephone or Internet for someone who is having a manic episode or is actively alcoholic with paranoid personality disorder may or may not be possible; however, thus far the empirical evidence is lacking.

Nevertheless, a patient may initiate such a process naively, lured by the psychologist's assurances, paying for consultations, and expecting to be helped. Instead, it is possible that little or no progress will occur or that the patient's mental health will decline, with the therapist attempting to use conventional interventions in the electronic medium.

Therapists should certainly be aware of new technology and creative ways of offering services to patients. However, they should evaluate new interventions with caution and always take positive steps to protect patients form harm while using them. Protecting patients while using new interventions and techniques for which no standards exist is discussed at the end of this chapter.

ASSESSMENT

Psychological assessment is an area that may invite going beyond one's area of competence, particularly in forensic settings. To provide guidance to psychologists, the APA first published *Technical Recommendations for Psychological Tests and Diagnostic Techniques* in 1954 and has been revising this document ever since. The most recent revision is the 1999 publication, *Standards for Educational and Psychological Testing*, a joint venture with the American Educational Research Association and the National Council on Measurement in Education (American Educational Research Association, APA, & National Council on Measurement in Education, 1999).

It is essential that psychologists use psychological tests in an appropriate manner and be fully aware of a test's purpose and limitations—reliability, validity, normative statistics, and other factors that inform its use. It is useful to consider using the Wechsler Adult Intelligence Scale as the sole basis for assessing a parent who is attempting to win custody of her 5-year-old son from her abusive ex-husband. By relying on an intelligence test for such an important legal case, the psychologist may be adversely impacting his client's case by failing to use instruments that would better evaluate her mental health and parenting ability. There are many valid assessment instruments that could be selected, and psychologists must always be cognizant of the test's purpose for which norms exist. Furthermore, when assessing those of a particular age, gender, race, ethnic or minority group, culture, or physical or mental disability for which the test has never been standardized, a psychologist must use cautious interpretations and disclaimers in his or her report.

TEACHING AND TRAINING

Remaining within one's professional boundaries while teaching in secondary school, college, or in graduate programs or professional schools of psychology can also be challenging at times. At the graduate level there may be risks of overextending oneself or venturing into areas of limited competence, such as the instructor who agrees to assume last-minute teaching responsibilities for a colleague who is unable to teach a course, although she has never taught the course before.

Another example of an ethical issue in teaching is the neophyte instructor who includes an experiential component along with the course work, such as an ongoing, self-disclosing "therapy group," ostensibly for the purpose of better understanding the theories of group process. The professor who is a didactic presenter in the classroom one day and a group therapist in his office on another places students in a potentially confusing situation. They are being asked to participate in a group therapy experience with the same authority figure who will be judging and grading their academic performance in the classroom the next day. This constitutes a multiple-role relationship for the instructor, whose objectivity in both roles may be compromised, and thus students coping with traumatic past events may be harmed more than helped to appreciate group dynamics.

CLINICAL SUPERVISION

Clinical supervision of pre- or postdoctoral trainees is a pivotal part of psychologists' training, and training and online resources are increasingly available for licensed psychologists to learn successful techniques involved in supervision. According to Rodolfa (2001), there are at least four different roles: teacher, therapist, consultant, and evaluator. In the role of teacher, the supervisor establishes clear goals for supervision and for therapy, provides instruction, comments on specific skills and case management, models intervention techniques, explains the rationale of various interventions, assigns and discusses readings, and interprets significant events in the therapy setting. The therapeutic role includes providing emotional support as needed, encouraging the supervisee to express feelings, exploring personal reactions to patients (either overidentifying or repellent reactions to patients), building trust, reflective listening, and modeling relationship skills. The supervisor as consultant monitors the overall system of therapist–patient–supervisor setting, intervenes at the strategic level (how the supervisee, not just the patient, changes), and collaborates with the supervisee to work out problems. And ultimately, the supervisor-as-evaluator assesses the attainment of goals and integration of suggested changes by the supervisee; follows up on patient and supervisee progress; helps the supervisee assess strengths and weaknesses; monitors the supervisee's awareness and application of ethical standards; and provides feedback on the supervisee's knowledge of theory, intervention skills, and personal qualities.

Supervisors of trainees in a practicum or internship setting could risk going beyond their level of competence whenever they encounter a clinical situation for which they have little or no experience. This is particularly true in high-risk situations requiring specialized experience in which supervisors may find themselves lacking needed skills. This might include a high-conflict divorcing couple who have already experienced physical assault; an expressed threat of violence to a third party that would necessitate breaking confidentiality; working with a lesbian or gay couple; or dealing with a psychotherapy patient from a different culture whose values, customs, and interpersonal style may be quite foreign to the supervisor. In any of these situations, the supervisor may opt to continue supervising, assuming that his or her skills may be adequate in spite of his or her inexperience or cultural difference. However, this may well constitute going beyond his or her professional boundaries of competence, with the possible result of a harmful or even catastrophic impact on the patient. A better choice, and one that would model exemplary behavior for his or her supervisee, would be for the supervisor to either seek consultation him- or herself or temporarily delegate supervision of work with this patient or couple to another psychologist who is experienced in these areas. In this way everyone benefits: The student therapist receives competent supervision with a difficult case; the patient likely receives better care; and the supervisor does not risk exercising poor judgment or advocating ineffective strategic interventions.

FORENSICS

Psychologists have become more engaged with the legal system by being called on to do forensic work in a variety of roles such as expert witness, child custody evaluator, worker's compensation evaluator, consultant to a lawyer for the plaintiff or the defendant, or consultant to a patient or former patient who is engaged in litigation with a third party as well as by either suing or being sued, contesting a will, or some other legal matter. Psychologists should not presume competence in these areas, particularly when a deposition will be taken or a court appearance is expected, because it is not a normal part of their educational training. Seeking training, supervision, or consultation for these nonclinical roles would help assure that psychologists remain within their boundaries of competence.

The forensic arena is dramatically different from the clinical consulting office in that it is fundamentally adversarial in nature, frequently subjecting psychologists to public scrutiny and even attacks on their credibility and professional work from opposing attorneys. By virtue of its adversarial context, a psychologist may feel demeaned or personally undermined and become defensive or hostile in return. A psychologist may also allow him- or herself to be manipulated into an advocacy role, such as making supportive statements or taking positions on behalf of his client that cannot be substantiated by the data. For example, a therapist who is being deposed in a child custody case may voluntarily advocate that the father have physical and legal custody of the child primarily because that individual has been a patient and the therapist happens to be very familiar with his strengths. However, the therapist may not be the one who carried out the evaluation of both parents and is certainly not objective; it would likely be improper for the therapist to make any recommendation about parenting, much less to volunteer it unasked. The assessment and testimony of the psychologist involved in a child custody case could have major, long-term implications for the lives of the parents as well as their children and extended family.

Incompetent testimony by an expert witness could result in a custody arrangement that would be harmful to children and possibly place them at significant ongoing risk were the custodial parent neglectful or abusive. In summary, keeping within one's boundaries while carrying out assessment is crucial in every area in which psychologists find themselves—forensic, neuropsychological, management consulting, school settings, or treatment settings (hospitals and clinics), to name a few—as it may strongly impact on the decisions and services delivered by other professionals.

Competence in Human Diversity

What is termed *competence in human diversity* consists of having a full awareness of the range of human diversity and acknowledging that (a) people differ greatly on a variety of criteria and (b) various skills and training, commensurate with these differences, must be acquired to successfully intercede in their lives. As mentioned in Chapter 3, the rich variety of human traits may be categorized as follows: age, gender, race, sexual orientation, ethnicity, national origin, religion, disability, socioeconomic status, or any basis prescribed by law. These are examined in detail in the sections that follow.

It is important for a therapist, researcher, or teacher to be aware of his or her own bias or outright bigotry and how it may impact others. An individual may hold a systematic prejudice against a member of a minority group, resulting in absence of objectivity, stereotyping, offensive humor, unfair treatment, hostility or some other unwarranted attitude or behavior, and ultimately, flawed psychotherapy or poorly designed research. Assessing one's own bias may be possible if one is aware of dysphoric feelings such as disgust, impatience, anxiety, resentment, shame, oversensitivity, powerlessness, or some other telling emotion when working with a particular individual or group. Unusual verbal or nonverbal behavior by the psychologist, such as poor eye contact, avoidance of topics that should be addressed, sarcastic humor, certain physical gestures, insensitivity or harshness, aggressiveness, or other rejecting behaviors that seem to be out of character, may be indicators that a problem exists. Such telltale signs of bias should herald a warning to remedy the situation by consulting a knowledgeable colleague, obtaining additional education or training (e.g., workshops, other training experiences), reading and studying, engaging in personal psychotherapy, or ultimately withdrawing from the setting altogether (treatment, research, or teaching) if the bias cannot be resolved. The areas of diversity are presented next.

AGE

Developmental issues manifest themselves continuously throughout the life of the individual, demanding that psychologists maintain their knowledge and skills commensurately. The needs of the infant are unique and differ greatly in the first and second 6-month periods. These needs continue to change throughout stages of early childhood, adolescence, adulthood, and old age. Psychologists who diagnose, provide treatment, teach, or do research with these individuals must be well-informed about these stages and not presume competence unless they have had proper education, training, supervision, or other life experiences.

Legal requirements may also pertain to those who are minors or in the elderly group. This is particularly important when seeking informed consent when counseling or conducting research with young children or adolescents, hospitalized mental patients, geriatric patients, or members of any disenfranchised group. Psychologists must always obtain informed consent from parents, legal guardians, or conservators before beginning any research or clinical work with these groups.

GENDER

Gender may be considered a subculture unto itself, one into which a person is born, with its own range of genetic predispositions, cognitions, perceptions, and behavior patterns conditioned by family and culture since birth. A researcher may unwittingly introduce gender bias into any phase of an investigation, including formulating the hypothesis to be explored, collecting data (the manner or extent of collection), interpreting data (what is systematically ignored or emphasized), and drawing conclusions (implications and recommendations).

Similarly, those engaged in teaching who do not accept males and females equally may reflect their bias in unfair evaluations and grades, unwarranted assumptions about abilities, demeaning verbal or nonverbal behavior, and inappropriate and damaging humor. Furthermore, they may subtly or explicitly sexualize their relationships with students, inviting a multiple-role relationship that is confusing, coercive, or otherwise destructive to the student. Sexualized behavior with students, supervisees, research participants, colleagues, or others over whom the psychologist has evaluative or other authority is fundamentally exploitative and considered a grave offense in the APA Ethics Code.

Therapists and organizational consultants with a gender bias harm patients and clients by what they do and what they fail to do. Assessment, psychotherapy, consulting with management, human relations work, and other direct services provide many situations in which differences in social power can result in exploitation of the opposite sex (more commonly, men exploiting women).

Other harm perpetrated by psychologists with a gender bias include making invalid formal assessments and recommendations, adversely influencing a employee's job, making inept recommendations about hiring or firing that are not warranted by any objective criteria, failing to make progress in treatment or contributing to actual deterioration in mental health, or siding with the husband or the wife in marital therapy.

Unfair gender discrimination has been a part of the fabric of our culture for many years—invisible to many men and women—as it is simply "the way life is." As a means of helping clinicians to understand these issues, the APA published *Guidelines for Psychological Practice With Girls and Women* in 2007, a lengthy document including eight guidelines that focuses on cultural issues, socialization, oppression, bias and discrimination, the sociopolitical context, health matters, education, and community resources (APA, 2007).[4]

SEXUAL ORIENTATION

Being familiar with and accepting the variety of sexual orientations is also a vital part of psychological training. As a part of educating psychologists, the APA published *Guidelines for Psychotherapy With Lesbian, Gay, and Bisexual Clients*, containing 16 guidelines addressing diagnosis, treatment, family relationships, social prejudice and discrimination, risks and

---

[4]An important book on this topic, including the writings of various ethicists, is *Practicing Feminist Ethics in Psychology* (Brabeck, 2000); it outlines the subtleties of the marginalization of women, how it has affected American society, and what steps need to be taken as a remedy.

challenges of being gay, health matters, obligations of the psychologist working with gay clients and patients, and other matters (APA, 2000). A systematic bias or fear of homosexuals (or heterosexuals) impairs a psychologist's work in the same way that gender bias does. A psychologist's vulnerable or panicky feelings, anger, avoidant or hostile behavior, or other signs of a homophobic response can adversely affect the working relationship with a gay patient or student. If therapists, consultants, or researchers are aware of their own bias against gays or lesbians, they should either limit their professional contacts or obtain supervision, consultation, psychotherapy, or some other rehabilitative experience to provide better coping skills.

In many situations, such as in the classroom or work setting (with colleagues), it may be impossible to limit one's contact with those with a different sexual orientation. Instead, it may be wise to welcome such exposure and increase one's knowledge and understanding through continuing education, training, supervision, and consultation as an opportunity for personal growth.

RACE, ETHNICITY, NATIONAL ORIGIN, AND LANGUAGE

The extensively diverse population within the United States poses a significant challenge for psychologists to learn of the values, norms, social customs, idiosyncrasies, and other attributes of those from other cultures. This topic is addressed in the APA publication *Guidelines on Multicultural Education, Training, Research, Practice, and Organizational Change for Psychologists* (APA, 2003).

Ignorance or prejudice about race or national origin of immigrants' or first generation Americans can impair a psychologist's ability to work competently and effectively in university, clinical, research, and management consulting settings. An example is the therapist working with a Mexican American man who wants to bring a family member into the consulting office. Although this might generally seem to be an unusual practice, personal boundaries among Hispanics are more inclusive of others, and it might be quite a natural practice to include a sibling or even a close friend. Likewise, the therapist working with a Japanese patient who is avoiding eye contact should remember that such a behavior may not be clinically significant but is more likely to represent the Japanese communication of respect for an authority figure.

Psychological assessment with language-based instruments can be compromised when evaluating individuals from other cultures. This is particularly true when the instruments have not been appropriately standardized or English proficiency of the client is limited. An example is a neuropsychological evaluation on a cognitively impaired Vietnamese woman who speaks broken English. In this situation an interpreter should be used, one provided by the hospital or institution for reasons of confidentiality and impartiality, instead of asking a family member to do the translating. Psychologists should consider using culture-fair tests, if available, or otherwise issue a disclaimer when the validity of an assessment is diminished as a result of inadequate norms, language proficiency, cultural bias, or other reasons pertaining to the client's race, ethnicity, or culture.

RELIGION

Religious differences can also detract from objectivity and competence if there is a pervasive bias on the part of the investigator, teacher, consultant, or therapist. Whether the bias is against atheists, Mormons, Jews, Muslims, or those of any other faith, the psychologist hobbled by such bigotry risks carrying out poorly conducted research, substandard teaching or supervision, and incompetent consulting or psychotherapy. It is useful to consider the therapist who has lost a brother in the Iraq war and cannot bring herself to make eye contact with a Muslim supervisee–trainee from a Middle Eastern country. Bias based on religion is particularly important when psychologists serve or assess members of the clergy; in addition to being impartial, the psychologist should also be familiar with beliefs, values, habits, and other attributes of the group with which he or she is working.

DISABILITY

In serving, teaching, or investigating those with physical or mental impairments, psychologists must be alert to the array of factors unique to each disability. The designation *special needs* includes sensory impairments (e.g., blind or hearing impaired), chronic pain or degenerative diseases, spinal cord or other severe injuries, fatal illnesses, or some other condition impairing daily functioning. The range of mental disorders includes mental retardation or pervasive developmental disorders (e.g., autism, Asperger's syndrome), schizophrenia, dementias, or other brain disorders resulting from accidents or illness (e.g., stroke, heart attack, or any event resulting in brain anoxia and subsequent permanent damage). Therapists, teachers, and researchers who work with impaired or disabled individuals must have the necessary education and training to address the special needs of these individuals. By so doing, they reduce the chance of harming students, clients or patients, or research participants by what they do or fail to do and enhance the likelihood of successful outcomes.

SOCIOECONOMIC STATUS

Sometimes special skills must be acquired for working with those from a lower or higher socioeconomic status. In practical terms, this could involve learning of any special needs or requirements of a student, patient, consultee, or research participant. For example, a woman who has been physically abused by her husband and is living in a housing project will have special needs of protection and safe refuge as well as concerns for the security of her children. She will be less motivated to begin a course of long-term psychotherapy focusing on the impact of early childhood experiences on her current circumstances. Likewise, the therapist working with a homeless person may need to first help him or her fulfill immediate requirements such as food and housing or getting a job and not press for psychological insight that fails to address the urgent issues at hand. Disregarding such exigencies runs the risk of jeopardizing the very safety of the patient or his or her dependents whom the therapist is attempting to help.

A different array of problems confronts the psychologist treating the very wealthy client or patient. For example, the millionaire who is willing to pay the full fee and more for visits to a therapist, regardless of the productivity of the sessions, may be functionally "buying a friend" once a week instead of resolving his life problems or learning more adaptive behavior. Or one might consider the wealthy patient who may wish to fund his clinic therapist's innovative research or donate a building to the hospital or university campus in exchange for public recognition of his philanthropy. This might constitute a strong inducement for this therapist to prolong treatment and continue working with this lucrative patient, regardless of the mental health benefits to him or her. In these situations, the therapist must monitor his or her own conflicting motivations and interests to avoid falling into a multiple-role relationship consisting of therapist and fundraiser. The Ethics Code specifically prohibits multiple-role relationships that could impair one's objectivity or competence because they can be confusing to all parties and ultimately result in conflicting loyalties that are not easily resolved.

Researchers who investigate those of lower or higher socioeconomic status must take steps to educate themselves about attributes of these groups that might affect the validity of the results. These attributes might include such things as dialects, dress, nonverbal cues, interpersonal style, and prejudices of the group under study, all of which could impact on the research hypothesis, experimental design, data gathering, interpersonal relationship with the investigator or research assistant, or other aspects of the study. Failure to pay attention to these factors could have direct consequences for the investigation and ultimately for the knowledge base by making a contribution that is biased, distorted, or inaccurate in some other way.

Protecting the Welfare of Others When Standards of Competence Are Lacking

Ideally, much of what psychologists do should be founded on evidence-based techniques or find support in their experience and training. However, there will inevitably be some emergent situations that the researcher, therapist, teacher, or consultant may not be prepared for and for which they lack specific guidance from their knowledge base, ethics code, legal statutes, or other sources. In these situations in which lack of education or training is the issue, one must use his or her best judgment to avoid harming the recipient–patient, supervisee, or other. This invokes the general principle of Beneficence and Nonmaleficence, and good ethical compliance would prompt psychologists to use all resources available—telephone consultation with other clinicians experienced in the emergent situation, use of online resource (e.g., journal articles and training experiences, training seminars and workshops), face-to-face consultation with those who are knowledgeable, and other educational experiences.

The Ethics Code allowed for these situations in the 2002 revision by adding two standards (APA, 2002). One standard allows psychologists to provide services in emergencies even though they do not possess the necessary competence as long as they discontinue when the emergency passes or another competent provider can take over. Another standard deals with nonemergency situations in which psychologists are asked to provide a service for which they are not specifically trained; this standard allows psychologists who are competent in a closely related area of practice to effectively address the situation. This might apply more commonly in a rural situation where few therapists are practicing and the therapist must be a "Jack or Jill of all trades" at times.

Even well-trained and experienced psychologists occasionally encounter situations for which standards may be lacking. It is useful to consider the therapist treating someone diagnosed with a disorder characterized by the *Diagnostic and Statistical Manual of Mental Disorders* (4th ed.; American Psychiatric Association, 2000) as falling outside of the usual range of symptoms for a particular syndrome such as Personality Disorder *Not Otherwise Specified*, or Depressive Disorder *Not Otherwise Specified* (italics added). Or one may consider the clinical researcher who thinks that the use of deception in his or her research is justified by the study's prospective scientific, educational, or applied value, as required by the Ethics Code, even though an objective colleague might view the study's value as falling well below the criterion justifying deception. What are psychologists to do when existing standards do not specifically address every situation that may arise in affecting the lives of others?

Avoiding harming or exploiting others, whether because of lack of competence or other factors, is a central feature of the Ethics Code and is the focus of Chapter 6. General guidance for psychologists concerning the ongoing obligation to protect the welfare of others and avoid harming them in the course of carrying out psychologists' work has been provided by every edition of the psychology ethics code since 1953. Where there is even a small possibility that another could be harmed, psychologists must take steps to protect recipients of their services.

The following should be considered a good beginning when there is a question of how to proceed as a result of inadequate standards or guidelines in one's area of work:

- Remain current about existing standards of practice, recent research, and changes in ethical rules that affect your area of work (e.g., participate in continuing education seminars and workshops, read journals, attend peer consultation groups).
- Provide adequate informed consent ahead of time about the attendant risk when standards are lacking (e.g., a therapist informing a patient that although the therapist has never treated this exact symptom before, he or she has worked with similar disorders).
- Consult with others who are knowledgeable about the area or situation about which you feel uncertain (e.g., experienced colleagues, former supervisors and mentors, institutional review boards, a university's or hospital's ethics or risk management office, the APA Ethics Committee or state ethics committees, state licensing boards, attorneys).
- Minimize the risk of foreseeable harm when it is unavoidable (e.g., not reporting a parent's HIV status in a child custody evaluation when it is irrelevant to the assessment).

Psychologists seek education, training, or supervision as preparation for working with individuals and groups and need additional training to work effectively with those who differ from them in important ways. It serves the science of psychology and the public for psychologists also to be well trained in multicultural factors, gender issues, and other important characteristics representing human diversity. Maintaining one's competence and pursuing learning should be an ongoing project throughout one's career, independent of legal regulations requiring continuing education, because the field of psychology continues to evolve.

Informed Consent 5

Dr. Newland was contacted by Fran, a 41-year-old woman with agoraphobia. Dr. Newland provided information at the outset of therapy about the length and frequency of sessions, fees and insurance reimbursement, and confidentiality and answered Fran's questions about the general treatment plan. She also explained that she used cognitive–behavioral therapy and some experiential techniques, but she did not note that these techniques included in vivo desensitization, during which Dr. Newland would accompany Fran to coffee shops, restaurants, and grocery stores.

At the fourth session, Dr. Newland informed Fran that on this day they would be going for a little "field trip" to the local coffee shop. This was the first time that Dr. Newland had described the nature of the in vivo desensitization part of the treatment. Fran's anxiety level began to escalate rapidly, and she developed unusual pains in both legs that made it impossible for her to walk any significant distance. She became increasingly anxious in the session and eventually asked to end early. Dr. Newland recognized that these symptoms were likely psychogenic but agreed to stop the session early, recommending that Fran contact her physician for an evaluation.

Fran phoned the next day to report that her legs were better, but she still planned to see her physician. She further stated that she wanted to temporarily stop treatment and would call back when she felt better. She never called back and did not return Dr. Newland's phone calls either. Dr. Newland realized that she should have provided more complete informed consent at the beginning, describing more fully what the treatment would entail.

Introduction

Providing informed consent about psychological services in advance has long been a fundamental duty of psychologists. In the 1959 edition of American Psychological Association's (APA's) "Ethical Standards of Psychologists," the principle titled Client Relationship required psychologists to inform prospective clients of the important aspects of the potential relationship that might affect the person's decision to begin treatment (APA, 1959). The standard went on to cite specific aspects of the experience that would likely influence a prospective patient's motivation to continue, such as (a) recording of an interview, (b) use of interview material for training purposes, or (c) observation of an interview by others. It even addressed the rights of those who are not competent—children, older people, or the mentally disabled—by requiring psychologists to provide informed consent to the responsible party.

Over the years there have been many refinements to the concept of informed consent addressing the various roles played by psychologists, such as therapist, researcher, supervisor, and consultant. In the 2002 Ethics Code, nearly 40% of the standards address some aspect of informed consent, and they are distributed throughout the code in eight out of the 10 sections. This book's supplemental website (http://pubs.apa.org/books/supp/essentialethics/) includes a list of the 35 ethical standards relevant to informed consent. The prevalence of this type of ethical standard in the Ethics Code reflects the pervasive nature of informed consent in the daily practice of psychologists, both at the outset and for the duration of professional contact.

In this chapter, I discuss what informed consent is and how psychologists should apply this concept to different roles.

Substance of Informed Consent

A review of the rights of inpatients and outpatients attests to the importance of the concept of informed consent. These include such things as the right to choose one's therapist without pressure from third-party payers (i.e., insurance companies and HMOs), the right to have continuity of care and not be abandoned by one's therapist, the right to terminate treatment if one is not benefiting or is being harmed, the right to discuss referral to a different therapist, the right to refuse medication as an inpatient, and the right to bring a grievance to a state licensing board (Cantor, 2005).

Standard 3.10, Informed Consent, in the 2002 Ethics Code begins as follows:

> When psychologists conduct research or provide assessment, therapy, counseling, or consulting services in person or via electronic transmission or other forms of communication, they obtain the informed consent of the individual or individuals using language that is reasonably understandable to that person or persons except when conducting such activities without consent is mandated by law or governmental regulation or as otherwise provided in this Ethics Code. (See also Standards 8.02, Informed Consent to Research; 9.03, Informed Consent in Assessments; and 10.01, Informed Consent to Therapy.)

There are four basic parts to this standard:

- stating and describing the obligation of providing informed consent,
- obtaining assent from those individuals who are minors or otherwise deemed legally incapable of providing consent,
- dealing with court-ordered or otherwise mandated services, and
- documenting informed consent in the clinical record or other appropriate place.

Providing Informed Consent

The process of informing recipients of psychological services varies with the type of service provided. The following are possible scenarios:

- providing psychotherapy to an Iraq war veteran who has post-traumatic stress disorder,
- offering marital therapy or premarital counseling,
- providing in vivo desensitization for those with phobias,
- providing group therapy for young adults with social anxiety,
- evaluating an 11-year-old boy for attention-deficit/hyperactivity disorder,
- performing a psychological assessment of an entire family because the parents are involved in child custody litigation,
- providing a specialized service such as hypnosis or biofeedback for a woman with chronic back pain,
- offering clinical supervision of a practicum or postdoctoral student in a college counseling center,
- carrying out a research project involving community volunteers who have lifelong depression,
- contracting with an attorney to testify as an expert witness in a case involving a patient suing her therapist for malpractice,
- providing management consulting to a Fortune 500 company,

- teaching a graduate-level class in clinical psychophysiology and biofeedback, and
- teaching continuing education workshops for mental health professionals.

Each of these roles played by a psychologist—therapist, biofeedback specialist, evaluator, clinical supervisor, researcher, forensic expert, management consultant, or professor—requires providing some manner of informed consent at the outset. Common to each role is giving information about what can reasonably be expected as a part of the anticipated experience, although the actual content of the informed consent might differ significantly with the role.

> Jennifer was a 33-year-old mother of two children, married to a narcissistic man who owned a small business. Because she was becoming increasingly depressed after the birth of her second child, she consulted a psychologist for help. In the course of therapy she learned about the causes of her depression and how to deal with anger and sadness in her marriage. As her mood and self-esteem improved, she began behaving more assertively with her husband and was less accepting of his intolerant views and criticisms of her. Unfortunately, this led to a worsening of the marital relationship as her husband became even more demanding and threatened to hit her on one occasion if she "didn't back off" and remember her "place in the marriage."

Marriage can be conceptualized as a complex interactive system involving two individuals, each of whom carries his or her own conditioning and expectancies from past experience. Therapists know that in some marriages as one spouse makes a significant personal change, such as recovering from long-term depression, the other spouse, instead of welcoming it, may well experience this as a stressful wave that seriously rocks the marital boat. Jennifer's husband preferred his wife to be more passive and depressed and felt threatened as her mental health improved. Adequate informed consent for Jennifer would have included a discussion of those possible anticipated changes in her marriage as her mood improved in response to treatment.

Although most practitioners might assume that informed consent generally pertains to the early stages of treatment, it is truly an ongoing process. Whenever the therapy or psychological service changes significantly over time, it is incumbent on the psychologist to discuss these changes with the recipient of his or her services. Recommendations to an ongoing therapy patient that he or she would benefit from couples counseling, group therapy, biofeedback, or mindfulness meditation training should be accompanied by an explanation of the risks and benefits associated with each. Now I turn to three common roles played by psychologists—therapist, researcher, and educator—and the informed consent process that accompanies each.

Informed Consent in Psychotherapy

Although informed consent for psychological treatment may cover many areas, depending in part on the type of practice one has, the age range of clients and patients (e.g., children, teenagers, adults, older people), degree of psychopathology and risk of harming self or others, and even theoretical orientation, the basic elements generally included are as follows. It should be noted that informed consent can be provided in written form, orally, or some combination of the two. If done orally, the psychologist must make an entry in the clinical record documenting the nature and extent of informed consent. What follows is a list of 13 common topics that may be discussed with clients and patients at the outset.

FEES AND INSURANCE REIMBURSEMENT POLICIES

This includes information about the cost of services (e.g., telephone consultations, being paged, e-mailing), whether the therapist accepts insurance, how payment is to be made (e.g., at each session or monthly, credit cards), fees for court testimony, fee scale for psychological evaluations, annual fee increases, and related matters.

INFORMATION ABOUT THE THERAPY PROCESS

Informed consent about the therapy process continues throughout treatment. At the outset this might include a brief statement about the length of sessions, theoretical orientation of the psychologist or his or her background experience, how treatment is likely to proceed, what is likely to be expected in the course of the consultations, the risks and benefits of treatment, frequency of consultation sessions, approximate duration if possible, and discussion of hospitalization options if required.

Later on, as the therapist introduces new strategies or techniques, the therapist must discuss these openly with the client. For instance, what does the new technique consist of? What will be required of the patient? If, for example, the therapist wishes to use hypnosis as a means of treating a patient's anticipatory anxiety concerning a pending medical procedure, the therapist must describe how hypnosis differs from conventional therapy, address the client's concerns or fears, and preferably obtain written consent before proceeding. If, on the other hand, the therapist makes the clinical judgment that his or her patient who has attention-deficit/hyperactivity disorder could best be served by consulting a specialist for neurofeedback, in addition to the ongoing psychotherapy, an explanation and rationale should be provided for this proposed intervention. A good rule of thumb might be to give the same information to one's client about the experiences that lie ahead that one, as a therapist, would want one's best friend to know.

SCHEDULING AND CANCELLATION POLICIES

This section addresses options about scheduling consultations (frequency of meetings), charges for missed sessions, the time frame for changing or canceling appointments, and absences by the therapist due to other professional work responsibilities (e.g., scheduled court appearances, regular teaching responsibilities, inpatient work, likelihood of clinical emergencies, related matters that would concern the frequency of meetings).

PRIVACY AND CONFIDENTIALITY

This section addresses confidentiality and its limits and exceptions. Although this topic is the subject of Chapter 6, it constitutes a basis for the professional relationships with clients and is briefly reviewed here.

Confidentiality and its exceptions must be thoroughly discussed at the outset of treatment because clients and patients hold misconceptions about their privacy. Patients must understand that no information must be revealed to a third party without written authorization, including other health care providers or using patients' identifiable information in public lectures or in writing (e.g., journal articles, books), barring specific exceptions. Patients must be informed about the nature of these exceptions to confidentiality—both what psychologists are allowed by law to reveal to third parties (e.g., a patient threatening to commit suicide) and what psychologists must reveal in accordance with the law to third parties (e.g., disclosures of child or elder abuse). Some of the finer points of privacy in the mental health arena are also explained to patients, such as the differences between confidentiality and patients' legal right of privileged communication. This is discussed in detail in Chapter 6.

AUDIOTAPING OR VIDEOTAPING

Patient consent must be acquired before a therapist may audiotape or videotape a consultation session, and this consent must be documented in the clinical record.

COLLABORATION WITH OTHER
HEALTH CARE PROFESSIONALS

This collaboration includes information about the therapist's consultations with a patient's referring primary care physician, specialists (e.g., neurologist specializing in chronic pain, gastroenterologist), or other psychotherapists (e.g., marital therapist, group therapist). It might also include referring the patient who may be in need of anti-depressant medication to a psychopharmacologist for evaluation. The patient, of course, must authorize such disclosures to other health care providers.

RECORD KEEPING

This section includes how records are maintained (e.g., written, computerized), what they consist of, where they are housed, how long they are retained, how security is maintained, who else may access them, and more. There may also be a statement about clients' rights to access their own clinical records, unless the psychologist thinks it could be damaging or upsetting to do so. This is explored more fully in Chapter 6.

PROFESSIONAL AVAILABILITY

Here the therapist provides information about how to make contact between sessions or in the event of an emergency on evenings or weekends (e.g., a suicidal patient, an adolescent with impulsivity). This might include emergency telephone numbers and other contact information, e-mail availability, use of a pager, or other means of making contact as needed. The patient or client must know what options are available at all times for dealing with emergency situations.

PATIENT RIGHTS

As appropriate for both inpatient and outpatient settings, there may be a statement describing the rights of patients and clients. This would include the right to review and request a copy of their clinical record, their right to bring a grievance to the appropriate body (e.g., state licensing authority, clinic director, ethics committee), and the right to be informed about interventions prior to experiencing them. State law or the clinic or hospital setting in which the psychologist is employed may have policies and procedures in place that address these matters.

CHILDREN AND ADOLESCENTS

Children or adolescents must generally have their parents' consent to begin treatment, with certain exceptions. However, they must be informed of psychologists' legal obligation to reveal clinical records to their parents or custodians on demand. State laws may vary on this requirement (Koocher, Norcross, & Hill, 2005).

UNTIMELY INTERRUPTION TO TREATMENT

The APA Ethics Code requires that psychologists have procedures in place for dealing with their own untimely incapacitation or death or other unplanned interruptions to services, such as illness or sudden absence or unavailability for any reason. These should not be relegated to several paragraphs in the therapist's last will and testament but should be part of the informed consent process and made known to others as well (e.g., director of the clinic, office staff, colleagues designated to provide assistance).

ANY OTHER RELEVANT INFORMATION

Other information that would likely affect the potential patients' decisions to enter treatment might include disclosing a limited specialty area, such as a practice limited to children and adolescents or a specialty in the issues of Asian clients. It could also include disclosing periodic absences during the year, such as those of a forensic psychologist who participates in depositions and trials or a pregnant therapist planning a maternity leave.

STATE AND FEDERAL LAWS

There are legal requirements that influence the practice of psychology, and all psychologists are obliged to remain knowledgeable about state and federal laws relevant to their work. States have differing laws concerning such things as creating and maintaining clinical records, dealing with a patient who reveals a sexual relationship with a prior therapist, or coping with a client who stalks or threatens harm to a third party. Federal laws regulate the actions of psychologists engaged in research (National Institute of Mental Health [NIMH]) or practice who meet the criteria for compliance with the Health Insurance Portability and Accountability Act (HIPAA). Because HIPAA includes so many rules for practitioners and researchers, it is useful to take a brief look at some of its history and implications for psychologists.

Health Insurance Portability and Accountability Act

HIPAA is a federal law that was implemented in 1996 and later amended to protect the privacy of patients receiving services from health care providers. It consists of three parts: (a) the Privacy Rule (compliance date: April 14, 2003), (b) the Transaction Rule (compliance date: Oct. 16, 2003), and (c) the Security Rule (compliance date: April 20, 2005). As technology became more commonplace in health care—using faxes, e-mails, or the Internet to communicate patient information (e.g., psychological reports, test data, invoices, insurance forms)—the protections for patients' clinical records also had to increase commensurately. The original intent of HIPAA was to provide stronger protections for the privacy of patients' medical and psychological records as employees moved from job to job. As technology became more commonplace in the storage, retrieval, and transmission of clinical records (or any patient information that includes identifiers), it triggered creation of the HIPAA regulations. Only those health care providers and institutions (e.g., hospitals, clinics) that use computers to store patient records and transmit these records by means of fax or the Internet are required to comply with this federal law.

The Privacy Rule states that at the outset of treatment, patients are to be informed that their records can be accessed and used (a) in the provision of psychological treatment and services, (b) to handle billing and receipt of payments for services, (c) for health care operations (e.g., assistants, technicians), (d) as required or permitted by law (e.g., disclosures about child abuse, elder abuse, intended harm to third parties), (e) in conjunction with business associates (e.g., billing agencies), and (f) for clinical research. They are also informed that they have certain rights during the course of their professional contact with health care providers; these are discussed in Chapter 6.

The Transaction Rule addresses the technical aspects, requiring standardized formats whenever health care transactions such as insurance claims were to be transmitted electronically. However, only those psychologists who actually participate in electronic filing and transmitting of their patient's protected health information are required to comply with the provisions of HIPAA. Hospitals, clinics, large group practices, and even some individual practitioners are generally required to comply with this federal law.

The Security Rule requires health care providers to use reasonable, state-of-the-art protective measures for computer security, such as limiting access to computers by clerical or other workers, using passwords or encryption, and backing up information before moving hardware. Many of these rules are more suitable for institutions than the individual private practitioner. However, the intent is the same: The privacy of patient information is paramount, and psychologists must both inform patients of their rights and take measures in their professional offices that keep patient data secure.

Informed Consent in Research

When in the role of research investigator, psychologists must give information to potential participants about the research and fully answer their questions at the outset without distorting, minimizing, exaggerating, or omitting important information. They must use simple language in attending to each factor involved in informed consent to adequately protect the rights and well-being of those who volunteer to participate. These factors are based on three sources: (a) federal law (NIMH and HIPAA requirements); (b) institutional review boards of universities, hospitals, and other institutions to which the investigator is attached or is researching; and (c) the APA or other professional associations to which the investigator may belong, which have ethical requirements pertaining to research.

Although consent forms may vary somewhat in form and content, they all include the following basic elements.

DESCRIPTION OF THE RESEARCH

This section informs participants about the nature and goals of the investigation, why it is important, and what will be expected of the participants in general.

SELECTION BASIS

This includes a clear statement about why the participant is suitable for the study, allowing the researcher to exclude a prospective participant if the researcher does not believe that the person meets the criteria for inclusion. Individuals must be told if they will be screened for inclusion and what the criteria are, if appropriate (e.g., history of panic attacks, failed treatment for nicotine addiction).

TIME REQUIREMENTS

This informs participants about the time frame of the research (e.g., hours, days, weeks) and what the duration of their involvement will be. This might include follow-up meetings involving testing, debriefing, or other matters.

CONFIDENTIALITY

This addresses the topic of privacy, how information will be stored and used or disseminated, audiotaping and videotaping and future use of the tapes, how participants' health care information will be used, the circumstances under which confidentiality might be breached (e.g., participant is at risk of harming him- or herself), special indications involved in Internet research that could compromise confidentiality, and more.

VOLUNTARINESS

Research participation must always be voluntary, and prospective participants must be so informed. They must also be informed that they may freely withdraw at any time without being penalized and be told of any consequences of dropping out (e.g., a Psychology 101 student expected to participate in research as a part of course credit may now be given the option of writing a paper, giving a presentation, or participating in some other project to obtain the same course credit).

RISKS

This section describes the potential risks of participation; essentially, this includes any factors that would likely affect participants' willingness to participate. These factors encompass any physical or psychological risks or discomforts, the range of possible adverse effects from unpleasant emotional or psychological stimulation (e.g., sleep deprivation, exposure to upsetting visual stimuli), medication effects, or any other factors that could be aversive and an explanation of compensation or medical and psychological treatments available if injury should occur.

BENEFITS

This section describes how participants might benefit from being involved in the research, for example, learning useful information about managing stress or anxiety, acquiring cognitive or behavioral skills that may have psychological benefits, or any other results that might increase their desire to participate.

ALTERNATIVES

This section describes alternative courses of treatment or therapies, if any exist, that might be helpful to the prospective participant who is symptomatic. For example, if an adult with depressive episodes was considering volunteering for a research protocol investigating new treatments for clinical depression, the person would have to be informed of existing treatments prior to agreeing to be a participant.

COMPENSATION

Some research projects involve compensating participants. This must be fully described at the outset (e.g., what the compensation will be, if any, such as the amount of money paid, fulfilling college course partial credit, receiving limited counseling).

MINORS

This clarifies and explains that parental consent is required for participation of parents' minor children in any research protocol. Furthermore, if the investigator will be seeking information from participants who are minors about any of the following topics, he or she must so inform parents or custodians at the outset of research: parents' political affiliations or beliefs, mental or psychological problems, sexual behavior or attitudes, illegal or antisocial behavior, self-incriminating behavior, appraisals of others with whom the minor has a familial relationship, relationship that is legally recognized as privileged (e.g., lawyers, health care providers, clergy), and religious affiliations or beliefs.

WHOM TO CONTACT

This section informs potential participants about whom they should contact for additional information at any time during the investigation or afterward. This addresses situations in which the participant may have a delayed adverse reaction, is seeking to learn the results of the study, or has some question relevant to the project.

PARTICIPANTS' RIGHTS

Some institutions may require investigators to give participants the names and contact information of administrators who can respond to complaints or questions concerning participants' rights that may have been violated during the course of the study. This might involve the institutional review board, the chairman of the psychology department, the university judiciary board, or some other entity. In addition to this, NIMH requires that investigators include six additional informed consent items if their research grant is funded by that agency. These are presented in simple language and are paraphrased as follows:

- a statement that the particular treatment or method used may not work as planned and may be risky for you,
- the reasons why the investigator might have to drop you from the study without asking you first,
- a list of any extra financial charges that you may incur in order to take part in the research,
- a description of what would happen if you decide to drop out of the study and what the researcher will do to make sure that you keep receiving appropriate treatment if you do drop out,
- a statement that you will be told of any important results of the research that may help you to decide whether to continue participating, and
- approximately how many subjects are in the study.

OTHER QUESTIONS

Investigators must remember to fully answer participants' questions when discussing their possible involvement in the study. These should be addressed with candor and without minimizing or exaggerating important information. This is particularly important when dealing with children, older people, those for whom English is a foreign language, and those with developmental disabilities or other mental impairments who may be prone to distorting or misinterpreting their experience. It is not always an easy task to evaluate the extent of potential research participants' comprehension of what will be expected of them. The research experience may be novel, and they may be naive about the subject at hand. It is the wise researcher who can determine "how much information is enough."

INTERNET-BASED RESEARCH INTERVENTIONS

The Internet vastly increases access to potential subject pools and can hasten data collection when timeliness is an independent variable. Shortly after the September 11, 2001, terrorist attacks, a researcher rapidly received responses from 7,000 participants from all 50 states and 39 countries by posting a research website on a secure Stanford University server (Butler et al., 2005). However, it should be noted that problems do present themselves when the Internet is used, such as biased sample selection, false information provided by participants, privacy breaches, and crisis situations (impending suicidal behavior or psychotic episodes).

NIMH has addressed these situations by citing eight research issues involved with data gathering and the Internet and proposing remedies for each one (U. S. Department of Health and Human Services, National Institutes of Health, National Institute of Mental Health, 2003). These issues are

- anonymity or falsifying of information by the research participant,
- bogus "individuals posing as researchers" seeking information from vulnerable persons,
- limited monitoring of a research participant's clinical status—no immediate access to treating clinician or facility in case of an emergency (e.g., suicidality),
- lack of in-person communication between researcher participant and investigator,
- limited information as to whether consent was informed,
- research participant's delay in seeking appropriate treatment (assuming that the research intervention will be sufficient to address their psychological symptoms),
- uncertainty regarding adequate debriefing, and
- unintended limits to privacy and confidentiality.

The last problem can be addressed by consulting with specialists, using state-of-the-art technology in computer security, and cautioning participants about privacy with their own computers (e.g., controlling access to their computer and e-mail by use of passwords, using a home computer rather than one at the office).

However, some of the other research issues present significant challenges that may require innovative solutions, such as requiring conventional mail confirmation of identity or credentials, requiring face-to-face visits or telephone consultations early on, or including explicit questions concerning a participant's immediate crisis assistance that would trigger direct notification of the researcher. More information is available on the NIMH website (http://www.nimh.nih.gov/) or the website of the Center for Information Technology (http://www.cit.nih.gov/security.html).

Informed Consent in Teaching and Training

The APA Ethics Code Principle E: Respect for Peoples' Rights and Dignity reminds psychologists that they respect the dignity and worth of all people and the rights of individuals to self determination. The autonomy required for self-determination of students and trainees depends on having adequate information about the anticipated didactic experience to make an informed choice. Therefore, the principles of informed consent clearly apply to those involved in teaching, training, supervising, and mentoring students as well as those who have already completed their formal studies but need continuing educational experiences.

Although there is not usually a contractual relationship between teacher and student in the same sense as there is between therapist and patient in mental health care settings or investigator and participant in research settings, there is still the expectation that students and trainees shall be informed in advance of what they will experience and what degree of participation will be expected of them (whether face-to-face or in an online course). One may consider the course syllabus as adequate documentation for informed consent, and it could be considered the equivalent of a contract (Thomas, 2007).

EDUCATION AND TRAINING

Psychologists who are responsible for education and training programs must verify that there is a current and accurate description of the program content, training goals and objective, stipends and benefits, and requirements that must be met for satisfactory completion of the program. This applies to professors teaching courses in college and graduate programs as well as those holding administrative positions, such as the chairperson of the psychology department or the director of training.

An accurate description of training program content includes an accounting of all required experiences that would materially affect a student's decision to apply to that program for a master's degree, a doctoral degree, an internship experience, postdoctoral training, or any other psychological training. Some require participating in community service or consulting, such as involvement in local schools or community mental health centers. Some programs require students to have individual counseling or psychotherapy or participate in an experiential group in addition to the ongoing didactic experiences. There are also programs that may require more extensive self-disclosure, either orally or in writing; however, psychologists are specifically prohibited from probing the personal aspects of a student's past, such as sexual history; history of abuse and neglect; history of psychological treatment; and relationship matters, such as with parents, peers, and spouses, unless the training entity has clearly identified this requirement in its admissions and program materials.

SUPERVISION

Professional supervised experience with therapy clients is an integral feature of clinical training, as mentioned in Chapter 4. In recent years there has been an increase in the use of letters, contracts, or other informed consent documents that clearly explain the nature of the intended supervision, including goals, frequency and duration of supervisory sessions, limits of confidentiality, and provision of informed consent to the supervisee's clients and patients (Saccuzzo, 2003; Thomas, 2007).

The Association of State and Provincial Psychology Boards (1998) published *Supervision Guidelines* that address the different settings of supervised experienced, qualifications of supervisors, and evaluation of the supervisee.[1] If the supervisor is paid for clinical supervision by the supervisee, he or she should attend carefully to the risks involved in this inherent multiple-role relationship; laws in different states address this matter differently. It also recommended that the supervision address any legal, ethical, social, and cultural dimensions impacting on the professional practice of psychology as well as the supervisory relationship. This is explored more fully in Chapter 12.

This book's supplemental website (http://pubs.apa.org/books/supp/essentialethics/) includes a sample contract describing the supervisor's

---

[1]These guidelines are currently under revision because they may not provide adequate guidance to licensing boards considering emerging issues related to supervision (J. Schaffer, personal communication, August 17, 2009).

and supervisee's responsibilities, including the following three sections: (a) joint agreements, (b) supervisor's agreements, and (c) supervisee's agreements (Sutter, McPherson, & Geeseman, 2002).

Providing informed consent honors the autonomy of others and enhances their security in interacting with psychologists. In being able to anticipate what to expect from a therapist, researcher, or supervisor, an individual has some degree of predictability and feels free to change course, stop, withdraw, or move in some other direction at will. It is important to note that with the advent of new technology in providing psychological services, teaching, and carrying out research, there will be novel questions and issues that will require even better informed consent to safeguard the public. This includes predictability about matters of privacy and confidentiality and their exceptions, which are discussed in Chapter 6 as a central feature of providing good informed consent in any role played by psychologists.

Privacy and Confidentiality 6

A 41 year-old man with depression was referred by his primary care physician to Dr. Teller for treatment. In the first session, the patient revealed that he had recently divorced and was experiencing chronic pelvic pain and many depressing thoughts. Dr. Teller described how therapy would proceed, discussed fees and length of sessions, and gave a general description of his theoretical orientation. He said little about confidentiality and its limits, however.

In the second session, Dr. Teller informed his patient that he had contacted his primary care physician to learn of his medical history. He had also revealed the patient's history to the physician, including disclosures about the man's experiences of childhood sexual abuse. The patient was distressed that the therapist had done so without first obtaining his authorization. It is true that he had consented to contacting his physician and obtaining additional medical history from him, but he did not want Dr. Teller disclosing details of his early sexual abuse to him. He abruptly terminated treatment with Dr. Teller, feeling that the trust had been broken.

Introduction

Maintaining privacy and confidentiality has long been an essential ingredient in the work of psychologists. This includes psychotherapy, management consulting, research, academic settings, and virtually any situation in which personal information is disclosed to a psychologist with the expectation that it will be held in confidence. Confidentiality was addressed in the very first Ethics Code, informing American Psychological Association (APA) members that safeguarding information about an individual was a "primary obligation of the psychologist" (APA, 1953a). In this chapter, I discuss what privacy and confidentiality are and how psychologists should apply this concept to different roles.

Privacy, Confidentiality, and Privileged Communication

It is important to note the differences between privacy, confidentiality, and privileged communication while complying with ethical and legal rules.

PRIVACY

Privacy speaks to the relationship between the psychologist and other individuals (e.g., patients, clients, supervisees). As a general concept, privacy is an integral part of the professional relationship; what is revealed in the consulting office must remain there. Even the fact that the consultation occurred is a private matter if the professional relationship is to be effective and helpful to the client. Although not unique to psychological or health care settings, privacy is also considered to be a right of all U.S. citizens and is inferred from the US. Constitution in Amendments I, IV, and V, albeit narrowly defined (http://www.law.cornell.edu/constitution/constitution.billofrights.html#amendmenti).

CONFIDENTIALITY

Confidentiality concerns the information that is gathered or held by psychologists. It includes the specific obligation, both ethical and legal, that private information must be safely maintained and never revealed to others, voluntarily or in response to a formal request (e.g. from family members, employers, other interested parties), unless certain conditions are met.

It is enforced by professional codes of ethics as well as legal statutes, and it was originally formalized in ancient times, approximately 2,500 years ago, by the Hippocratic oath, requiring physicians to pledge to the following:

Whatever, in connection with my professional service, or not in connection with it, I see or hear, in the life of men, which ought not to be spoken of abroad, I will not divulge, as reckoning that all such should be kept secret. (http://www.euthanasia.com/oathtext.html)

The APA has been in the forefront in defining and promulgating confidentiality in its Ethics Code, casebooks, and ethics committee adjudications since the first Ethics Code was published (Caudill & Kaplan, 2005). However, legal statutes defining confidentiality on a federal or state basis have been relatively recent. These address the concept of privileged communication and form the basis for rules concerning compelled discovery of the clinical records of mental health providers. There are many exceptions to confidentiality as well, such as disclosures concerning one's intention to harm oneself or another or revelations of child abuse; these are explored later. Although the Ethics Code does not specifically require psychologists to disclose these exceptions in writing to new patient and clients, many states do have such a rule.

PRIVILEGED COMMUNICATION

Privileged communication refers to the legal right of an individual to shield confidential disclosures made to a psychologist from any judicial proceedings or court of law. These include trials, depositions, and subpoenas for examining clinical records (Kaplan, 2005). Two cases of importance are the 1970 California Supreme Court decision *In re Joseph E. Lifschutz* (1970) and the 1996 U.S. Supreme Court decision *Jaffee v. Redmond* (1996). In the latter case, the U.S. Supreme Court reversed the ruling of a lower Illinois court ordering the release of the psychotherapy records of a police officer who shot and killed a man who was about to stab another man with a butcher knife. Following the shooting, a wrongful death action was initiated against police officer Mary Lu Redmond, who was treated by a clinical social worker for a total of 50 therapy sessions after the shooting. By upholding the confidentiality of the psychotherapists' records, the Supreme Court strengthened the concept of privileged communication, which by 1996 had been addressed by all 50 states (Caudill & Kaplan, 2005).

The California Evidence Code provides a good example of how privileged communication is defined:

The patient, whether or not a party [to a legal proceeding] has a privilege to refuse to disclose, and to prevent another from disclosing, a confidential communication between patient and psychotherapist if the privilege is claimed by: (a) the holder of the privilege [e.g., the client or patient]; (b) a person who is authorized to claim the privilege by the holder of the privilege [e.g. parent or legal guardian]; or (c) the person who was the psychotherapist at the time of the confidential communication, but such person may not claim the privilege if there is no holder of the privilege in existence or if he is otherwise instructed by a person authorized to permit disclosure (e.g., the client, patient, or legal guardian). (Cal. Evidence Code, § 1014, 2009)

The term *psychotherapist* is defined rather broadly in most states and includes a psychiatrist; a person whom the patient reasonably believes to be a psychiatrist (whether or not such person is in fact licensed to practice medicine); a licensed psychologist; a licensed clinical social worker; a licensed marriage, family, and child counselor; a credentialed school psychologist; and other health care providers, interns, and certain agencies and other health care providers (Cal. Business and Professions Code, § 2909, 2009; Cal. Family Code, § 6924, 2009).

And finally, the term *patient* is defined as

a person who consults a psychotherapist or submits to an examination by a psychotherapist for the purpose of securing a diagnosis or preventive, palliative, or curative treatment of his mental or emotional condition or who submits to an examination of his mental or emotional condition for the purpose of scientific research on mental or emotional problems. (Cal. Evidence Code, § 1011, 2009)

Such a sweeping definition of patient clearly opens the door to legal protection for those who volunteer to participate in psychological research as well.

Privacy and Confidentiality in Research Settings

Investigators have been obliged to maintain the privacy of individuals and protect the confidentiality of any information gathered about them in the course of data gathering since the very first code was written in 1953. It stated that "only after explicit permission has been granted is the identity of research subjects published" (APA, 1959, p. 280). Since then, the concepts of privacy and confidentiality have expanded in scope far beyond protecting the identity of research subjects, as have the threats to safeguarding them, as a result, in part, of the complexity of research and the innovations in technology. To review, privacy pertains to one's interest in controlling others' access to information about one, whereas confidentiality pertains to the psychologist's obligation to safely maintain private information that is revealed in the course of a professional relationship with a researcher. Let us examine these two concepts as well as the risks to each.

PRIVACY IN RESEARCH SETTINGS

Privacy is not only a relevant concept for individual research participants but also has implications for the outcome of research and, ultimately, the body of research knowledge in psychology itself. Participants who feel their privacy is not secure may have anxiety about the consequences of revealing their personal information and responses in the course of an investigation, doubting that their anonymity will be respected. And in addition to increased anxiety about participating in research, these participants may be evasive in their responses or withdraw from the research altogether, resulting in biased sampling as well as a threat to the validity and usefulness of the data (Folkman, 2000).

The few constitutional or federal laws relating to privacy in social and behavioral research focus on protecting the rights of school-age children (Sieber, 1992). In 1974, the National Research Act was passed, requiring all research funded by the U.S. Department of Health, Education, and Welfare to be reviewed by institutional review boards (for a legislative chronology, see http://history.nih.gov/research/sources_legislative_chronology.html). It also required that research involving children must be authorized by their parents and assented to by the children. In 1985, the Buckley Amendment to the Family Educational Rights and Privacy Act of 1974 was passed, prohibiting access to children's school records without parental consent (Folkman, 2000). And in 1994, the Goals 2000: Educate America Act was enacted, prohibiting researchers from even asking children questions about religion, sex, or family life without parental permission. This act begins to address a central theme of privacy that pertains to human subjects of all ages, namely, how they may be affected by intrusions into their privacy if they elect to participate in research.

Current understandings of privacy consist of two elements that go far beyond simply protecting the identity of the participant. The first pertains to participants' freedom to select the time and circumstances under which facts about them and the extent to which their attitudes, beliefs, behavior, and opinions will be revealed to or withheld from others (Kelman, 1972). This freedom is largely dependent on providing comprehensive informed consent, allowing prospective participants to learn about any aspect of the research project that might affect their willingness to volunteer as a subject. The second aspect of privacy protects participants' right to avoid receiving information that they might not want to know about (Sieber, 1992). This might include feedback about their own HIV status, their performance or score on a competitive task compared with other participants, personality traits assessed during the course of the investigation, or information that might be considered offensive or anxiety provoking (e.g., learning that they scored higher on measures of paranoid thinking or willingness to lie or cheat compared with the norm). Another example would be receiving information that a participant might consider to be pornographic, such as research involving sexual attitudes or behavior (Folkman, 2000).

CONFIDENTIALITY IN RESEARCH SETTINGS

Confidentiality pertains to the agreements psychologists make with research participants about the use of their data. Researchers are expected to protect the privacy of participants' data (i.e., not share with others) unless they are authorized to do so or there is some other justification. For example, investigators commonly assign code numbers instead of using actual names of participants. Video or audio recording of participants presents somewhat more of a challenge to the investigator because the study may involve raters evaluating the recordings and, obviously, the necessity of seeing clear images of the facial expressions or hearing sound recordings that could also clearly reveal the identity of the participant. Here the concept of *informed consent* would be tightly linked to confidentiality because the prospective participant would be made aware early in the explanation of the research protocol that his or her image will not only be captured but also revealed to others. It would also add an additional level of security for the participant to be informed of the identity of those who would actually view or evaluate the video- or audiotapes in advance; in that way, the participant would know if there was a risk of revealing his or her private information to a person already known to him and could opt out of participating in the project.

Breaches of confidentiality can have serious consequences for some participants. For example, (a) a child's observations about a parent that are disclosed to that parent could negatively impact the child later, (b) revelation of a participant's positive HIV status to his or her employer or significant other could have strong implications for his or her career or domestic relationship, or (c) information about a participant's illegal alien status revealed to a court or other authority could jeopardize his or her current living situation (i.e., a specific violation of the concept of *privileged communication;* Folkman, 2000). Unauthorized sharing of research data with another researcher can also constitute a breach of confidentiality if the participant's contact information or other identifying information is included in the data.

On the other hand, investigators who are members of the APA are ethically required to share their data with any "competent professional" who might wish to verify the substantive claims by reanalysis for a period of 5 years after publication (APA, 2010). Complying with such a rule might mean taking extra steps to delete all identifying information about the participants before releasing the data to another investigator for statistical reanalysis to preserve the anonymity of the participants.

Although it is permissible, and even mandated, to break confidentiality when patients reveal certain information to licensed mental health providers (e.g., child abuse, serious suicidal threats, or credible threats to harm a third party) a similar requirement does not necessarily always apply in research settings. Furthermore, those who carry out research are frequently not clinically trained and may not be skilled in evaluating possible dangerous situations that may surface in the laboratory, such as whether a participant who verbalizes a suicidal or homicidal intent is really at risk of acting on it. A young college student who is dejected about having lost his part-time job 2 days before beginning his participation in the research project may write that his mood is low and he feels like dying but have no actual intention or concrete plan to carry out suicide. Much more problematical are responses culled from data gathered from large numbers of anonymous participants, such as over the Internet, that seem to present ambiguous threats to the safety of self or others. How does an investigator determine when to take such threats of harm seriously and intervene by quickly referring the participant for treatment or calling the emergency psychiatric team or police to help with involuntary hospitalization? These situations are likely to emerge more frequently in research concerning sensitive topics or participants with physical or mental health issues, such as investigations focusing on violence, child maltreatment, substance abuse, AIDS, and sexuality (Appelbaum & Rosenbaum, 1989).

Historically, ethics complaints brought against researchers for privacy or confidentiality violations are rather infrequent. Nevertheless, it is essential for researchers to always be knowledgeable about current relevant state laws or institutional requirements regarding mandatory reporting in these gray areas as well as ethical standards concerning research, privacy, and informed consent. They should also have ready access to consulting with a mental health provider when in doubt about what course of action to take with a research participant who raises their level of concern.

Privacy and Confidentiality in Academic Settings

Psychologists who hold academic or training positions are also expected to respect the privacy of their students and supervisees, including instructors, teaching assistants, clinical supervisors in training settings, and anyone else involved in teaching students of any age or stage of development. Those teaching graduate students or supervising training in clinical settings must avoid certain personally sensitive subjects, such as the student's or supervisee's sexual history; history of abuse and neglect; psychological treatment; and relationships with parents, peers, spouses, and significant others (APA, 2010).

There are two exceptions to this ethical rule allowing educators to broach these topics if (a) the training program has disclosed such requirements of self-disclosure in its admission materials or (b) the information being sought is essential to help students with personal problems that are interfering with their current training and professional duties (e.g., the competent rendering of personal counseling or therapy) or pose a threat to fellow students or others. The first exception specifically has to do with informed consent—what the student entering the program or signing up to take a class was informed of about requirements concerning revealing such private information by the instructor at the outset or in the course catalogue. The second exception clearly addresses the situation in which a teaching assistant, practicum student, or therapist trainee under supervision is experiencing impairment in mental health (e.g., major depression, anxiety disorder) or a life event (e.g., illness or chronic pain, divorce, death of a family member) that diminishes his or her ability to carry out his or her work as a psychology trainee. In these situations the trainee's personal stress may prevent a trainee from completing professional responsibilities or impair his or her ability to maintain professional boundaries, resulting in the befriending of clients or patients or seeking solace by engaging them in romantic relationships.

When client or patient information is used for didactic purposes, such as a professor's clinical vignette from his or her therapy practice to describe obsessive–compulsive personality, great care must be taken to adequately disguise the patient whose private information is now being put on display. This can be done by altering identifying information such as the gender, age, ethnicity, and details of the patient's situation before presenting it in public. It is also wise to inform listeners that this necessary deception has occurred, lest they believe that confidentiality is being disregarded. Whenever clinical data are used in publications, such as journal articles or books, it is essential to obtain specific consent from patients to do so; otherwise, the author must carefully disguise salient details of patients' situations to protect their privacy.

Privacy and Confidentiality in Clinical and Consulting Settings

Psychologists offering psychotherapy, assessment, or consulting services must consider the following: (a) ethical rules concerning privacy and confidentiality, (b) relevant state and federal laws, (c) institutional rules (e.g., established policies of the hospital, clinic, university, or other setting where the clinical services take place), and (d) the nature of the professional or scientific relationship (e.g., patient or research participant). It is important to have a thorough understanding of confidentiality because different demands are placed on the psychologist offering individual therapy, marriage counseling, family therapy, court-ordered neuropsychological assessment, or management consulting.

I now examine the ethical and legal rules that guide or restrict psychologists' professional conduct.

ETHICAL RULES CONCERNING PRIVACY AND CONFIDENTIALITY

Ethically, psychologists must inform new clients and patients about their rights to privacy and the exceptions to confidentiality at the beginning of services, unless this is contraindicated or not feasible (e.g., emergency situations). With individual clients this is a relatively straightforward process. Adult recipients of services are told that, apart from the list of exceptions, everything they discuss and reveal in the course of treatment or psychological assessment will remain confidential, including the fact that the consultations occurred. They are free to discuss any aspect of their treatment with anyone of their choosing, but psychologists must always protect their privacy, refuse to acknowledge the identity of their patients and clients, and reveal nothing of the patient's or client's disclosures, commonly referred to as *protected health information* (PHI), unless at least one of the conditions for such a revelation is met.

When psychologists write psychological reports engage in authorized communications with others about their patients (e.g., other therapists, group or marital; high school teachers of a boy with oppositional defiant disorder; or parents of a minor), they must limit their communications to that information that is germane to the request; no gratuitous information is to be included. For example, a psychologist responding to a request of his or her patient who is filing a worker's compensation claim might reveal information to the employer about his or her patient's cognitive impairment or other metrics of his or her disability that directly impair his or her ability to work but would not reveal his or her patient's positive HIV status or history of childhood physical abuse unless these had a direct bearing on the case.

When there is more than one patient or client in the consulting room at a time, the requirements of confidentiality can become more complex. In couples therapy, with either a gay or straight couple, how would the therapist deal with a private revelation by one party that he or she was having an outside relationship? Or what if one party informed the therapist privately that his or her partner was not being honest in the course of their counseling sessions? The Ethics Code of the American Association of Marriage and Family Therapists takes an unambiguous stand by prohibiting therapists from revealing individual client confidences to the other party or family members unless that client so authorizes in writing (American Association of Marriage and Family Therapy, 2001). The APA Ethics Code does not have an analogous standard, although it does require written authorization for disclosures in general. These situations are best handled by providing a clear understanding of privacy at the outset. As noted in Chapter 5, good informed consent, preferably in writing, allows all parties to know and agree about what the privacy rules will be. The marital therapist may advise his couple of a "no-secrets" rule at the outset, basically refusing private unilateral discussions with the therapist, with all sessions being joint sessions. Or the therapist may allow one-on-one meetings and permit confidential disclosures that are never shared with the spouse or partner if this reflects the couple's theoretical orientation or addresses the clinical needs of the moment (i.e., strategic individualized sessions with one spouse related to the marital situation, such as safety issues concerning management of hostility or rage, or individual consultations related to something other than the couple's treatment, such as panic attacks).

Providing therapy to children and adolescents offers a different array of privacy concerns to be reviewed at the outset. Therapists should clearly explain privacy and confidentiality to parents as well as the child in treatment at the beginning of therapy: what is required by law and maximizes clinical benefit. Legally a parent or custodian of a minor is entitled to know what occurs in the course of his or her child's treatment, but clinically it is generally considered unwise for the therapist to be fully transparent about every detail of the therapy process.

A simple example of the therapist using his or her judgment about how much to disclose to a parent is the case of an adolescent boy who is actively contemplating suicide and has developed a detailed and specific plan for ending his life. In this case the therapist would have an obligation to take steps to maximize the boy's safety. This might include some combination of the following: informing the parents of the risk of suicide, engaging their cooperation in maintaining his safety, referring the boy for a psychopharmacological evaluation, hospitalizing him on a voluntary basis, or calling the police or emergency psychiatric team for hospitalizing on an involuntary basis. However, the therapist treating a 16-year-old girl who has been experimenting with sexual activity may have less of a clear mandate to inform her parents or none whatsoever. The parents may be legally entitled to have access to the therapist's clinical records on their daughter, but would it serve the best interests of the daughter if she knew that her parents were going to be privy to all that is revealed in treatment? On the other hand, the therapist would also be obliged to assess the potential risk of harm connected with ongoing casual sex, considering the possibilities of physical assault, pregnancy, and sexually transmitted diseases with potentially fatal consequences. In this case, given sufficient risk of harm to the girl, the therapist may opt to include her parents in treatment at some point. Again, the therapist establishes, at the outset, what the limits of confidentiality will be, apart from legal entitlements, and helps the parents grasp the concept of privacy in therapy as an essential core condition for progress with their child. Ultimately, one goal of treatment, in some cases, may be to help the patient feel secure enough to broach important topics with her parents, if that is feasible, rather than the therapist serving as a conduit of information to the parents of an adolescent client. It should also be noted that individual states vary in mandated reporting laws for patients who are legally defined as minors, with at least two important variables being (a) the relative ages of the two parties (i.e., a minor who is having sex with an 18-year-old as opposed to a 26-year-old), and (b) the specific type of sexual activity involved (e.g., oral, anal, vaginal).

Family therapy and group therapy create an additional layer of complexity involving confidentiality. Not only must the therapist be mindful of the usual ethical and legal constraints, but agreements must also be in place for every single participant in the treatment to honor each other's privacy and in language that is developmentally appropriate for children if they are participating. Again, what are the provisions for privacy in individual discussions with the therapist, and what are the agreements about honoring family secrets?

The APA Ethics Code requires couples and family therapists to provide clear informed consent about who is considered to be the client or patient at the outset and also to describe the type of relationship that he or she will have with each member of the family. This standard also addresses confidentiality by cross-referencing a standard requiring psychologists to discuss the limits of confidentiality so that each party understands his or her rights and obligations. The American Group Psychotherapy Association addresses this topic in its ethics code by requiring participants as well as the group psychotherapist to safeguard everyone's rights of privacy, regarding both information that is revealed in the group as well as the identity of group members: "The group shall agree that the patient/client as well as the psychotherapist shall protect the identity of its members" (American Group Psychotherapy Association, 2007, para. 2.1).

LAWS CONCERNING PRIVACY AND EXCEPTIONS TO CONFIDENTIALITY

Laws regulating psychologists' records and disclosures emerge from cases that have been litigated in state courts (as mentioned previously) or enacted by the state or federal legislature. An example of a state law protecting patient privacy is the California Confidentiality of Medical Information Act enacted in 1979 (Cal. Civil Code, § 56–56.37, 2008). This law requires that psychologists properly maintain patient records under their control. The language of the law is wide-ranging: "Every provider. . . who creates, maintains, preserves, stores, abandons, destroys, or disposes of medical records shall do so in a manner that preserves the confidentiality of the information contained therein" (Cal. Civil Code, § 56.101, 2008). This law prohibits psychologists (and other health care providers) from unauthorized release of their patient records, including any patient's individually identifiable information (name, address, e-mail address, Social Security number, etc.). It also states the situations under which psychologists may or must disclose patient information.

An example of the requirement to break confidentiality arose from case law emerging from a 1976 California Supreme Court decision, *Tarasoff v. Regents of the University of California.* A graduate student by the name of Prosenjit Poddar, who was attending the University of California, Berkeley in fall 1968, became infatuated with a young woman, Tatiana Tarasoff, with whom he had developed a friendly relationship over a period of months. As time went on it became clear that Tatiana was not interested in pursuing an intimate relationship, despite Prosenjit's ardor, and his mental health began to deteriorate as a result. Ultimately he sought treatment at the university's health facility, where a clinical psychologist diagnosed him with paranoid schizophrenia. During his brief course of therapy he revealed his intention to kill Tatiana, at which time his therapist summoned the police for an involuntary hospitalization; however, he was quickly released from custody by the police, who found him to be sane and warned him to keep his distance from the object of his affection. He stopped his therapy; however, 2 months later Prosenjit followed through with his earlier threat and murdered Tatiana in October 1969. Her parents sued the university, the police, and the psychologist for negligence and were awarded $600,000.

Following this landmark case, laws were enacted in most states requiring psychologists to warn those at risk whenever a serious threat of physical violence to a reasonably identifiable victim is communicated to a treating therapist. Furthermore, therapists are not liable for physical violence perpetrated by their patients unless certain conditions are met, namely, that (a) there was a fiduciary relationship between two individuals (i.e., a contractual relationship existed that is recognized by law as one of trust and confidence between two parties, such as between doctor and patient, in which the patient can communicate without fear of disclosure; Crocker, 1985), (b) the danger was foreseeable (i.e., the threat of physical violence was directly revealed to the therapist, although the therapist bears no obligation to personally investigate the threat), and (c) the victim or victims were identifiable (i.e., the patient revealed the actual name of the intended victim or supplied sufficiently detailed information so that the individual could be readily identified). It should be noted that some states require the therapist to notify both the intended victim and the local police of an intended physical threat, and some states permit the therapist to use his or her own discretion in these matters (Werth, Welfel, & Benjamin, 2009).

This rule was expanded in California in 2004 in the case of *Ewing v. Goldstein* (2004), which extended the therapists' duty-to-warn statute to include communications about the patient from an immediate family member. This case also involved a frustrated lover, although there were salient differences from the Tarasoff case. A despondent man revealed to his father that he intended to murder his ex-girlfriend's new boyfriend, Keith Ewing, and asked his father to loan him a gun. The father refused and instead contacted his son's therapist, Dr. David Goldstein, to report the threat. Dr. Goldstein thereupon hospitalized the man on a voluntary basis. The man agreed to being hospitalized, was held overnight, and then released. He then proceeded to shoot and kill Ewing and then turned the gun on himself (Ewing, 2005).

The APA dissented from this ruling, stating that requiring a therapist to warn intended victims when notified by a family member of the patient would have a "chilling effect" on patients, discouraging them from trusting their therapist if they knew that private conversations with family members could be used against them. The new California law passed nonetheless.

Federal laws have been enacted from time to time that have a bearing on patients' privacy and confidentiality of their clinical records (i.e., their PHI). In 2003 the Privacy Rule of the Health Insurance Portability and Accountability Act (HIPAA) was implemented, requiring all health care providers who used electronic means of storing, retrieving, or transmitting patients' PHI to comply with specific rules concerning patient privacy. HIPAA required psychologists to take measures concerning patient rights and privacy protection in addition to state regulations or the APA Ethics Code (which, technically, applied only to those who held membership in APA). These measures included informing patients at the outset of treatment about exactly how their personal psychological records might be used and disclosed to others and their prerogatives concerning them. These include the rights of patients

- to inspect and obtain a copy of their psychological record (with certain limitations),
- to make corrections in their record if there were factual errors or to make an addendum,
- to receive an accounting of disclosures that their therapist made to third parties (e.g., other therapists, physicians),
- to request restrictions on certain uses or disclosures of their psychological record,

▪ to request that their psychologist communicate with them in a certain way or location (e.g., e-mail, cellular phone instead of office telephone),

▪ to receive a complete version of the HIPAA Notice of Privacy Practices as implemented by their psychologist, and

▪ to be informed about whom to contact with questions or complaints.

Also, they must be informed about exceptions to confidentiality, such as when disclosures could or must be made to third parties (e.g., child or elder abuse, threats of physical harm to identifiable victims, suicidal threats) and how to receive confidential information or be contacted by their therapist (e.g., sending invoices to an address other than their house if they do not want family members to know of their treatment or using an alternate telephone number).

Additional features were added to the HIPAA requirements in subsequent years requiring providers to disclose security measures that were in place for computerized record keeping, such as the use of firewalls, means of backing up PHI, and other relevant safeguards and procedures whenever the electronic manipulation or transmission of patient data occurred, such as using e-mail or fax machines to transmit records.

Exceptions to Privacy and Confidentiality in Clinical and Consulting Settings

Psychologists are ethically obliged to inform clients and patients about the limits of confidentiality at the outset of services unless it is not feasible or contraindicated. A patient just admitted to the hospital emergency room because of a thwarted suicide attempt or a schizophrenic patient with auditory hallucinations likely does not have sufficient cognitive ability to process a presentation on the limits of confidentiality. However, in less emergent situations, clients and patients are entitled to an explanation of confidentiality and its exceptions in all settings. Examples include a patient undergoing treatment, a high school student beginning counseling with a school psychologist, or a recent graduate from the police academy who is being assessed for his first job.

In the legal arena it is also essential to reveal the exceptions to confidentiality unless prohibited by the situation, as discussed previously. Common examples include the defendant being held on a felony charge who is about to undergo a psychological evaluation for competency to stand trial or parents who are litigating for full custody of their children and both will undergo court-ordered psychological evaluations. In such cases the individuals would also be informed that a report will result from the assessment and that the court and others will view that report; in addition, they would be told about any other likely consequences relevant to privacy and confidentiality that will flow from the evaluation.

Although some of the confidentiality exclusions have already been mentioned, I briefly review the common exceptions next. It should be noted that the list that follows reflects California law, and legal statutes vary by state concerning what is discretionary on the part of the psychologist (i.e., what may be reported) as opposed to what is mandatory (i.e., what must be reported). This book's supplemental website (http://pubs.apa.org/books/supp/essentialethics/) contains a list of the legal exceptions to confidentiality in the state of California as it might be presented to a new patient or client.

DANGER TO SELF

This includes the client or patient who reveals his or her intent to harm or kill him- or herself. An example is the patient who discloses to his therapist that he or she has a clear intent to inflict harm on him- or herself or commit suicide, that he or she has a detailed plan to do so, and that he or she has the means (i.e., has purchased a weapon, has access to lethal drugs, or has some other obviously risky or lethal plan). In addition, the psychologist would also consider the patient's prior history of suicide attempts, the presence of a psychological disorder such as major depression or a personality disorder, concurrent drug or alcohol abuse, family history and current living situation, and other variables that might be likely to increase the risk of self-harm. But regardless of the presence or absence of other risk factors, the patient's verbalizing his or her serious objective in ending his or her life would be sufficient grounds for intervening rapidly by voluntary hospitalization or other means to maintain the patient's safety. If the patient refused and was actively suicidal, then the therapist would contact the police or an emergency psychiatric team for involuntarily hospitalization, necessarily breaking patient confidentiality by revealing information to law enforcement authorities and hospital personnel.

DANGER TO OTHERS

When a troubled patient discloses to a therapist a serious intention to harm a third party, such as a former lover, boss, or professor, the patient has generally sacrificed his or her right to privacy. However, federal circuit courts have differed on the extent of the duty to report or warn when such a threat surfaces. In 1998, the 10th Circuit Court of Appeals in *United States v. Glass* held that a therapist could disclose a serious threat if the disclosure was the only means of averting the transference of harm (Caudill & Kaplan, 2005). Then, 2 years later, the Sixth Circuit Court of Appeals in *United States v. Hayes* (2000) asserted that therapists may have a duty to warn the intended victim but ruled that the psychotherapist–patient privilege continued to hold later on, preventing therapists from testifying about the threats in a subsequent prosecution (Caudill & Kaplan, 2005). In 2004 in California, as mentioned previously, the *Ewing v. Goldstein* case broadened the duty to warn by resolving that psychotherapists must break confidentiality if they receive information from a family member about their patient's intention to seriously harm a third party. Although state laws differ on the specifics of notifying the intended victim and the local police department, for the most part psychologists are required take proactive measures when a patient reveals a serious intention of harming another individual.

REVELATION OF HARM TO CHILDREN OR ELDERS

Some situations, such as child or elder abuse, invoke state laws requiring a psychologist to notify the police or appropriate county or state agency. Psychologists who reasonably suspect that their minor patient is the victim of child abuse are required to make a report to the governmental agency responsible for child protective services. By example, *child abuse* in California is defined as "unlawful corporal punishment or injury," meaning a situation in which a person deliberately inflicts cruel or inhumane corporal punishment or an injury resulting in a traumatic condition (Cal. Penal Code § 11165.4, 2009). Even if psychologists learn of an adult patient's past abuse, psychologists may be required to report if they know that the perpetrator currently lives with minors and therefore continues to pose a threat to children.

Child abuse by neglect is defined as the negligent treatment or maltreatment of a child by the parent or legal custodian resulting in harm or threatened harm to the child and also triggers reporting by the psychologist.[1] And in the event of suspected childhood sexual abuse, psychologists are generally required to promptly make both an oral and a

---

[1]According to California law a more extreme form, *severe neglect*, is defined as neglectful failure of the parent or custodian to protect the child from severe malnutrition or medically diagnosed nonorganic failure to thrive. *General neglect* is defined as the failure to provide adequate food, clothing, shelter, medical care, or supervision but does not include physical injury to the child (Cal. Penal Code §11165.2, 2009).

written report with documentation to the appropriate agency, resulting in an investigation of the situation by that agency.[2]

Elder abuse generally refers to a patient over the age of 65, usually a dependent adult, who the psychologist believes is the victim of abuse that is physical, sexual, emotional, or financial in nature. States vary in reporting requirements for elder abuse, with some permitting psychologists to break confidentiality and file a report and some requiring that they do so.

DEPENDENT ABUSE

A patient between the ages of 18 and 64 who is mentally or physically dependent on another (e.g., family member, caretaker, conservator) may disclose that he or she has been abused by his or her caretaker(s), again, according to California law. If the therapist believes that these claims are true, then the therapist must report them to the appropriate governmental agency, either county or state (Cal. Penal Code § 15630, 2009).

CHILD VICTIM OF A CRIME

If a child under 16 years of age has been the victim of a crime, such as assault or rape, and discloses this to his or her psychologist, the child has yielded his or her right to confidentiality because the therapist may be required to report this information to the authorities.

ASSISTING IN COMMITTING A CRIME

An individual who seeks psychological services to enable him- or herself or another to commit a crime yields his or her right to privacy concerning the details of the intended crime. This includes an individual seeking psychological services to avoid detection or apprehension concerning a crime.

COURT APPOINTMENT

Whenever a psychologist is appointed by a court to evaluate an individual, the resulting report is submitted to the court and the individual forfeits his or her right of confidentiality.

---

[2]*Childhood sexual abuse* in California law is defined as sexual assault or sexual exploitation including statutory rape, rape in concert (aiding or abetting a perpetrator), incest, sodomy, and any sexual contact between genitals or anal opening of one person and mouth or tongue of another as well as any intentional touching of the genitals or intimate parts with the clothing covering them, for purposes of sexual arousal or gratification (Cal. Penal Code 11165.1, 2009).

SANITY PROCEEDINGS

This includes the situation in which a patient has been arrested and is involved in a criminal proceeding. If his or her sanity is directly at issue, a court-appointed psychologist will evaluate him, and a report will be submitted to the court.

PATIENT LITIGANT EXCEPTION

This occurs when a court orders a patient's psychological record to be examined because the patient has filed a lawsuit placing his or her emotional state at issue. An example is a woman who is suing her surgeon for malpractice because of permanent damage resulting from a relatively simple operation (e.g., a nerve was cut) and the diagnosis of major depression that ensued. In this case the psychologist's records and testimony might constitute a central part of the supporting evidence for his or her lawsuit (Cal. Evidence Code §1016, 2009).

COMPETENCY PROCEEDINGS

When a patient is being evaluated for his or her competence, such as in a proceeding for guardianship (e.g., child custody) or conservatorship (e.g., a patient with dementia), the patient does not have the right of confidentiality. Again, the psychologist performing the evaluation writes a report that is submitted directly to the court as a guide in making a legal determination about the mental status of the individual being assessed.

LAWSUIT AGAINST A THERAPIST OR PATIENT

Confidentiality is voided in both of these cases: (a) a patient suing a therapist for breach of duty (e.g., the patient sues the therapist for incompetent practice or for having a sexual relationship with the patient) or (b) a therapist litigating against the patient for his or her behavior (e.g., the therapist sues a patient in a small claims court for nonpayment of a bill or sues a potentially violent patient who has been stalking the therapist or damaged his office or car). Information in the psychologist's clinical record sufficient to resolve either dispute will be subject to disclosure.

DEEDS, WILLS, OR OTHER LITIGATION

The psychologist may release information in the clinical record of his deceased patient concerning a deed of conveyance, will, or other writing executed by the patient concerning his interest in property (real estate claims). Also, any information in the record that is relevant to pending litigation with a deceased patient could be subject to disclosure (Cal. Evidence Code §1021, 1022, 2009). However, it is important to note that in general, clinical records remain confidential even after the client or patient dies, and psychologists have an ethical duty to refrain from releasing them to anyone unless coerced by a valid subpoena or court order.

PUBLIC RECORDS

Sometimes a patient may require that a psychologist file a report with a public agency on his or her behalf, in which case his or her PHI is only as secure as the confidentiality of that agency. An example of this is releasing details of a patient's mental health for a patient who has been injured or is ill and is filing for long-term disability with the state division of workers' compensation. It is possible that clinical records may be predisclosed by the agency receiving the PHI. Sometimes psychologists are asked to reveal generic patient data in response to ongoing research. Examples include clinical research by investigators conducting epidemiologic studies, health care research organizations, and accredited public or private nonprofit educational or health care institutions for bona fide research purposes (Cal. Civil Code 56.10(c)(7), 2009). In such cases, the psychologist may comply with requests received but must obtain the patient's signed consent before responding.

PATIENT AUTHORIZATION

If a client or patient signs an authorization for release of his or her PHI to a certain entity, the client or patient is consenting to the transmission of his or her PHI to that entity. However, the authorization itself must comply in form and content with (a) state law, if any applies, and (b) the federal regulations of HIPAA. Regulations may include important details such as including an expiration date, stating the rationale for the release of records, including the fact that the patient is entitled to receive a copy of the consent form, and printing the authorization form in 14-point letters, which are easier to read.

Two exceptions to releasing records have been legally authorized with a signed consent form (California law). These both pertain to potential harm that might result if (a) a patient requests to view his or her own clinical record or (b) a parent or guardians request to view their child's clinical record.

In the first scenario a patient requesting to see his or her therapist's notes or assessment results is legally and ethically entitled to receive them if she so authorizes in writing. However, the therapist may decline to release the record to the patient if the therapist judges that the patient could be harmed in some way, such as by learning of his or her formal diagnosis too early in treatment (e.g., narcissistic or paranoid personality disorder), seeing test results that could be confusing, or reading his or her therapist's notes written in technical language that could be interpreted as criticism or in some other negative way.

In the second scenario parents generally legally have access to their minor children's therapist, including the clinical record. Although state laws vary concerning inpatients and outpatients, parents could be declined access if the health care provider judges that releasing the records to them would have a detrimental effect on (a) the provider's professional relationship with the minor patient, (b) the minor's safety, or (c) the minor's psychological well-being (Cal. Health and Safety Code § 123115(a)(2); 2009). This includes potential endangerment situations, as spelled out in federal law, in which the therapist reasonably suspects domestic violence, abuse, or neglect and releasing information about the therapy might further risk the child's safety (Uses and Disclosures of Protected Health Information: Personal Representatives, 2002, revised 2003).

An interesting question arises when a couple has participated in marital or family therapy and subsequently decides to end their relationship. In the ensuing decision making or litigation about physical and legal custody of the children, one parent may authorize the release of clinical records concerning the marital therapy under the impression that the psychologist's notes might help him or her win custody of the children (e.g., the notes might reveal both his or her strengths as a parent and the weaknesses or psychopathology of his or her former spouse). However, unless the second parent also authorizes such a release, the psychologist is ethically and legally bound to withhold all clinical records. In short, both parties involved in couples counseling must agree for the psychologist to release the PHI. If the treating therapist even acknowledges that the dissenting parent was ever a participant in treatment, even without releasing any specific clinical information about that person, the therapist is breaching that patient's confidentiality as well as violating both an ethical rule and state law.

Technology and Confidentiality

Information technology continues to advance at a rapid rate, and it is incumbent on psychologists who use such technology to be current in their understanding and application of effective means of protecting patient privacy. Increasingly hospitals, universities, mental health clinics, and individual psychologists use technology in the course of their work that may jeopardize privacy. This technology includes audio- or video-taping clients and patients, a procedure long used for research, clinical, and training purposes. The problem also applies to record keeping by computer, using e-mail and cell phones with patients and other health care providers, using fax machines for patient data, and even delivering individual psychotherapy by means of videoconferencing. Each of these poses its own risks to privacy, and clients must be so informed in advance.

Computers holding clinical records can be lost, stolen, immobilized by viruses, or corrupted by hard drive crashes. Some state and federal laws, such as HIPAA, require health care practitioners to take measures to maximize the security of patient records. Examples are the routine use of password protection for files, secure off-premise external backup systems, and having well-understood protocols in place for the psychologist and support staff using technology that minimizes the possibility of error (e.g., accidentally sending patient records to a wrong fax number or e-mail address).

E-mail is an extremely convenient tool for rapid exchange among health care providers, clients, and patients, but it has its risks. For example, other people using the same computer or server (e.g., family members, work colleagues) may be able to read confidential material. Clients must be informed of these risks to confidentiality in advance, and psychologists should avoid using technology in which the risk to privacy and confidentiality outweighs the convenience or possible benefit to the consumer.

Consulting With Other Health Care Providers

It is common, and even advisable at times, for psychologists to consult with peers either in person, by telephone, or by some other electronic means. Some therapists attend a monthly peer-consultation group where patients are anonymously discussed and therapeutic issues and strategies are explored. In these situations, of course, details that would reveal the identity of a client or patient must never be shared without prior authorization.

When psychotherapists share information with other treating health care providers, such as a marital therapist or a referring primary care physician, only the information that is essential to the consultation should be disclosed and, naturally, only with signed authorization. For example, a psychologist treating a woman individually, who was consulting with the patient's group therapist, would not reveal that the woman was currently in litigation for tax evasion unless it were directly related to the matter at hand and the patient authorized such a disclosure. As a general rule, only the minimal amount of information from the patient's clinical record, sufficient to address the clinical need, should ever be conveyed to others.

It is generally important for clients and patients to be able to verbalize their painful and destructive life experiences, rather than just ruminate about them privately, if they are to make progress in treatment. Psychologists' maintenance of their ethical duty of privacy and confidentiality creates a safe and productive environment for those consulting with them to make such progress. In considering privacy and confidentiality, however, therapists must always balance their obligation to patients with their duty to society, hence the exceptions to privacy and confidentiality. It is also important to note that what is revealed in private to a therapist or supervisor may increase the psychologist's interpersonal power over the other. Every psychologist must be vigilant and well trained to avoid exploiting that power, and this is the subject of Chapter 7.

Avoiding Harm and Exploitation 7

Jason's wife of 4 years left him because of his increasing compulsive sexual behavior with Internet pornography. Jason would commonly spend 3 to 4 hours each day searching for new websites and participating in online social networks focused on sex. This habit was interfering with work, the couple's financial security, and their personal relationship.

Jason was upset by his wife's departure and decided to initiate treatment with Dr. Tauss, a local therapist who was well-known in treating sexual addiction. Dr. Tauss was confident of his innovative treatment and felt entitled to charge exorbitant fees, given the power of this particular addiction. He charged $3,000 for the initial 90-minute evaluation, and each subsequent 45-minute session was $600. Jason was initially shocked by Dr. Tauss's fees but went along with them because he was feeling desperate. He had just spent the past week staying in his house each day for 14-hour sessions in front of his computer and had received a warning from his employer that he would be fired unless he returned to his job immediately.

Jason made such excellent progress in treatment after 4 months, with only one relapse early in therapy, that his wife decided to return to him. However, she questioned the high therapy fees that Jason was paying and noted that they were far higher than any other therapist. She convinced Jason to seek a reduction in fee from Dr. Tauss because the couple now had diminished financial resources. However, Dr. Tauss denied Jason's request for a lower fee, pointing out that his job was secure now that his sexual addiction was gone and saying he would have to terminate treatment if Jason could not pay his fee. Jason followed his wife's advice and opted to stop treatment, even though he was at significant risk of relapsing.

Introduction

The American Psychological Association (APA) Ethics Code has always contained a rule against inflicting harm on others as a basic value underlying both practice and research. Whether in the role of researcher, professor, supervisor, clinician, or management consultant, psychologists follow Principle A: Beneficence and Nonmaleficence, which states as the highest goal that they must avoid harming others and attempt to safeguard the welfare and rights of those with whom they interact. The ethical standard that is the corollary to this principle does not specifically address beneficence but focuses exclusively on avoiding harm. Standard 3.04, Avoiding Harm, is short and simply states the following: "Psychologists take reasonable steps to avoid harming their clients/patients, students, supervisees, research participants, organizational clients, and others with whom they work, and to minimize harm where it is foreseeable and unavoidable" (APA, 2010).

Of the 89 ethical standards in the 2002 Ethics Code, approximately 72% are concerned with harming or exploiting others. This book's supplemental website (http://pubs.apa.org/books/supp/essentialethics/) contains a list of the 64 ethical standards relevant to harm and exploitation in the 2002 code. The vast majority of these prohibit exploitation per se, and relatively few address harmful activities of psychologists that are not necessarily exploitative. Exploitation may be seen as a subset of harm. Although every dog is an animal, not every animal is a dog, and although every exploitative act is harmful, harm can also occur when there is no exploitation. How does one then define exploitation and harm?

In this chapter, I discuss what exploitation and harm are and how psychologists should apply this concept to different roles.

Harm Versus Exploitation

Inflicting harm on the recipient of psychological services may not always be an intentional act. A psychologist who harms someone may be unaware that he or she has done so and certainly may never have deliberately engaged in the behavior or failed to fulfill the responsibilities that resulted in harm. The incompetent therapist who fails to involuntarily hospitalize a patient who discloses a plan, means, motivation, and immediate intent to commit suicide harms the patient by his inaction. Likewise, a psychologist may harm a patient applying for long-term disability by using an obsolete form of an assessment instrument instead of the most current edition or by attempting to formally assess a client who has such poor fluency in English that the assessment's validity would be flawed. The results of testing could be inaccurate and not serve the best interests of the client, despite the assessor's best intentions. In each of these cases the resultant harm was more attributable to incompetence or lack of awareness by the practitioner. The psychologists had nothing to gain and, possibly, had something to lose in the form of future complaints or grievances that could be brought by the clients or family members in each case.

To *exploit* means to make use of unfairly, or benefit unjustly from the work of another (Compact Oxford English Dictionary, 2009). Exploiting another invariably means that the psychologist has deliberately introduced a secondary role—he or she is about to engage in a multiple-role relationship in which his or her own wants or needs might be gratified in addition to the primary role of carrying out the work of clinician, supervisor, professor, or other. A conflict occurs when the expectations attached to one social role are incompatible with those of another role (Kitchener, 1988). Kitchener (1988) developed three guidelines for determining when relationships have a high probability of leading to harm: (a) As the incompatibility of expectations increases between roles, so will the potential for harm; (b) as the obligations associated with different roles diverge, the potential for loss of objectivity and divided loyalties increases; and (c) as the prestige and power differential between the professional's and the consumer's roles increases, so does the potential for exploitation. The author makes the point that therapists should increase the ethical prohibitions against engaging in the questionable relationship as the risk of harm increases.

An example of exploitation is the researcher who attempts to attract more participants for a study by omitting important details of the protocol in the informed consent that participants would possibly experience as embarrassing, offensive, or otherwise aversive. The researcher selfishly benefits by duping prospective participants into taking part in this research, which they might well have refused to do had the researcher revealed certain critical details of the protocol.

Another example is the professor who encourages a romantic relationship with a current student who has expressed such an inclination. Even though the student may have initiated it, the professor knows that such a relationship is judged to be exploitative by the profession, given the inherent power differential between teachers and students, and that such a relationship is specifically forbidden by the Ethics Code as well. The professor also may be indirectly harming other students in the class, not only by modeling behavior that is prohibited by the Ethics Code but also by eroding his or her objectivity in evaluating and grading students' academic performance (i.e., playing favorites).

HARMFUL BUT NOT EXPLOITATIVE

Comparatively few ethical standards address inflicting harm that does not necessarily constitute exploitation. These consist of the following topical areas: (a) the psychologist's own personal problems and conflicts, (b) unfair discrimination, (c) third-party requests for services, (d) cooperation with other professionals, and (e) informed consent (APA, 2010).

The first of these addresses situations in which a psychologist experiences a psychological or health problem sufficiently serious to compromise his or her ability to work. As noted in Chapter 4, psychologists are subject to the same range of stresses, loss, trauma, and dysfunction that affect the rest of humankind. A psychologist who is grieving the loss of a parent may find, to his or her surprise, that he or she has developed blind spots and is unable to be vigilant about his or her own biases or prejudices any longer. The psychologist finds, to his or her chagrin, that he or she periodically has lapses in complying with the standard prohibiting unfair discrimination. This standard forbids psychologists from acting in a biased way with clients, patients, students, and others on the basis of age, gender, gender identity, race, ethnicity, culture, national origin, religion, sexual orientation, disability, socioeconomic status, or any basis proscribed by law.

Third-party requests for services introduce a multiple-role relationship right at the outset and therefore can be confusing or even harmful to the recipient of psychological services. The third party could be (a) a parent referring a child to be treated for attention-deficit disorder, (b) the court referring a defendant for a determination of mental competency to stand trial, (c) a therapist referring a patient to a neuropsychologist for diagnostic evaluation concerning a head injury, (d) an employer referring one of his or her best employees for treatment of alcohol dependency, or (e) a neurologist referring a chronic pain patient for treatment of depression and pain management. In each of these situations the psychologist has a relationship both with the patient and the referring third party and must "attempt to clarify at the outset of the service the nature of the relationship with all individuals or organizations" (APA, 2010, Standard 3.07, Third-Party Requests for Services). The psychologist must also identify who the client is and the probable uses of the services provided or information acquired and disclose the fact that there could be limits to confidentiality, more frequently in forensic settings.

Psychologists must cooperate with other professionals to serve their clients and patients effectively unless prohibited for some reason. Here, too, one could inflict harm on a client or patient inadvertently, but not deliberately exploit them, by simply failing to collaborate with a health care professional who referred someone for treatment. The press of daily work might result in a failure to return phone calls or triage appropriately—requesting and reviewing the records of a new patient, following up with authorized requests from others who are also treating the patient (e.g., marital or group therapists, medical specialists), or collaborating and following up in a timely manner with a student's high school teachers in response to a referral for an evaluation.

Finally, the requirement to provide informed consent, as discussed in Chapter 5, is ubiquitous throughout the Ethics Code, and failure to honor this rule could be harmful to others but is usually not intentionally exploitative. Psychologists in nearly every role are required to provide informed consent—as researchers, therapists, evaluators, supervisors, and even professors.

HARMFUL AND EXPLOITATIVE

Most serious harm caused by psychologists is also exploitative in nature; the psychologist somehow stands to benefit at the expense of the other and has made a deliberate decision to do so. This is most evident with the therapist who preys on patients by initiating sexual activities; the therapist gratifies him- or herself on a variety of levels and clearly exploits the dependency and vulnerability of the patients. There may be what appear to be "justifiable exceptions," such as the lonely, recently divorced therapist who falls in love with a patient and rationalizes that this constitutes a valid exception to the no-sex rule. This psychologist may not be fully aware of the potential for harm or exploitation inherent in the multiple role that is about to commence and may even view the ensuing relationship as beneficial for both his or her patient and him- or herself.

According to Gabbard (1994), psychoanalysts who engage clients and patients in a sexual relationship generally all have narcissistic issues and may be grouped into four categories: (a) the psychotic-disordered clinician, (b) the predatory psychopathic and paraphilic clinician, (c) the self-destructive clinician, and (d) the "lovesick" clinician. The psychotic clinician experiences a loss of contact with reality characterized by delusionally depressed or manic states with odd or bizarre ideas; this therapist may believe that a sexual relationship with his or her patient is the only way to effect change in the patient's life. The psychopathic therapist may be charming and intelligent but lacks a conscience or sense of guilt, is unable to tell the truth, takes needless risks, is incapable of real love or attachment, and fails to learn from unpleasant experiences (Corsini & Auerbach, 1998). This therapist exploits and preys on clients and patients, with no capacity for empathy for their needs, driven by paraphilic urges (i.e., abnormal or extreme sexual desires frequently involving risk). The self-destructive therapist responds to unconscious self-punitive needs prompting him or her to make decisions and engage in activities that could lead to ruin as a practicing therapist, such as jeopardizing his or her license by engaging in sex with a patient. And the lovesick therapist is one who feels that he or she has genuinely fallen in love with a "special" patient; sometimes this individual may have recently had a major personal loss (e.g., divorce, death of a child) and is experiencing depression and attendant impaired judgment. Understanding the psychological nature of these individuals who sexualize the therapeutic relationship helps with diagnosing and rehabilitating the abusing therapist.

Sometimes the theoretical orientation of a psychologist and the nature of the treatment being offered play a role in helping to determine what may be experienced by the client or patient as being harmful and what is not. It is interesting to note that what appears to be the same intervention performed by psychologists with different informed consent at the outset and different levels of competence may result in harming one patient but helping another. For example, an experienced, behaviorally oriented psychologist uses in vivo desensitization with a patient who is agoraphobic and unable to enter a public place such as a restaurant without experiencing overwhelming anxiety. The therapist practices exposure therapy with the patient by walking into a restaurant with him, sitting down at a table, ordering something from the menu, and then waiting for the patient's anxiety level to decrease to a reasonably comfortable level before eventually leaving the restaurant with him at the end of the meal. The patient is informed in advance of the treatment modality and understands the theoretical approach prior to experiencing it.

What follows is a different scenario. A recently licensed, classically trained psychoanalyst who read a journal article on the topic of exposure therapy impulsively decides to offer the in vivo restaurant intervention to a patient whom she is treating in psychoanalysis. However, she fails to adequately prepare him for the experience in advance and does not process the meaning of the experience afterward back in the office, which is a departure from her normal practice. This is experienced as confusing to the patient and increases his anxiety about the treatment process, and he now feels that his therapist was being seductive with him by inviting him to lunch.

The analyst had not adequately prepared the patient or thought through the process of how to integrate her first application of a behavioral technique within ongoing psychoanalysis. There was inadequate informed consent with the patient, a lack of shared expectations about this particular intervention, and inadequate processing of the experience afterward. Hence, what appeared to be the same intervention—meeting a patient for lunch in a restaurant—was experienced quite differently by the two patients; this might have been due less to the therapists' differing theoretical orientations and more to a lack of competence. The psychoanalyst should be commended for experimenting with an approach that would not be acceptable to many of her peers, but she requires additional training for its competent application to patients.

Review of Harm and Exploitation by Ethical Topic

I now briefly review each section of the Ethics Code for topics addressing harm and exploitation, although these topical words may not always be mentioned in the ethical standards themselves. These topics are explored more comprehensively in the chapters that follow; they are presented here for the purpose of focusing on those specific interventions that could result in harm and exploitation of others.

COMPETENCE

The standards discussing competence generally require that psychologists (a) be competent at what they do, including providing services, teaching, and conducting research, and (b) avoid areas in which they are incompetent. Although these may seem to be two sides of the same coin, there actually are some differences between the two. For example, a therapist in private practice treating a new patient who presents with major depression has good skills at diagnosing and treating depressed patients and feels competent to offer the requested clinical services. However, after four sessions, when the therapist learns that her patient is a Gulf War veteran and had been a prisoner of war enduring months of torture, she may have some doubts about her competence level to treat him, never before having worked with a patient who had such an extreme history of trauma resulting in posttraumatic stress disorder.

What began as practice within the psychologist's area of competence soon expanded into an area that she felt ill equipped to treat. Nevertheless, she may be motivated to continue treating because of a combination of incentives: ethical concern for the continuity of care with her patient (i.e., continuing the treatment she began with him) and also her private financial motivation to maintain her income by retaining as many patients as she can. Unfortunately, the business motive can be confounding and lead to a decision that could be exploitative in nature.

If the patient would be better served by referral to another practitioner when the treating therapist doubts her own capacity to provide ongoing clinical services, then she should make such a referral if there are other competent therapists available. However, if she continues treating when she could refer or fails to obtain consultation or additional training to upgrade her skills, then she places the patient at risk of harm. By allowing her role as a businessperson (private practitioner) to influence her clinical judgment (as a treating therapist), she falls victim to a duality that could be exploitative of her patient.

HUMAN RELATIONS

This section of the Ethics Code focuses on the nature of the personal and professional relationships that psychologists establish with colleagues, clients and patients, students and supervisees, research participants, organizational clients, and others with whom they work. It includes Standards 3.04, Avoiding Harm, and 3.08, Exploitative Relationships, as well as related standards on harassment and sexual harassment, conflict of interests, multiple relationships, unfair discrimination, and others. Certainly it is abusive to harass or demean another person on the basis of factors such as age, gender, gender identity, race, ethnicity, culture, national origin, religion, sexual orientation, disability, language, or socioeconomic status. Harassment based on gender is not only prohibited by the Ethics Code but has legal ramifications as well; it has been characterized as a form of sex discrimination by the U.S. Equal Employment Opportunity Commission (2002) that is a violation of Title VII of the Civil Rights Act of 1964. *Sexual harassment* is defined as

> unwelcome sexual advances, requests for sexual favors, and other verbal or physical conduct of a sexual nature when submission to or rejection of this conduct explicitly or implicitly affects one's employment, unreasonably interferes with their work performance, or creates an intimidating, hostile or offensive work environment. (U.S. Equal Employment Opportunity Commission, 2002, para. 2)

The APA Ethics Code includes this language but adds the concept of *intentionality* by requiring ascribed motivation on the part of the harasser, thus creating a higher threshold for violation than the law. It defines sexual harassment as (a) behavior that is unwelcome, offensive, or creates a hostile workplace or educational environment, *and the psychologist knows or is told this* (italics added), or (b) behavior that is sufficiently severe or intense to be abusive to a reasonable person in the context. It concludes by stating that sexual harassment may be conceived of as a single intense or severe act or multiple persistent or pervasive ones (APA, 2010, Standard 3.02, Sexual Harassment). Hence, a harasser might plead ignorance to having transgressed and if the harasser was never "told" by the victim might escape being found in violation of the ethical standard, even though this individual might have violated the federal statute. The second part of the ethical standard, admittedly, may strengthen the rule by citing the "reasonable person" argument.

Sexual harassment and multiple-role relationships culminating in sexual activities are viewed with extreme gravity by ethics committees and state licensing boards, resulting in expulsion from the APA, loss of license, and other sanctions. This includes sex with students and supervisees (see the Education and Training section, which follows), sex with current patients and clients, sex with their family members or significant others, and sex with former patients (see the Therapy section later in this chapter).

Other nonsexual multiple-role relationships can also result in harm and exploitation, such as concurrently participating in the following with an adult recipient of psychological services:

- a business venture (e.g., opening a joint website on eating disorders with a client or patient),
- any other service (e.g., tutoring in an academic course, giving tennis lessons, providing a therapeutic massage as a licensed masseuse),
- hiring one's patient or bartering with him or her for psychological services in a manner that constitutes a potentially risky multiple relationship (e.g., gardening, secretarial work at one's office, babysitting, odd jobs around one's house, helping with computer problems), and
- friendship (e.g., meeting one's patient for dinner, including one's client or patient on family outings).

In each of these activities the psychologist is initiating a secondary role or relationship in addition to the professional one, sometimes in the role of employer (e.g., hiring the patient to babysit or do odd jobs) and sometimes as a service provider (e.g., tutor). Moreover, this secondary role invariably meets his or her own needs in some fashion—growing a business, bringing in more income, or meeting the social needs of a psychologist.

The psychologist's objectivity may be reduced when a secondary role is added, and that can impair competence in any psychological service or activity. The psychologist who begins a business venture online with his or her patient but several months later has a disagreement with the patient about the business plan or strategy may find that he or she has lost effectiveness as a therapist. If that role bleeds into the other, boundaries are forever compromised, and it may be impossible to ever recover the original therapeutic alliance, thus harming the patient by truncating treatment. What began as a business venture in good faith, ended in exploitation of the patient's vulnerability. Psychologists have many patients and have learned through experience about boundaries between their personal and professional life. Patients often may have only one therapist and usually are quite naive about professional boundaries, trusting and relying on the experience of their therapist. Exploitation of the trust may surface with certain dyads under certain circumstances whenever the psychologist contemplates a secondary role in addition to the therapeutic one.

It should be noted that not every multiple relationship is unethical or destructive to patients. In fact, it may be commonplace in rural areas with limited psychological resources for treating therapists to also know their patients in another context, such as the cashier in the local grocery store or the teacher of their junior high school age daughter.

PRIVACY AND CONFIDENTIALITY

In clinical settings, ethical rules as well as state and federal laws protect the privacy of patients and clients. There are many examples in which harm may occur without exploitation, such as when patient privacy is violated, either accidentally or with the best intentions of an unskilled clinician. It is useful to consider the marital therapist who reveals to the wife a private disclosure by the husband about a felony conviction prior to their marriage. Although the disclosure may reflect the therapist's commitment to a policy of "no secrets in therapy," this had never been discussed in advance or authorized by the husband, and it may cause significant harm to the marital relationship.

There are many examples of both harming and exploiting others by violating their privacy. The psychologist both harms and exploits the patient about whom the psychologist writes a journal article or a book without first discussing it with the patient and obtaining prior authorization. It would be best to wait until the termination of treatment to initiate discussion of such a joint project because the power differential inherent in the treatment setting could weaken the patient's ability to decline.

Even psychologists working in educational and training settings must safeguard the privacy of their students and supervisees, as discussed in Chapter 6. Psychologists must avoid inquiry about certain personal topics unless certain conditions prevail (e.g., prior consent, significant impairment, risk of harming others).

ADVERTISING AND OTHER PUBLIC STATEMENTS

Advertising includes promotional messages for products or services in newspapers or other print media (e.g., ads for clinical or consulting services, books, workshops or seminars for mental health professionals or the public), in telephone yellow pages, over the Internet, on radio or television, or elsewhere. Even if a third party creates the advertising message, the psychologist still assumes full responsibility for its content. It is harmful and exploitative, as well as illegal, to attempt to influence the thinking and behavior of others by falsely presenting one's clinical skills, such as claiming unattainable results. The psychologist who guarantees outcomes (e.g., lasting weight loss from a single session) or who claims to cure medical illness in the absence of clinical or experimental data supporting such assertions is giving false hope to gullible patients. The psychologist offering innovative treatment (e.g., individual psychotherapy by e-mail) that lacks validating empirical support also risks exploiting others. Innovation and experimenting with creative methods for change are ethically acceptable only if the psychologist makes a good-faith effort in clinical or research settings to offer full disclosure of any risks and any other information that would affect one's willingness to participate and obtains informed consent as well. By such transparency the psychologist allows consumers to make an objective choice that will best meet their needs while minimizing the risk of exploitation.

Advertising that includes testimonials by current patients or clients is a clear example of a multiple-role relationship that has a high potential for harm and exploitation. The therapist immediately adds a secondary role—that of advertising or business executive—the moment he or she asks a current patient to supply a testimonial about treatment. The power differential inherent in clinical settings usually precludes a patient from refusing such a request. It may feel both flattering and coercive to the depressed patient engaged in psychotherapy to be asked by his or her therapist to comment publicly on therapy effectiveness. It may also be burdensome to decline such a request, disappointing the very person who has helped the patient so much, without feeling additional guilt or shame, the very feelings that the patient has already been struggling with in depression.

Public statements include everything that is said, written, or communicated in any way to another while in the role of a professional psychologist. This includes résumés (e.g., affiliations, degrees), grants or licensing applications, psychological reports, disclosures in depositions or other legal proceedings, informed consent documents describing treatment or research protocol, description of academic courses or training experiences (e.g., including clinical supervision or workshops), media interviews (e.g., print or electronic media—radio, television, Internet, e-mail), public lectures and oral presentations, as well as journal articles and books.

The potential for harm and exploitation comes with obvious examples of conflict of interest, such as the psychologist reporting his or her positive research findings about a new antidepressant medication but failing to disclose that the research was funded by the very pharmaceutical firm that produced the antidepressant and that the psychologist had given lectures or media statements in support of its use that were paid for by the pharmaceutical firm. The public is led to believe that this psychologist has empirical support for the statements and does not know about the $100,000 or more the psychologist has already received as an incentive.

Even academic settings pose risks of harm and exploitation. An example is the inexperienced college instructor who teaches a new course in group therapy but neglects to inform students in advance that it will involve an experiential component that includes participation in group therapy with truthful self-disclosure and will be led by another faculty member. The instructor may fear students would avoid selecting the course were he or she to be completely accurate in describing this requirement in the course catalogue. The harmful aspect is exposing students to the pseudotherapy group without informing them in advance, and the exploitative aspect meets the instructor's needs by assuaging his fears that too few students would select the course unless he or she deceived them about its content and format.

FINANCIAL ARRANGEMENTS

Clients and patients have a right to know about the complete cost of psychological services in advance, and psychologists have an ethical obligation to inform them. This is true in clinical and forensic settings, whether or not health insurance or some other third party is being relied on for payment. The client or patient must be informed, even if the person does not inquire about cost. A neuropsychological evaluation can be costly, ranging from $2,000 to $10,000 or more, and a psychological evaluation in a child custody setting could be even more, ranging from $5,000 to $20,000, depending on the region of the country, the complexity of the assessment, and fees required for depositions and court appearance.

Bartering products or services in exchange for psychological services may be a creative way of transacting business in rural communities or with low-income patients. The lobster fisherman in Maine who exchanges part of his catch for a therapy hour is using products as currency for which a fair market price has been established. The psychologist accepts the lobsters and, at the end of the year, completes the appropriate Internal Revenue Service form documenting the transaction. However, bartering for services may expose the patient and therapist to the complications of a harmful multiple-role relationship. The licensed electrician in Boston who agrees to rewire an aging electrical system in his therapist's Victorian house in exchange for treatment faces a much more complex business arrangement. Now his therapist has also become his customer with whom he is engaged in a contractual relationship for professional services. A multiple role has been established that may confound the therapy relationship if things do not go quite right. It is useful to consider the scenario of the patient–electrician who makes a critical error in judgment when rewiring the children's room. While standing on a radiator to switch on the electric light, the therapist's young child receives a serious electrical shock. How would the therapist feel about such a mishap, and how might this interfere with the ongoing psychotherapy relationship? In a worst-case scenario the new wiring could start a fire that destroys the house, resulting in serious injury or loss of life.

These may seem to be unlikely situations, but they draw attention to the problems that can occur while bartering for services. The psychologist may be dissatisfied with the work carried out by a careless or impaired patient, at best, and harmed by it, at worst. And the potential for harm to the therapeutic work may increase for other reasons as well because the patient now has taken on the secondary role of employee of the therapist. The patient who becomes familiar with his or her therapist's living situation, family members, religious affiliation, political preferences, and intimate day-to-day habit patterns and quirks, as can happen with a workman who visits a house over a period of days or weeks, may experience changes in the therapy relationship that irrevocably alter the treatment process. The patient may begin to feel like "one of the family," or the therapist may also develop this feeling, thereby losing objectivity in the therapy hour and impairing competence to diagnose and treat. On the other hand, a decidedly negative result may emerge. The politically conservative Roman Catholic patient may be disappointed to learn that his or her therapist is a liberal Democrat and a member of the American Civil Liberties Union who supports policies formally opposed by the patient's church (e.g., stem cell research, abortion) after seeing literature or other telltale signs taped to the therapist's refrigerator door. This patient has learned more than he or she ever wanted to know about the therapist's private beliefs and values by simply entering the therapist's home to carry out work and has certainly learned more than the patient would have inquired about during therapy. The impact on therapy could be immense or minimal, depending on the theoretical orientation of the therapist, diagnosis of the patient, and other factors, but the risk is obvious.

EDUCATION AND TRAINING

The power differential inherent in academic and training settings presents a variety of potential risks of harm and exploitation. Providing thorough informed consent is an important part of avoiding harm, and instructors and supervisors are required to inform students and trainees about the educational experiences they are about to have in advance. For instructors, this includes information about course or program content, training goals, objectives, and requirements to be met, as well as any compulsory personal counseling, psychotherapy, experiential groups, consulting projects, or community service. An example of harm without exploitation is the student who was not informed at the outset of a course requirement to participate in a discussion group in which self-disclosure about emotional past losses is the focus. For the student with unresolved major trauma such a requirement may be retraumatizing, and the requirement certainly should have been disclosed in advance in the course catalogue or by some other means.

For supervisors, avoiding harm includes informing the trainee about the theoretical orientation of the supervisor as well as terms of the agreement—frequency and duration of supervisory sessions, nature of the patients or clients who will be seeking services, training goals and expectations, details of scheduling (e.g., weekly quotas, anticipated vacations), and any financial arrangements (if appropriate). The Association of Psychology Postdoctoral and Internship Centers is an important professional association for those involved in training predoctoral and postdoctoral psychologists as well as for those involved in the national match program.[1] One of the most destructive experiences for students and supervisees over the years has been engaging in multiple roles that include sexual relationships (Pope, Levenson, & Schover, 1979). Both harmful and exploitative, sex with one's own student or supervisee, regardless of who initiates it, clouds the objectivity and judgment of the senior psychologist. Beginning with the 1992 revision of the Ethics Code, there are no exceptions to this rule. Whether both parties experience this as an emotional commitment or merely a casual affair, sexual acting out with students or supervisees in the same department, agency, or training center over whom psychologists have or are likely to have evaluative authority is strictly prohibited.

The student gains a lover but loses a supervisor because objectivity and competence begin to erode. Mentors, instructors, and supervisors are ideally positioned in the course of a student's academic training to model good boundaries, yet they may not have had much training, guidance, or life experience themselves in how to carry this out. Many if not most universities and other academic institutions have sexual harassment and related policies. This book's supplemental website (http://pubs.apa.org/books/supp/essentialethics/) provides Stanford University's statement on consensual sexual or romantic relationships.

RESEARCH

Exploitation or harm in research can take several forms. The researcher who fails to provide potential participants with adequate information about the nature of the research in advance or fails to indicate that they will be videotaped is at risk of harming or exploiting. For example, a participant could be harmed if not informed that the research protocol on marital relationships would include exposure to sexual content and imagery, some of which the participant might find disturbing or offensive. If the researcher deliberately omits this information from the informed

---

[1]The monthly newsletter of the Association of Psychology Postdoctoral and Internship Centers is freely available online and is filled with useful information about training and supervision matters (http://www.appic.org/).

consent document, fearing that full disclosure might alienate potential participants, the researcher is making a deliberate decision that will benefit him or her and possibly harm a participant, thus both harming and exploiting.

Using deception with research participants is acceptable only if certain criteria are met (see Chapter 11, this volume). And candidates should never be deceived about the details of their expected participation, such as monetary inducements, the duration of the protocol, anticipated experiences of the protocol (while preserving participants' naiveté), or other specifics that would influence their decision about participation. If the investigator uses deception in the course of the protocol, the investigator must debrief each participant as soon as is feasible after the data collection is completed. The researcher who is short staffed or delays debriefing for some other reason for months after the conclusion of data collection would be harming participants by allowing them to remain deceived for so long a time and would be in violation of the ethical standard concerning deception.

PUBLICATION

Plagiarizing consists of copying the words or using the concepts obtained from another without citing the source or attributing authorship. It is both harmful and exploitative to an author if his or her published theoretical concepts or research results are lifted by another and used in a professional context—journal article, book, professional lecture, or media presentation—without acknowledging the source. In addition to violating certain standards of the Ethics Code, such actions may also be in violation of legal statutes, such as federal copyright laws involving the protection of intellectual property.[2]

Another form of exploitation and harm in the area of publication consists of deliberately claiming publication credit for a journal article, book chapter, or professional presentation in any public forum for work that was essentially created by others. Although seemingly related to plagiarism, it differs in the scope of the misrepresentation as well as the intent. The senior psychologist who deliberately claims primary authorship in a multiply authored article when he or she actually did none of the writing and participated little in the research itself may be in violation of this rule. The senior psychologist may feel entitled to be listed as the first author because he or she contributed toward conceptualizing the investigation as well as toward writing the grant that funded it. But it might be more

---

[2]The first copyright law in the United States was enacted by Congress in 1790 on the initiative of President James Madison, and within 2 weeks, the first work was registered at the U.S. Copyright Office (U.S. Copyright Office, 2005).

appropriate for the senior psychologist to be listed as a junior author and credited in the acknowledgment section or cited in the reference section for contributions rather than to be listed as the primary author.

ASSESSMENT

The area of psychological assessment includes both the construction and scoring of instruments of assessment as well as their use in a diversity of settings and purposes. Psychologists who perform assessments evaluate students in primary and secondary schools, perform child custody evaluations for divorcing couples who are in litigation, evaluate patients in clinical settings who present for treatment, evaluate candidates for work in a variety of settings, perform workers' compensation evaluations for employees with injuries and disabilities, evaluate decisional capacity for the infirm, and work in business and industry with management evaluating job performance of employees.

In each of these settings there is always a potential for harm when the evaluation is substandard and a potential for exploitation if the psychologist is remunerated for incompetent work. The candidate applying for a job with the county fire department could be harmed if the psychologist is careless in administering or scoring a test, carrying out a structured interview, or writing a report. The Vietnamese mother seeking custody of her young children could be harmed if the psychologist is not objective and methodical in evaluating both parents—using evidence-based techniques, using the proper instruments of assessment for a Vietnamese woman, using the same instruments with both parents, spending the same amount of time assessing both, and more She could lose access to her children if the assessment is not done properly, and the children could be harmed for years by mistakenly being placed with an abusive father. After parents receive an adverse judgment from the court, it is not uncommon for them to sue a psychologist who has performed an evaluation, claiming that that it was carried out incompetently, regardless of any actual wrongdoing.

Exploitation in assessment could come in the form of a psychologist who constructs a new instrument without adhering to the well-established scientific standards of test construction. This might include failing to properly evaluate each item for its discriminatory value, failing to establish validity and reliability for the test, and failing to adequately standardize the instrument by gender, age, and ethnicity. The psychologist may then market his instrument in a manner that exaggerates its usefulness, further adding to the exploitation of others—particularly to psychologists who believe the inflated claims and purchase the test in good faith. Such an instrument could harm individuals who take the test (e.g., an adolescent being evaluated for a learning disability) because its validity would be questionable. It could also harm the psychologists who administer the test because their professional work could be legitimately questioned by their clients and patients and, ultimately, could result in ethics complaints, licensing board investigations, or even lawsuits if the harm were sufficiently severe.

THERAPY

Ethical standards concerning harm and exploitation by therapists include (a) multiple-role relationships of a sexual nature and (b) improperly terminating therapy. As mentioned in Chapter 2, although the very first Ethics Code never mentioned the word *sex*, Principle 3, Moral and Legal Standards, required psychologists to show a

> sensible regard for the social codes and moral expectations for the community in which he [sic] works, recognizing that violations of accepted moral and legal standards on his part may involve his clients, students, or colleagues in damaging personal conflicts, and impugn his own name and the reputation of his profession. (APA, 1959)

Presumably sex with current patients would have fallen into the category of violating accepted moral and legal standards, as is addressed by Hare-Mustin, later, in her classic 1974 journal article. Even more relevant, perhaps, was Principle 8, Client Relationship, requiring a psychologist to inform "his prospective client of the important aspects of the potential relationship that might affect the client's decision to enter the relationship" (APA, 1959).

Although no ethical standard specifically addresses hugs, handshakes, pats, massages, or other forms of physical touch in the treatment setting, there are eight that address sexual intimacies, sexual harassment, disclosure of sexual history or current sexual relationship, and related abuses of those in professional relationships with psychologists. Most of these are in the Therapy section, discussed in Chapter 10. There is no accompanying glossary defining *sexual activity* in the Ethics Code, but if there were, it would likely include the following characterization, in some form, stated it in a teleological manner (e.g., a rule of conduct that takes the situation into account—is based on supposed goals and outcomes) rather than a deontological (a rule of conduct considered valid regardless of the situation or outcome) manner. Prohibited sexual activity would include any verbal, nonverbal, or physical activity (i.e., touching oneself or another) on the part of the therapist that has as its goal sexual arousal, sexual gratification, or satisfying of sexual needs of that therapist with a client or patient, regardless of the client's or patient's willing participation. Such a definition would, of course, include physical touching of any part of the body that could be considered sexually arousing to the therapist or patient as well as unwarranted (a) drawing attention to the patient's body (e.g., staring, ogling), (b) inappropriately questioning a patient about his or her sexual behavior, and (c) self-disclosure of the therapist's sexual history or any behavior that is intended to create sexual stimulation or sexual pleasure of any participant in the consulting room (e.g., therapist or patient).

By using a teleological definition, rather than a deontological one, one can concisely create a decision rule for therapists that is easy to follow. Basically, if what the therapist is about to say or do is intended to increase the probability of sexual pleasure, erotic interest or arousal, or romantic relationship with the client or patient, it is off limits and must be avoided. Specific standards concerning sex with current and former patients are presented in Chapter 10.

The standard concerning termination of treatment requires that (a) psychologists end treatment when it is clear that the client or patient no longer needs it, is not likely to benefit, or is being harmed by continued service and (b) psychologists provide pretermination counseling and suggest alternative services as appropriate (APA, 2010). It is likely exploitative and harmful, financially and in other ways, to continue with a patient long after the patient has resolved his or her original complaint and wishes to terminate. Conversely, it could also be harmful to abruptly end therapy simply because treatment met a temporary impasse, or for some other reason that met the therapist's needs rather than those of the patient, without providing pretermination counseling and offering alternative services. However, it is important to note that a therapist may end treatment if the therapist feels threatened or endangered by the patient or someone with whom the patient has a relationship.

The overarching teleological question to be repeatedly addressed by therapists is, Whose psychological needs are being met in the course of carrying out treatment? Certainly therapists may have insights about their own problems as well as derive emotional satisfaction from the process of providing counseling and psychotherapy. But that satisfaction must stop short of using individual clients and patients for social or sexual gratification or for increasing their income long after the therapy goals have been met.

When psychologists harm or exploit others it may be due to a lack of knowledge, poor training, inexperience, incompetence, an adverse life situation resulting in impaired mental health, or even deliberate or predatory motivations. Sometimes psychologists may see a red flag, recognizing that they are confronting a gray area, but may find little guidance from the Ethics Code or legal statutes as to which course of action to take. The next chapter addresses models of ethical decision making that help address these issues so as to avoid exploiting and harming the recipients of psychological services in therapy and other settings.

ETHICAL DECISION MAKING IN PRACTICE, RESEARCH, AND TEACHING

T his section presents a range of models for solving ethical dilemmas, including contemplating the worst-case scenario; the Canadian model; several five-step models; and finally, models by Keith-Spiegel and Koocher (eight-step model), Gottlieb (three-factor model), and Sonne (four-factor model). It also addresses ethical issues that surface in a variety of roles and settings—practice, research, academic settings, and clinical supervision—and how to anticipate and cope with these issues.

Approaches to Ethical Decision Making   8

Dr. Fox's close friend Tony was concerned about Gemma, his 15-year-old daughter, and her use of marijuana and possibly other drugs. He also had been covertly monitoring her computer use with spy software and had discovered that during the past week she had been e-mailing a man she had met online in another state and had sent a partially nude image of herself to him. Tony wanted Dr. Fox to treat Gemma because she already knew him, and that would add to his credibility.

Dr. Fox appreciated his friend's distress and wanted to help. However, he knew from past experience that accepting a family member of a friend might constitute a multiple-role relationship and impair his objectivity. He postponed making a decision at once and consulted with a senior psychologist who was experienced in ethical matters. The consultant advised that accepting Gemma into treatment could have a negative effect on the treatment and on the friendship as well. His prior knowledge of the teenager and his close friendship with Tony might have an inhibiting effect on Gemma's willingness to trust and disclose in treatment. And more important, engaging both parents in Gemma's treatment at some point would be impossible for Dr Fox, given their prior friendship. Finally, the necessary confidentiality of treatment would alter the normal camaraderie that the two men had enjoyed for years. Dr. Fox decided to refer Tony to a trusted colleague, thereby maximizing the treatment outcome for Gemma and keeping the friendship intact.

Introduction

In recent years much has been written about ethical decision making for addressing situations commonly encountered by psychologists. This chapter focuses on a variety of ethical algorithms, approaches for decision making and addressing the problem of selecting the most ethical choice in complex situations. First, I review the need for such a process when ethical standards already exist that broadly address many areas of psychological work.

Ideally, ethical standards provide clear guidance for psychologists working in many settings and roles. As discussed in the beginning of this book, the language used must be sufficiently generic to address the work of the management consultant, supervisor, and clinician while, at the same time, sufficiently precise to solve specific dilemmas that are encountered in each of these areas of work. It is useful to consider how an ethics code might address the following questions:

- Is a licensed therapist competent to try out a new clinical intervention with a married couple after attending a 4-hour workshop, or should the therapist have additional training and study (e.g., an advanced workshop, individualized consultation)?
- What topics should a researcher include in an informed consent form? Are they to be found in the Ethics Code, or is it an individualized matter determined by the nature of the research, the population under study, and the institution where it occurs?
- How long after ending therapy could a therapist wait before striking up a nonromantic friendship with the client or patient or beginning a business venture with him or her?
- How much should a psychologist reveal about his or her personal life to a student, patient, supervisee, or consultee?

There are many gray areas that neither the Ethics Code nor professional guidelines can adequately address because it is virtually impossible to take into account every variable in each situation involving an ethical dilemma. A partial answer is to combine general, guiding ethical principles and specific rules of conduct in the same document. As I have noted, the American Psychological Association (APA) Ethics Code attempts this by including both a set of core values providing the general context titled General Principles as well as specific rules of professional conduct titled Ethical Standards. The synthesis of these two sections helps address the gray areas that are inevitable in any professional setting.

However, this is not always sufficient, and additional means of addressing ethical uncertainties are needed. There are times when ethical standards may conflict with each other or with laws or institutional policies and procedures. An example of such an inconsistency is the ethical rule that psychologists must take reasonable steps to avoid harming those with whom they work yet they are obliged to notify the police if a therapy patient discloses his intent to assault or kill a third party. Does it not feel "harmful" to the patient for a therapist to notify the police about a patient's private disclosures in the therapy office given that the police will then deprive the patient of his or her freedom and likely take him or her into custody for questioning? How are psychologists to proceed when a situation falls in the middle of two inconsistent rules (e.g., law vs. ethics, ethical standard vs. another ethical standard) or in a gray area outside of the rules altogether?

In this chapter, I present approaches for ethical decision making, with an emphasis on multiple-role relationships because these constitute the most serious risks of harm to others.

Conflicting Ethical Standards

It is sometimes true that ethical principles or ethical standards come into conflict with each other. A common example is (a) the ethical requirement for psychologists to be accurate in filing a diagnosis on a patient's managed health care form and (b) an apparently conflicting requirement for psychologists to avoid harming their patients. Unfortunately, accuracy in diagnosis on an insurance form might also result in the patient's being excluded from financial reimbursement for treatment and thus being harmed by depriving him or her of needed therapy (certain diagnoses, such as personality disorders, are routinely excluded from coverage by some health insurance policies). On the other hand, if the psychologist would simply alter the diagnosis (downgrade to a diagnosis that generally requires far less time in treatment and hence is less costly)—knowing that it would be covered by insurance—the patient could presumably remain in treatment and receive reimbursement from the insurer. A specific example is failing to report that a patient meets the criteria for a diagnosis of borderline personality disorder and reporting, instead, that the patient has an adjustment disorder with anxiety, a diagnosis of less severity requiring far less treatment. However, providing an erroneous diagnosis violates the ethical imperative of avoiding false or deceptive statements. I discuss how to address this dilemma while exploring ethical-decision-making models later in this chapter.

Recognizing an Ethical Dilemma in Professional Work

Before psychologists can address ethical decision making, they must first have the awareness that the situation encountered may indeed invoke a moral question. Detailed in this section, the following 13 questions that a psychologist can readily pose to him- or herself are helpful in identifying when a choice point may involve ethical decision making that should be more formally addressed (Nagy, 2005).

BOUNDARIES OF COMPETENCE

Am I working within my boundaries of competence, according to my formal education, training, supervision, or experience? Psychologists work in many different settings (e.g., academic, clinical, forensic, industrial, military, prison, religious) and professional roles (e.g., supervisor, consultant, researcher, teacher, therapist, media presenter) with a broad range of people (e.g., adults of all ages and occupations, couples and families, children and adolescents, people who are gay and lesbian, people with physical or mental disabilities—both inpatients and outpatients, people who are racially, ethnically, and culturally diverse). Although graduate academic training and postdoctoral educational experiences prepare psychologists for the work they do, including preparation for the state licensing exam (if required for their work), these experiences cannot always address every situation or adequately address questions of judgment. Ethical violations concerning competence are frequently cited by the APA and state licensing boards when processing complaints by consumers. In 2007 the APA Ethics Committee adjudicated 32 ethics complaints, 16% of which found the psychologists operating beyond their areas of competence (APA, 2008).

STATE AND FEDERAL LAWS AND REGULATIONS

Am I up to date on current state and federal laws concerning psychological research and practice? State laws regulate the conduct of health care providers in the following areas: confidentiality and its exceptions; a duty to protect, as reflected in mandated reporting of child abuse and sometimes elder and spouse abuse and mandated reporting of a threat to a third party that is revealed to a psychotherapist; requirements for training and licensure of psychologists as well as continuing education; record keeping and the use of computers; advertising of psychological services and products; and the business aspects of practice. In addition, some state licensing boards are showing an interest in formalizing policies concerning termination and referral of patients, closing a practice, maintaining a professional will, and psychologists' activities on the Internet.

The APA Ethics Code has jurisdiction over APA members only, but as mentioned in Chapter 3, states are incorporating the APA Ethics Code into law, thereby investing each ethical standard with the force of law. If psychologists violate a rule, they may be held accountable to both the APA Ethics Committee and the licensing authority in their home state.

Federal laws pertain to both research and practice activities of psychologists. Researchers obtaining federal funding must comply with policies articulated by the U.S. Department of Health and Human Services as well as the granting agency, including such matters as informed consent for research participants, confidentiality and privacy, deception in research, debriefing participants, and care and use of animals in research, to name a few. These are commonly published in the *Federal Register,* a single uniform publication for executive agency rules and notices (published daily) and codified in the *Code of Federal Regulations,* published by the U.S. Department of Health and Human Services. Licensed psychologists must also be knowledgeable about the Health Insurance Portability and Accountability Act. As discussed in Chapter 5, this act, in part, describes policies and procedures for providing information to clients and patients seeking psychological services concerning informed consent, privacy and confidentiality, record keeping, and other matters.

INSTITUTIONAL ETHICS

Am I up to date on the current policies and procedures of my institution? Institutional policies provide important guidelines and standards for researchers and practitioners working in hospitals (private, public, or federal installations such as the U.S. Department of Veterans Affairs hospitals), clinics, universities, public school settings, or other institutions. Those doing research must submit proposals to the institutional review board and comply with its recommendations for the protection of research participants. Any additional changes to the research protocol must again be submitted for approval before being implemented. Those doing clinical work must comply with the institution's policies over and above any ethical or legal requirements. These might include policies about record keeping (e.g., requiring a certain format for record keeping), informed consent for treatment (e.g., informing patients that the facility is a training institution and that some therapy sessions will be observed through a one-way mirror or videotaped), or business matters (e.g., informing patients that payment is expected at the time of treatment).

ETHICS CODES AND PRACTICE GUIDELINES

Do I know the ethical standards of the APA Ethics Code or those of any other professional association of which I am a member that may have a bearing on what I am about to undertake? No ethical standard can determine competence for a practitioner, but by understanding the standards relevant to competence a psychologist can minimize the risk of harm. For example, there is an ethical standard that allows for practicing when not fully trained in a particular intervention; however, that standard also requires limiting one's practice and discontinuing as soon as the emergency has ended or appropriate services are available. This standard provides guidance for psychologists who suddenly encounter an emergency situation, such as with a family member of a patient. Those in rural areas may be particularly affected when there is no other mental health provider in the area to whom to refer.

Certainly psychologists have training in the APA Ethics Code, but how rigorously do they study ethics codes and practice guidelines from other professional associations which they join? An example is the publication *Practice Guidelines for Effective Treatments of PTSD* from the International Society for Traumatic Stress Studies (Foa, Keane, & Friedman, 2000). Psychologists belonging to a professional association should learn of any rules, regulations, policies, or practice guidelines promulgated by that association. If they choose to ignore or depart significantly from a practice guideline, they must have a rational, preferably evidence-based reason for doing so. In contrast, there is no choice about departing from an ethical standard; these are rules that must be followed under all circumstances.

INNOVATIVE PROTOCOL, INTERVENTION, STRATEGY, OR APPROACH

Am I about to engage in a new activity, research design, or clinical intervention for which I have had little or no training or professional experience? It was highly innovative thinking in research that led to the controversial experiments conducted by social psychologist Stanley Milgram at Yale University in 1961 concerning obedience to authority and individual responsibility (Milgram, 1973). The protocol inflicted significant emotional stress on the research participants, who were asked and prompted to administer increasingly strong electric shocks to supposed volunteers in the study. This would not be considered ethically acceptable now. However, the results of the study illuminated a human tendency in two thirds of the participants to "follow orders" when responsibility for personally inflicting extreme pain on another was displaced to those who were conducting the research. This was considered pivotal research by Milgram and others in the context of the post–World War II Nuremberg

War Crime Trials in an attempt to contribute to understanding the behavior of the perpetrators of the Holocaust. Regardless of the presumed prospective value of the research, investigators are always obliged to strike a balance between that and the risk of harm to research participants. Awareness of this balance has increased over the past 45 years, and changes in the APA Ethics Code have reflected this as well.

Certainly evidence-based treatment is not intended to discourage creativity or innovation by psychologists offering services to consumers, but it is intended to reduce risk and maximize the benefits of treatment. A tragic story of therapist innovation that was far from evidence based occurred in 2000 when two Colorado therapists, April Watkins and Julie Ponder, diagnosed a 10-year-old girl, Candace Newmaker, with attachment disorder and devised a treatment strategy that turned out to be fatal ("Attachment Therapy on Trial," 2003). As the child's mother and a pediatric nurse practitioner looked on, the two therapists provided the young child with a supposedly corrective rebirthing experience. They required her to assume a fetal position on the floor, wrapped her up tightly in a flannel sheet, piled many pillows on top, and added their own weight on top. In spite of panicky cries from Candace that she could not breathe, the therapists continued the "treatment" until such time as she fell silent, 50 minutes into the session. They waited an additional 20 minutes, urging the child not to be a "quitter" in the rebirthing process. When they finally checked on her, they found that she had suffocated, and all attempts to revive her were unsuccessful. To be sure, rebirthing therapy was innovative, but no institutional review board would have approved such a dangerous intervention if it had been submitted as a clinical research protocol, and no research existed that would support exposing participants to such a traumatic or risky experience.

UNCERTAINTY ABOUT THE IMPACT ON OTHERS OF THE INTERVENTION OR RESEARCH

Do I have misgivings or concerns about how to proceed because of how others will be affected? Feelings of uncertainty or anxiety about an intervention, strategy, or research design can be useful cues and should not be ignored. They can prompt the desire to take a specific kind of action, such as (a) consulting with someone who is knowledgeable about the topic; (b) beginning some independent study through books, journals, or the Internet; (c) seeking out workshops and other continuing education experiences; or (d) in some cases, beginning psychotherapy when personal life stresses or long-standing issues interfere with judgment or competence. These feelings can also help raise a variety of other questions concerning the adequacy of the theoretical approach or the data obtained, professional competence of the psychologist, the population being served or addressed, the nature of the professional relationship, or the risk of harming or exploiting another. I now address each of these.

RISK OF HARM TO ANOTHER

Is there a possibility of harm, however small, to an individual, group, or organization as a result of my conduct? An investigator plans research and devises a consent form in such a way so as to minimize the risk of harm to participants. A therapist uses interventions with a patient with bipolar disorder that are evidence based and minimize the chances that the patient will stop taking his or her medication and comply with treatment. A professor teaching an experiential course in psychology is careful to avoid coercing self-disclosure from students that might precipitate reliving a traumatic episode. A forensic psychologist evaluating a man charged with homicide for competency to stand trial performs a thorough and competent examination, regardless of the heinousness of the crime or pressures from the defense or prosecution to arrive at certain conclusions. And a media psychologist being interviewed about African Americans' performance on intelligence tests is careful to base his or her comments on the research and avoid drawing conclusions that are not warranted by the data. In each of these situations the psychologist uses good judgment to avoid actions that could harm another person or group. If there are alternative courses of action that would provide greater safety or minimize the risk of harm even further, then the psychologist would be expected to at least consider such a choice.

ADEQUACY OF DATA ABOUT THE OTHER PERSON TO MINIMIZE THE RISK OF HARM

Have I gathered the right kind of information from the other person to proceed with research, therapy, consulting, or other intervention with reasonable certainty that no adverse reactions will result? In many roles that psychologists play they perform careful evaluations of individuals and situations before intervening. This involves seeking information from the individual as well as collateral sources—those who know the individual in a different context, such as parents of minors; previous therapists; parole officers; teachers; referring physicians; or in the case of management consulting, managers or supervisors—after the individual has authorized contact. Research settings demand vigilance by investigators who provide thorough informed consent as a means of helping potential participants self-screen before volunteering to take part in research.

A therapist treating a woman with major depression would want to know if she had ever had suicidal thoughts or previous attempts. A Caucasian therapist treating an Asian client would need to know if his or her patient's avoidance of eye contact is diagnostically significant—

avoiding the truth—or if it is simply a cultural sign of respect. And a psychologist evaluating a divorcing mother and father for competency in parenting would need to select an accurate means of assessment, using tests, clinical interviews, collateral interviews, and other resources that provide valid and reliable data on which to base his or her decision. Selecting an evaluation tool or procedure simply because one is more familiar with it, rather than using instruments or procedures that are more likely to provide relevant and useful data for the question at hand, raises the ethical question of competence. Such a practice might degrade the accuracy of the evaluation, overlooking serious deficits in one parent, ultimately influencing the court's decision regarding custody, and potentially resulting in a risky child placement judgment by awarding custody to the parent who is more impaired rather than the one who is more capable.

LOSS OF OBJECTIVITY, IMPAIRED JUDGMENT, AND AVOIDANCE OF IMPORTANT INFORMATION

Do I systematically avoid addressing certain topics with this particular client or patient, such as the client's constant sarcasm or obviously seductive behavior toward me and others? A therapist may have feelings of anxiety, sadness, shame, resentment, or some other emotion when interacting with a particular client or patient that make it difficult for the therapist to carry out psychotherapy with objectivity and competence. Or the therapist may have negative feelings about certain individuals with particular personal qualities or values that could impair objectivity, such as feelings about gays or lesbians, African Americans, Jews, Asians, overweight people, those with physical disabilities, arrogant men, histrionic women, Republicans, those who engage in casual sex, seductive men or women, or those who remind the therapist of a difficult mother or father.

Certain individuals may evoke thoughts, feelings, and responses from psychologists that interfere with an objective appraisal or intervention. These reactions could be caused by either negative or friendly feelings (both impairing judgment). Examples of negative feelings include personality traits of the psychologist (e.g., childhood conditioning or long-standing prejudice), more recent negative or traumatic episodes (e.g., a physical assault on a family member of the psychologist by a member of a minority group), personal impairment of the psychologist for health reasons (e.g., chronic pain with cognitive-impairing medication, sleep disorder, or any medical condition that may affect judgment), psychological impairment and increased vulnerability due to a major life transition (e.g., divorce, death of a family member, or financial difficulties), or personal impairment due to an ongoing untreated mental disorder (e.g., dysthymic disorder or chemical dependency). Examples of positive or friendly feelings involve an unwarranted positive prejudice (e.g., a favorable bias toward Eastern Europeans because the psychologist himself is Polish) or the blind spots that emerge from offering psychological services to a family member (e.g., niece, son-in-law, or cousin).

Loss of objectivity for any reason can result in impaired judgment and unfair discrimination that degrade professional assessments and interventions. Ethical practice does not require psychologists to be fully objective or fair with everyone with whom they interact, as this would likely be impossible. However, psychologists should aspire to fairness and justice with all and try to recognize when they are unable to accomplish this. After acknowledging that their competence may potentially be threatened, psychologists are required to take some action to remedy the situation. This might include consulting with an experienced peer about the matter, obtaining training to upgrade professional skills, entering psychotherapy to address long-standing prejudice, or withdrawing and referring the recipient of their services to another.

RELINQUISHING STANDARD OPERATING PROCEDURES

Am I departing from my usual ways of dealing with others, such as spontaneously extending the length of therapy sessions without discussing it or agreeing to meet a research participant for drinks or dinner while still in the data-gathering phase of my investigation? Any psychologist engaged in research, practice, training, or consultation has developed evidence-based procedures and routines that help maintain efficient and competent work. These may include such things as providing informed consent at the outset of contact, taking a history and gathering information as needed, keeping thorough records, taking steps to preserve privacy and confidentiality, maintaining professional boundaries, and remaining up to date on current research.

Becoming lax about such matters, becoming careless, and taking risky shortcuts increase the risk of harming others. Such lapses may be due to a decline in physical or mental health, time pressures, financial stresses, feelings of exhaustion or burnout, vulnerability to certain clients and patients, changing career interests, or other factors. The psychologist who discusses his or her latest neuropsychological patient within earshot of other patients in the waiting room is being neglectful, not willfully exploitative, yet is nevertheless failing to safeguard his or her patient's privacy. And the therapist who has become careless about record keeping—sometimes making minimal entries of just a few words and other times a few paragraphs—ultimately may be harming his or her patient. If those records are needed by another health care professional or a court (e.g., in the case of litigation involving the patient and another health care provider), then it would be important to have a comprehensive history of the patient's diagnosis, treatment, progress, and more. Whenever standard professional habits begin to fall by the wayside, it could be a signal that the recipients of psychological services are at risk of harm and the psychologist is at risk of an impending ethical transgression. At the very least it is a reminder to carry out some self-scrutiny.

MULTIPLE-ROLE RELATIONSHIP WITHOUT EXPLOITATION

In addition to my formal relationship as a clinician, do I also have a secondary social role with someone, such as family member (daughter-in-law), my friend's father, my dentist, or my next-door neighbor? Not all multiple-role relationships can be avoided, particularly in rural areas where mental health providers may be few and far between. If someone is the only psychologist living in a small town in Oklahoma and the owner of the local pharmacy wants to consult the psychologist for marital problems, will the psychologist be able to keep his objectivity and fairness in working with the pharmacy owner and her husband, even though the psychologist has gone fly fishing with the husband several times and has known the pharmacy owner casually for several years? Or consider the scenario of a psychologist whose husband's boss knows that the psychologist specializes in anger management and wishes to consult her for some strategies to help with a quick temper with employees who underperform. Or consider the alcoholic neighbor down the street who seeks out the psychologist for family therapy because the neighbor has a young adolescent experimenting with marijuana and an older one who is anorectic. In these situations extra measures might be taken at the outset to provide clear boundaries and a safe environment, as discussed in Chapter 10. Remaining objective when in a multiple role can be daunting, and to be sure, not all multiple roles are destructive, but they require some awareness of the pitfalls that may have a bearing on informed consent and the therapeutic strategies that will be used.

A general rule of thumb might be to avoid multiple-role relationships at the outset whenever possible. This approach may be considered overly conservative by some, but there may be benefits in avoiding a multiple-role relationship. By referring the client or patient to another at the outset, the unforeseen problems that can occur by accepting a therapy patient with whom one has a previous social relationship can be avoided. In many parts of the country, particularly in metropolitan areas, there are an adequate number of therapists, and consumers can readily consult with someone they do not already know.

MULTIPLE-ROLE RELATIONSHIP FOR PERSONAL GAIN AND EXPLOITATION

Do I have something to gain personally by using the other for his or her knowledge or expertise, money, status, sex, or some other attribute? A psychologist who has such a private motivation may alter customary boundaries, limits, or normal operating procedures hoping or planning on developing a secondary role with a client, patient, consultee, or other with whom the psychologist has a professional relationship. The psychologist may initiate the process by encouraging the person to think about participating in a secondary role, such as coauthor for a journal article or book, donor to ongoing clinical research, romantic partner, or business associate for a web site. The steps to engaging another in an exploitative multiple relationship may be cleverly tailored to take advantage of perceived weaknesses and decrease the normal social distance by being inappropriately friendly, familiar, or casual (e.g., prematurely encouraging use of first names, meeting after hours, sharing a meal).

Sexual attraction to one's client or patient is not uncommon and, if not addressed, can impair objectivity and competence. When there is sexual "chemistry" between a psychologist and the recipient of his or her services, it may be useful to consult with a peer, former supervisor, or therapist to help grapple successfully with this stressful situation. It does not always mean that the professional relationship must end, although at times this may be the most responsible choice.

In clinical situations, the Ethics Code prohibits sexual relationships with clients or patients until 2 full years have past following the formal termination of services. Even then, there is a long list of conditions that must be met to assure that exploitation does not occur. Probably the best rule of thumb for psychologists is to eschew forever the possibility of a romantic relationship with any therapy patient they have ever treated, regardless of how much posttermination time has passed. This is discussed further in Chapter 10.

CONFLICT OF INTEREST

Am I caught between two opposing goals or incompatible loyalties over which I have little control? A special form of exploitation or harm is a conflict of interest situation that results from trying to comply with two opposing contexts or rules simultaneously. In this situation the therapist may not necessarily stand to gain anything directly from the client or patient but participates in harming the person nevertheless. An example of such a situation is the military psychologist who was reportedly pressured to underdiagnose posttraumatic stress disorder in returning war veterans (Citizens for Responsibility and Ethics in Washington, 2009). Such informal coercion was reportedly motivated by the economic demands placed on the U.S. Department of Veteran Affairs to rehabilitate troops who have seen the worst of active duty. It placed the psychologist in a multiple-role dilemma: In his role as therapist he had a duty to competently diagnose and treat returning soldiers seeking treatment for posttraumatic stress disorder, but in his role as an employee of the federal government he must also comply with the requirements of his employer, the U.S. Department of Veteran Affairs, which allegedly exerted pressure on him to minimize or change the diagnosis. One role inevitably conflicts with the other, resulting in either (a) a risk of harm to soldiers by depriving them of needed services by falsifying diagnostic statements, thereby violating a number of ethical standards, or (b) a risk of possible harm to his career or himself by challenging the administrative culture of the system and encountering censure by a commanding officer or some other punishment. Either choice results in potential harm, and oddly enough, both parties, patient and therapist, may feel exploited. The veteran feels exploited by the therapist who downgrades his diagnosis, making it unlikely that he will receive needed treatment, and the therapist feels exploited by being coerced to make inaccurate diagnostic statements and withholding evidence-based treatment.

General Ethical-Decision-Making Models

Some of the most exploitative behavior, sometimes under the guise of therapy, has involved engaging in multiple-role relationships with patients (e.g., adding a secondary or tertiary role such as business partner, friend, or lover) and resulted in expulsions from the APA, court actions, and loss of license. Each of the decision-making models I consider next helps the psychologist to decide on the wisdom of adding a secondary role to the initial primary role of client or patient. And each model assumes that it is being used by a competent professional who is able to make rational decisions independent of his or her own needs. When this is not the case, outside consultation is important in providing an objective appraisal.

In reviewing various models for ethical decision making, readers will see similarities at times in the recommended steps for psychologists to take in recognizing and resolving ethical dilemmas.

WORST-CASE SCENARIO

Posing a worst-case scenario by asking the question, "What could possibly go wrong as a result of this choice, even though the probability is low?" can often be helpful in reducing the potential for harm to consumers. It is important to continuously balance the risk of an adverse outcome with the likelihood of a beneficial one.

If the psychologist in an urban or rural area decided to accept a patient whom the psychologist knew in another context, a clear multiple-role relationship might arise that could impair the therapist's objectivity and confidence. Consider the following scenario.

> Louise, a psychiatric nurse working at her first postgraduate job, has just become pregnant by her boyfriend. She works at the same hospital as Dr. Taylor, a psychologist, and decides to seek her out for treatment for her depression and burgeoning cocaine dependency. She trusts Dr. Taylor because they have known each other for 3 months and have worked as cotherapists in a therapy group with outpatients who have chronic illness.
>
> Dr. Taylor agrees to see Louise for psychotherapy in her clinic office, and on some days she plays the role of Louise's therapist in the morning and cotherapist with Louise in the therapy group in the afternoon. The multiple role of being Louise's psychotherapist and her colleague treating other patients eventually becomes confusing to both. In the group setting the normal interplay between two cotherapists dealing with patients with mental illness soon becomes disrupted as Louise, slipping into her "patient" role, develops the habit of deferring to Dr. Taylor and overvaluing her opinion instead of continuing to trust her own therapeutic skills, as she had done in the past. Dr. Taylor, on the other hand, begins to become overprotective of Louise in the therapy group at times, particularly when the psychotherapy session early in the day may have covered difficult material for Louise, such as early life trauma or current problems with her boyfriend. It is a strain for both to keep the individual therapy relationship separate from their professional collegial one. Increasingly, Louise's psychotherapy seems to focus more on her performance in the group therapy and her relationship with the other patients there and less on the resolution of her life issues that led to her depression.
>
> The situation becomes more complicated when Louise discloses her sexual attraction to a male patient in the group and begins to have obsessive thoughts about him. After a while it becomes clear to Dr. Taylor that one of the two roles must cease— either the therapy or the professional collaboration as group cotherapists. Both roles are suffering, that of therapist and that of colleague, and Dr. Taylor feels that her objectivity and competence were no longer adequate to address Louise's issues. Although resistant at first, Louise eventually accepts the logic of Dr. Taylor's point of view and sees the importance of ending one of the roles.
>
> Ultimately it would have been preferable to avoid creating the multiple relationship at the outset because it simply added another layer of problems to address, which neither therapist nor patient foresaw. If Dr. Taylor had identified this as a potential ethical dilemma and consulted a colleague about potential worst-case scenarios before accepting a colleague as a patient, she might have arrived at a wiser decision from both a clinical and ethical standpoint.

Often a decision is made without even considering the risks or impact on others, simply because circumstances may arise quickly and psychologists may be prompted to act from a variety of incentives that may not always reflect sound judgment. Examples of therapists' compelling motivation are the personal motivation to be helpful to everyone who seeks their services (regardless of competence level or problem type), to increase income by accepting all new patients and rapidly enlarging their new private practice, or to do a favor for a colleague or friend who refers a family member for treatment.

NINE QUESTIONS FOR PSYCHOLOGISTS CONTEMPLATING INITIATING A MULTIPLE-ROLE RELATIONSHIP

A simple but effective model for helping therapists identify the important factors when contemplating beginning a multiple-role relationship was developed by Younggren and Gottlieb (2004), who developed nine short questions on which the therapist should reflect. They are rank ordered in importance and should be answered one by one.

1. Is the multiple-role relationship necessary? Sometimes it is, especially in rural settings where there may be very few choices because of the scarcity of mental health care providers.
2. Is the multiple-role relationship exploitive? Examine the risk of harm in any way—financially, sexually, or in any other way.
3. Who does the multiple-role relationship benefit? Ascertain who stands to gain more from the multiple-role relationship—the therapist or the patient.
4. Is there a risk that the multiple-role relationship could damage the patient? Determine how the patient might be harmed in a worst-case scenario, even though unlikely.
5. Is there a risk that the multiple-role relationship could disrupt the therapeutic relationship? Determine how the secondary role might undermine the treatment, such as hiring a patient to do clerical work in the psychologist's office.
6. Am I being objective in my evaluation of this matter? This may be a difficult or impossible question to honestly answer, and it is wise to seek consultation.
7. Have I adequately documented the decision-making process in the treatment records? Thorough record keeping is the best defense in case there is ever a complaint or grievance brought by the patient later.
8. Did the patient give informed consent regarding the risks of engaging in the multiple-role relationship? Take the time to discuss all the possible risks with the client ahead of time.

9. Does the documentation reflect that the patient has been informed and consents to the relationship? Be sure to chart the ongoing discussion of these matters and resulting decision and the consent of the patient to proceed with the secondary relationship.

Although this is a useful model for assessing whether a psychologist should move ahead with a contemplated multiple relationship, and it might well have helped Dr. Taylor in the previous vignette to make a better decision in advance, it does not always provide enough decision-making information, particularly with Questions 2, 4, and 5 in the list. How is the therapist to decide whether the contemplated secondary role will be exploitive, damaging, or disruptive to treatment?

To understand how to gauge the likelihood of future harm to a client or patient, one must consider Gottlieb's (1993) comprehensive earlier model, which is discussed in the subsequent section, Gottlieb's Three-Factor Model for Addressing Contemplating a Multiple Role. To provide a perspective on the evolution of the process of analyzing risk while honoring the rules of ethics, I first review earlier models of ethical decision making in general, not just those focusing on the risks of beginning a secondary role. These include Keith-Spiegel and Koocher's eight-step model, The Canadian Code of Ethics 10-step model, and several five-step models of decision making. The chapter concludes with Sonne's four-factor model for addressing multiple roles, incorporating elements of Gottlieb and Younggren's work along with important additional factors.

KEITH-SPIEGEL AND KOOCHER'S EIGHT-STEP MODEL FOR ETHICAL DECISION MAKING

Keith-Spiegel and Koocher (1985) created an early eight-step model for ethical decision making that was based on Tymchuk's (1981) original guidelines from several years earlier. Keith-Spiegel and Koocher's model consists of the following steps to take when psychotherapists are faced with an ethical question.

1. Describe the parameters of the situation (including data from the involved parties, colleagues, and the relevant psychological literature as well).
2. Define the potential issues involved (deducing the critical issues on the basis of Step 1).
3. Consult the guidelines, if any, already available that might apply to the resolution of each issue (e.g., Ethics Code, federal or state law or policy, APA guidelines).
4. Evaluate the rights, responsibilities, and welfare of all affected parties (including institutions and the general public as well as the individual client or patient).

5. Generate the alternative decisions possible for each issue (regardless of feasibility).
6. Enumerate the consequences of making each decision (e.g., psychological, economic).
7. Present any evidence that the various consequences or benefits resulting from each decision will actually occur (estimate the probability of such occurrences).
8. Make the decision (and share this decision with all people affected by the decision, and solicit their input; if this is impossible, at least take steps to ensure that their welfare is protected).

If every psychologist followed these steps when sorting through an ethical dilemma, psychologists would likely make better choices, resulting in minimizing the risk of harm and maximizing beneficial outcomes for those with whom they work as well as prompting fewer ethics complaints from clients and patients who felt that they had been harmed.

CANADIAN CODE OF ETHICS 10-STEP PROCESS FOR ETHICAL DECISION MAKING

In its ethics code, the Canadian Psychological Association includes 10 steps for ethical decision making that help psychologists to arrive at a resolution of a conflict after it has already been identified as an ethical issue (Canadian Psychological Association, 2000). The complete code, including the 10 steps, is available online (http://www.cpa.ca/cpasite/userfiles/Documents/Canadian%20Code%20of%20Ethics%20for%20Psycho.pdf). A synopsis of these steps follows:

1. Identify individuals and groups potentially affected by the decision.
2. Identify ethically relevant issues and practices, including interests, rights, and any relevant characteristics of (a) the individuals and groups involved and (b) the setting (system or circumstances) in which the ethical problem arose.
3. Consider how personal bias, stress, or self-interest might influence your choices between various courses of action.
4. Develop several courses of action.
5. Analyze likely short-term, ongoing, and long-term risks and benefits of each course of action on the individual(s) or group(s) likely to be affected (e.g., client, family, employees, employing institution, students, research participants, colleagues, the discipline of psychology, the professional association, self).
6. Choose a course of action after conscientiously applying existing principles, values, and standards.

7. Take action, and be ready to assume full responsibility for the consequences.
8. Evaluate the results of acting.
9. Assume responsibility for the consequences of acting, correct any negative consequences, and reengage in the decision-making process if the ethical issue is not resolved.
10. Take action as is warranted and feasible to prevent future occurrences of this dilemma (e.g., communicate with colleagues, problem solve with them, change your procedures and practices accordingly).

Canadian psychologists are reminded that this is a time-consuming deliberation, and they are encouraged to consult with parties who ,are affected by the ethical problem (if appropriate) and also with colleagues and advisory bodies. This is a carefully crafted model that helps neophyte and senior psychologists alike. As with the previous model, if every psychologist followed these steps when sorting through an ethical dilemma, psychologists would likely make better choices, resulting in minimizing the risk of harm and maximizing beneficial outcomes for those with whom they work as well as prompting fewer ethics complaints from clients and patients who felt that they had been harmed.

FIVE-STEP MODELS FOR ETHICAL DECISION MAKING

A variety of five-step models have evolved in the field of biomedical ethics that have application for psychological decision making. Bransford and Stein (1993) developed a five-step model for decision making with the acronym IDEAL—identify, develop, evaluate, act, and look back. And similarly, Härtel and Härtel (1997) developed the SHAPE system of decision making—scrutinize, develop hypothesis, analyze proposed solution, perform, and evaluate—while researching how small groups engage in decision-making behavior.

Knapp and VandeCreek (2006) further elaborated this as a "principle-based" model for ethical decision-making whereby psychologists can engage in a sequence of activities that incorporate much of the Canadian model. Their model uses the five steps of IDEAL and facilitates decision making that is specifically linked to defined ethical principles in a variety of ethics codes. These steps also address the specific problem of ethical rules that may conflict with each other. They are as follows:

I: *Identify or scrutinize the problem.* Activities that violate or threaten to violate an ethical principle are identified as ethical concerns.

D: *Develop alternatives or hypotheses.* The alternatives should be based on, or at least be consistent with, general moral principles.

E: *Evaluate or analyze options.* The option chosen depends on which one strikes the optimal balance or ranking of moral principles.

A: *Act or perform.* Although one moral principle may be violated, efforts are taken to minimize the harm to that principle when the rule or standard conflicts with another rule or standard.

L: *Look back or evaluate.* The outcome of the action is evaluated according to the extent to which it fulfills, balances, or minimizes harm to the offended moral principle.

The third step—evaluate or analyze options—specifically asks the psychologist to examine moral principles that may conflict with one another and how one resolves such a conflict by upholding the values of one at the expense of the other(s). Before infringing on or violating a particular moral principle, however, the psychologist must satisfy the following six conditions:

1. The psychologist must be able to offer better reasons for acting on the overriding moral principle than the infringed one.
2. The chosen course of action must have a realistic chance of succeeding.
3. There must be no morally preferable alternative that could be substituted.
4. The infringement chosen must be the least possible, commensurate with achieving the main goal of the action.
5. The psychologist must seek to minimize any negative effects of the chosen course of action as a result of infringement on or violation of the other moral principle(s).
6. The decision must be made impartially regarding all affected parties; it must not be influenced by morally irrelevant information received about anyone involved in the situation (Beauchamp & Childress, 2001).

Summarized, these six conditions require that psychologists must be able to give a better reason for selecting choice *a* than choice *b;* the choice must be likely to succeed; there must be no better moral option; the choice must be an option that does the least damage; psychologists must then take steps to minimize any damage that could happen; and psychologists' decision must not be affected by details of the players that are not relevant to the moral principles at stake.

A detailed analysis of the vignette about Dr. Taylor and Louise using the IDEAL decision-making model is available online (http://pubs.apa.org/books/supp/essentialethics/).

GOTTLIEB'S THREE-FACTOR MODEL FOR ADDRESSING CONTEMPLATING A MULTIPLE ROLE

Gottlieb developed an excellent decision-making model in 1993 that identified three factors in any professional relationship that are metrics for deciding about entering a multiple role with a recipient of one's services—power, duration, and clarity of termination. His general assumptions are as follows: (a) This model is to applicable to all professional relationships and to consumers of any psychological service; (b) the goal of striving to avoid all multiple-role relationships is unrealistic in many circumstances; (c) as a result of the inherent risk, every additional relationship with consumers should be evaluated to assess potential harm; (d) not all multiple-role relationships are exploitative per se—some are beneficial, but all must be avoided if they may prove harmful; (e) the model sensitizes psychologists to the relevant issues and makes recommendations for action; (f) the model is to be used when contemplating the addition of a second relationship to an existing one, not for situations in which the duality already exists; and (g) the model requires that the professional attempt to make judgments about the following three dimensions from the consumer's perspective: power, duration of the relationship, and clarity of termination.

Power refers to the amount or degree of power or influence that a psychologist holds over a consumer (e.g., the psychologist giving a public lecture on stress management holds relatively little power compared with a psychotherapist engaged in insight-oriented psychotherapy with a patient).

Duration of the relationship is an aspect of power, and it is assumed that power increases as the duration also increases (e.g., the power differential experienced by a clinical supervisee after a single session would be much less than after 10 months of weekly supervision).

Clarity of termination addresses the likelihood that the consumer and psychologist will have further professional contact in the future, addressing such questions as, When is therapy over? Is there an unambiguous ending of the professional relationship? Is there an option for beginning treatment or supervision again on an as-needed basis?

This model contains formulaic steps that help the psychologist charter these murky waters when considering adding a second relationship to the existing one.

First, the psychologist must assess the current relationship according to the three dimensions of power, duration, and clarity of termination. If two out of these three factors already exist—higher power, longer duration, or no clear termination—then the potential for harm is high, and the psychologist should reject initiating the contemplated relationship. An example is the therapist who will be ending treatment soon with a patient who has been in therapy for 2 years and decides to invite the patient to serve as his or her research assistant. Power and duration are high after 2 years of treatment; therefore, the contemplated role should be rejected.

Second, the psychologist must examine the contemplated relationship along the same three dimensions—power, duration, and clarity of termination. Again, if the contemplated relationship would also fall into the category of either higher power, longer duration, and uncertain termination, then, again, the potential for harm is high, and the psychologist should reject initiating the contemplated relationship if the existing relationship also falls into a high category (e.g., either has a stronger power differential, is longer in duration, or has no clear termination). An example is the therapist inviting a current patient to coauthor a book with him. In this situation the role of coauthor also contains a long duration and no clear termination, so the contemplated role should be rejected.

Third, the psychologist must examine both current and contemplated relationships for role incompatibility if they fall within the midrange of those same three factors. It has been found that role incompatibility generally increases when there are also increases in power differential, differences in expectations of the two roles, and divergence of the obligations of the two roles (Kitchener, 1988). If the two roles are highly incompatible, then the contemplated relationship should be refused. An example is the therapist who is asked by the chairman of the department of psychology in which the therapist serves as an adjunct clinical professor to treat him and his wife in marital therapy. The expectancies of the two roles—treating therapist and professor in the psychology department, who has accountability to the chairman of the department—may have a high degree of incompatibility, and the contemplated role should be rejected.

Fourth, the psychologist should obtain consultation from a colleague and make a decision on the most conservative basis; this provides an unbiased and fresh look at the situation and should be a routine option when faced with these decisions.

And fifth, the psychologist must discuss his or her decision with the consumer if the psychologist decides to proceed with the additional relationship. The psychologist must review the essence of this decision-making model, its rationale, the relevant ethical issues, available alternatives, and potential adverse consequences as a matter of informed consent. If the consumer is competent and chooses to engage in the contemplated relationship, the psychologist may proceed. However, if the consumer is unable to recognize the dilemma or unwilling to consider the issues before deciding, he or she should be considered at risk, and the contemplated secondary relationship should be rejected.

SONNE'S FOUR-FACTOR MODEL FOR ADDRESSING CONTEMPLATING A MULTIPLE ROLE

This model is partly a synthesis of the work of previous ethicists but also introduces new variables to consider, such as gender and culture. It examines four factors that contribute to the therapist's decision-making process, with each factor consisting of a variety of elements—therapist factors, client factors, therapy relationship factors, and other relationship factors (Sonne, 2006).

Therapist Factors

Therapists differ on a variety of criteria as bases for making good ethical decisions in clinical situations. Sonne (2006) identified the following 10 therapist factors as primary:

- ethical sensitivity,
- willingness to expend cognitive effort,
- guiding ethical principles,
- gender (men and women tend to differ on the bases of their moral reasoning),
- culture,
- religion and spirituality,
- profession (psychologist, marriage and family therapist, social worker, psychiatrist),
- theoretical orientation,
- years of experience as a therapist, and
- character traits (a therapist with a strong need to please may, i.e., comply with a patient's request to enter a business venture together).

Client Factors

The five client factors to consider are[1]

- gender,
- culture (e.g., American, Asian, European),
- religion and spirituality,
- psychosocial strengths and vulnerabilities (more caution is required if the patient has a narcissistic or borderline personality disorder), and
- history of prior boundary violations (e.g., childhood abuse or incest, inappropriate boundary crossings with others such as teachers, physicians).

Therapy Relationship Factors

Therapists establish a broad variety of relationships with their clients and patients, affected by their theoretical orientation and the type of

---

[1]Some of these client factors were identified in the APA Ethics Code to be considered by therapists when considering entering a romantic relationship with former patients (Standard 4.07b, Sexual Intimacies With Former Therapy Patients, APA 1992; Standard 10.08b, Sex With Former Therapy Clients/Patients, APA, 2010).

service being rendered. The following five relationship factors are considered fundamental to ethical decision making:

- nature of the therapeutic relationship (partly as defined by informed consent and partly the patient's emotional reaction to the therapist),
- power differential,
- duration of therapy (weeks, months, or years),
- practice setting (e.g., solo practitioner, outpatient clinic, group private practice, inpatient facility), and
- practice locale (e.g., small town, big city, specialized communities such as military, university setting, deaf community, sports athlete communities).

Other Relationship Factors

The following nine factors concern what the therapist anticipates (or may already know) will be part of the secondary relationship with the client:

- clarity of change in nature and function of relationship (how will the relationship actually be different?),
- professional's motivation for engaging in the other relationships (whose needs are being met or enhanced?),
- professional's affective response to the potential additional relationship (e.g., what feelings are evoked in the therapist—intrigue, excitement, pity, anger?),
- potential for role conflict (e.g., could the two roles become incompatible at some point, such as the therapist's protecting his or her own financial interests in a business role while still trying to preserve the patient's welfare in treatment?),
- potential for benefit for the client,
- potential for harm to the client,[2]
- potential for harm to third parties (e.g., other interns or staff members, confusion or resentment in family members of the therapist or client, or emotional reactions of other clients and patients),
- setting of the other relationship (e.g., considering employing a current patient in zone's own office as opposed to a business setting in another town), and
- locale of the other relationship (e.g., rural area, large metropolitan area, or a specialized community).

---

[2]According to the APA Ethics Code, there are four domains of potential harm that, if present, would define the multiple relationship as unethical: (a) impaired objectivity of the therapist, (b) impaired competence of the therapist, (c) impaired ability of the therapist to safeguard the client or patient in therapy, and (d) exploitation of the client or patient (see APA, 2010, Standard 3.05, Multiple Relationships).

This level of analysis in a model of decision making helps one to consider specific factors that are frequently overlooked. When used in conjunction with the nine questions posed by Younggren and Gottlieb (2004) and the three factors of Gottlieb's (1993) model, it helps one to better estimate the risk of harm to a client by considering a broad range of variables. At this point the reader may practice using any of the decision-making models outlined previously to analyze vignettes presented throughout this book.

Using a formal ethical decision-making model can help a psychologist arrive at a decision that minimizes or eliminates harm to a recipient of services. By so doing in situations of conflicting ethical rules, the psychologist also will determine which standard is the primary one with which to comply while at the same time honoring the values of the infringed secondary standard as much as possible. Simply being familiar with a problem-solving process also helps increase the awareness of ethical dilemmas in the first place, permitting the psychologist to address situations that otherwise might never have been noticed or simply have been deliberately ignored. In Chapters 9 through 12, I discuss psychological assessment, psychotherapy, research, publishing, teaching, and supervision as the key settings in which one can effectively apply models of ethical decision making.

Ethics in Psychological Assessment   9

Dr. White was contacted by the general counsel of a manufacturing company to do a blind review of the test results of a woman who is making a disability claim against the company. He was provided with the results of her Minnesota Multiphasic Personality Inventory— 2 (MMPI–2) by the attorney, who pointed out that the "fake bad" scale was elevated and that the profile had a high score on the F scale and low score on the K scale. Such scores indicate signs of possible exaggeration, or faking, especially in the context of litigation. The attorney lacked information about how and why the test was administered, but she asked Dr. White to write a brief report stating that the woman is very likely exaggerating her disability. The attorney also indicated that Dr. White's court testimony would not be necessary— only the report is needed.

Dr. White was experienced in forensic work. He was well aware of the attorney's obvious attempts to persuade him to state that the woman was exaggerating her disability. However, he was concerned that making such statements in the absence of additional information about the woman and the circumstances of testing would be overreaching and knowingly doing something with the test results that would be deceptive to the court. He informed the attorney of his reservations and withdrew from the case.

Introduction

Assessing human behavior with a variety of instruments has long been an important part of psychological work, with standards providing guidance in the very first edition of the American Psychological Association (APA) Ethics Code (APA, 1953a). That edition had three principles concerning assessment—Test Security, Test Interpretation, and Test Publication—and listed eight separate paragraphs, most of which can still be found in some form in the Assessment section of the Ethics Code today (APA, 2010).

Another publication, the *Standards for Educational and Psychological Testing*, a joint venture of the APA, the American Educational Research Association (AERA), and the National Council on Measurement in Education (NCME), provides a comprehensive review of the pragmatics and ethics of assessment. It consists of a glossary, three sections (Test Construction, Fairness in Testing, and Testing Applications), and 264 standards (AERA, APA, & NCME, 1999). These standards are prescriptive only; there is no specific entity responsible for enforcement and no consequences for violating them. They promote the highest standards in sound and ethical use of tests and provide optimal criteria for the evaluation of tests, testing practices, and the effects of test use.

Psychological tests are commonly used for four different purposes: (a) diagnosis, as at the beginning treatment; (b) intervention planning and outcome evaluation, such as evaluating a child suspected of having attention-deficit/hyperactivity disorder and planning a course of treatment for the child; (c) legal and governmental decisions, such as evaluating a suicidal patient who wishes to sign him- or herself out of the hospital against medical advice; and (d) personal awareness, growth, and action, helping clients to learn more about themselves. I now discuss how these apply to a variety of patient populations and settings.

Instruments of Assessment and Their Application

Psychological assessment is carried out in a variety of settings with clients and patients of any age who find themselves in many different life situations. These settings include outpatient clinics and private offices of psychologists (e.g., diagnostic testing, treatment evaluation), hospitals (e.g., mental health evaluation for organ transplantation, end of life decisional capacity), schools (e.g., assessing learning disabilities), industry (e.g., employment, performance appraisal), the courts (e.g., evaluating capacity to stand trial, child custody evaluations), and research (e.g., using a broad array of assessment instruments for the study under way, screening out research participants with mental disorders or those inappropriate for the study).

The types of psychological tests commonly used by psychologists fall into five categories (AERA, APA, & NCME, 1999). These are (a) cognitive and neuropsychological testing; (b) social, adaptive, and problem behavior testing; (c) family and couples testing; (d) personality testing; and (e) vocational testing. I briefly examine each of these categories of tests.

Cognitive and neuropsychological testing is usually carried out by a psychologist who specializes in assessment and provides measures of the following abilities: cognitive ability; attention; motor functions, sensorimotor functions, and lateral preferences; perception and perceptual organization and integration; learning and memory; abstract reasoning and categorical thinking; executive functions; language; and academic achievement. This testing is useful in evaluating patients who have had head injuries, organic brain damage from some other cause, significant learning problems, or pervasive developmental disorders.

Testing for social, adaptive, and problem behavior provides measures of the individual's ability and motivation to provide self-care and have social relationships with others. This assessment is beneficial for those with mental retardation, dementia, or cognitive deficits that may significantly impair one's ability to thrive independently.

Family and couples testing provides information about interpersonal relationships, compatibility, shared interests, and intimacy. It is used by couples and family therapists for assessing parents who wish to adopt a child, parents who have remarried and may have problems in their relationships with the stepchildren, or even extended family members who may be living under the same roof.

Personality testing provides information about an individual's formulation and expression of thoughts, attitudes, emotions, and behaviors. It is commonly used in clinical settings to assist with treatment, in employment settings to assess suitability for work, and in forensic settings to assess competence to stand trial and custody issues. The formats of these instruments vary considerably and may consist of asking the test taker to respond to multiple-choice questions (e.g., self-report inventories) or placing the client in a novel and partly unstructured situation (e.g., responding to visual stimuli, telling stories, discussing pictures or other projective stimuli).

Vocational testing assesses clients' interests, work needs, and values and may be used with college students or young adults or with older clients undergoing career transitions. It uses interest inventories; work values inventories; and measures of career development, maturity, and indecision.

Use of Computers in Testing

Computers have been used for psychological testing for nearly 50 years for the administration of tests, test scoring, and computer-generated interpretations of test results. In 1966, the APA published its first guidelines for psychologists using computers: *Automated Test Scoring and Interpretations Practices.* By 1986, this document had developed into *Guidelines for Computer-Based Tests and Interpretations* and consisted of two sections: The User's Responsibilities and The Developer's Responsibilities (APA, 1986). These guidelines continued to evolve as psychologists relied more heavily on computers and eventually were absorbed in modified form in the 1999 publication mentioned previously, *Standards for Educational and Psychological Testing* (AERA, APA, & NCME, 1999).

Competence in the use and application of computers is of critical importance in each area of testing—development, administration, scoring, and interpretation. Comprehensive knowledge of the instrument being used and evidence-based clinical judgment about the patient being evaluated are both prerequisites for competently assessing a patient. Psychologists should only use computer-generated interpretive reports for explaining test results with clients when they have a good understanding of the variables on which the interpretations were derived. Test users should not rely on computer-generated interpretations of test results unless they have the expertise to consider the appropriateness of these interpretations in individual cases. There is no substitute for sound clinical judgment, and test users must understand how to interpret conflicting data between test results and personal evaluation of the client being assessed.

Selection and Use of Assessment Techniques

Competent use of assessment techniques is spelled out in a general way by the Ethics Code; psychologists must consider the research and evidence of usefulness of a particular test for a particular situation. They must use the right test for the job. A neuropsychologist evaluating an adolescent boy who had a head injury from playing football 6 months previously would carefully select appropriate instruments to evaluate the presence of organic brain damage. If the young man was Latino and his understanding of English was limited, the evaluation should be conducted with the assistance of a Spanish-speaking interpreter who is familiar with psychological assessment, and a Spanish edition of any printed materials should be used, if possible.

The onus is always on psychologists to use assessment instruments with demonstrated validity and reliability for members of the population being tested. A newly released instrument for evaluating couples and families that was standardized on a population of Caucasian men and women in the United States may have diminished validity for use with a family who has recently emigrated from Japan.

Administering and scoring tests must also comply with established procedures, with no shortcuts or delegation of these tasks to unqualified persons (e.g., clerical workers or untrained graduate students). Psychological tests are generally meant to be administered by the psychologist on the premises where the psychologist's office is located in a reasonably quiet, well-lighted, and comfortable setting that is free from distractions. Giving a client a test to take home not only compromises test security but may also increase the likelihood of other factors that could affect performance, such as fatigue (e.g., taking the test late at night), distractions (e.g., going online or talking to others while taking the test), or interruptions that could affect performance (e.g., telephone calls, eating, or drinking alcohol). It also erodes the integrity of the assessment process by allowing the possibility of an individual other than the patient to complete the test unbeknownst to the psychologist.

Informed Consent for Assessment

Before beginning any type of assessment, psychologists must obtain informed consent from the client, whether it is a paper-and-pencil test, structured clinical interview, projective test, behavioral observation, or any other form of personal evaluation. An excellent and concise statement from the Science Directorate of the APA reviewing the rights and responsibilities of test takers may be accessed online (http://www.apa.org/science/programs/testing/rights.aspx).

Informed consent normally consists of a discussion with the client in simple language disclosing and explaining the nature and purpose of the test, any fees that must be paid, the fact that feedback about the results will be provided, any involvement of third parties (e.g., using the services of a psychologist specializing in assessment or responding to a court order for psychological assessment), and limits to the usual expectations of confidentiality concerning test results. The limits of confidentiality change when a client is ordered by the court to undergo assessment, such as in cases of competency to stand trial or child custody evaluations.

It must be explained to the client in these situations that the psychologist will generate a psychological report based on the assessment procedure and submit it to the court to be used in the ongoing judicial procedures. Clients and patients must also be allowed to ask questions about the anticipated testing and receive answers as a part of the informed consent process, and all authorization must be documented as well in the clinical record.

If the client is unable to authorize assessment, either for legal or psychological reasons, such as in the case of a child or psychotic patient, then the psychologist must obtain informed consent from a parent or legal guardian before proceeding. The psychologist must also inform those with a questionable capacity to consent about the nature and purpose of the proposed assessment, using nontechnical, reasonably understandable language.

There are situations in which full informed consent is not required, such as (a) when testing is mandated by a court order or governmental regulations (e.g., applying for a government position such as working as a police officer or in the Central Intelligence Agency); (b) when informed consent is implied, as in routine educational, institutional, or organizational activity (e.g., a person voluntarily agreeing to assessment when applying for a job); and (c) when evaluating decisional capacity (e.g., with moribund patients contemplating a choice of medical interventions). However, even in situations described in the first exception, court orders and government regulations, psychologists must inform testees of the nature and purpose of the proposed assessment, although they are not required to provide full informed consent (e.g., disclosures about exceptions to confidentiality, third-party involvement).

> Mr. Hirting, a new client with chronic back pain who was beginning treatment both for pain management and relationship problems with his wife, was asked to undergo testing by his therapist early in treatment. It included the following: (a) The West Haven Yale Multidimensional Pain Inventory to assess the impact of pain on his life, (b) the Melzack Pain Questionnaire to assess the subjective severity and type of pain, (c) the Millon Clinical Inventory to assess psychopathology, (d) the Beck Depression Inventory to screen for the presence of depression, and (e) the Symptom Checklist-90 to evaluate the frequency and intensity of certain cognitions, emotions, behavior, and physical symptoms. The therapist then explained how using such instruments could help with diagnosing and treating Mr. Hirting, likely resulting in more efficient therapy and useful strategies in treatment. The therapist also explained the format of each test— whether it consisted of multiple-choice answers, a rating scale of frequency or intensity, diagrams to be filled in, or open-ended oral questions. Mr. Hirting was then told that the results of the testing would remain confidential, as are all clinical records, with the usual exceptions. He was also informed that the results of the

assessment would be shared with him, and he was encouraged to ask questions in advance about any aspect of the testing.

If the situation were slightly different and the client not only had a history of chronic pain and marital difficulties but had actually initiated a legal separation from his wife, the confidentiality disclosure might be different. If the couple should divorce and there was conflict about the terms of custody of the children, it is possible that the therapist's records of assessing and treating Mr. Hirting could be subpoenaed in the course of resolving the dispute. It would be important to inform him of this possibility because it might affect his decision to proceed with the assessment. If he believed that psychological testing might reveal personal deficits that could weaken his role in custody litigation and reduce his chances of obtaining custody of his children, he might choose to delay the testing and only proceed with psychotherapy at this time.

Basis for Assessments and Explaining Assessment Results

Psychologists are required to use current editions of tests and base their findings and recommendations on current test data of clients and patients. Psychologists generally must not rely on obsolete editions, outdated measures, or evaluations of clients that may no longer be valid because so much time has past since the assessment was completed.

They also have an obligation to interpret and explain assessment results to their clients, whether they score and interpret the tests themselves or use computer narrative printouts or other automated services. When doing so, they must take into account a variety of factors that could influence the results, including (a) the situation, (b) the milieu, and (c) personal attributes and the language of the client being tested. Situational factors include such things as the purpose for taking the test (such as a voluntary vocational test battery, a timed aptitude or intelligence test, a mandated personality assessment by a court, an optional evaluation at the outset of treatment, or employment screening for a new job). The testing milieu includes lighting, ambient noise, use of a computer for test administration, the physical presence of others (such as in group testing), or other distractions that could influence the outcome. Personal variables can also influence the validity of a test and should be addressed in advance and in providing interpretations later; these include physical disability, reading level, test-taking ability, language (English as a foreign language), and culture (using a personality test for a Vietnamese immigrant only if the test has been standardized for that culture).

Psychologists' opinions in formal recommendations, reports, diagnostic or evaluative statements, and forensic testimony must be based on sufficient information and assessment techniques. Psychologists must always disclose when the validity of the assessment might be diminished, as with the personal factors listed previously with the Vietnamese client.

Another example is the forensic psychologist who is testifying about the parenting ability of a lesbian woman based solely on the psychologist's extensive review of the woman's psychological tests performed by another psychologist but not including a personal evaluation of the woman by the psychologist him- or herself. In such a situation the psychologist would clarify the likely impact of limited information (e.g., failure to personally evaluate the woman) or situational factors that would affect the reliability and validity of his or her opinions, and the psychologist must also exercise caution about his or her formal conclusions and recommendations. Hunches and opinions not based on the assessment data must always be identified as such. A psychologist may harm patients by giving opinions that are not sufficiently based on well-established assessment techniques, such as testifying, drawing conclusions, and making recommendations on the basis of data from an unvalidated or obsolete test. This could impact major aspects of a client's life, such as competency to stand trial or eligibility for long-term disability compensation.

Dr. Palmer had recently stopped doing clinical work and was transitioning to doing fitness-to-work evaluations for employees of a company. He was offered a contract if he could do them at a cost that would include a 2-hour interview and administering the MMPI–2 and the Millon Multiaxial Clinical Inventory—III (MCMI–III). After he agreed, the employer indicated that a substance abuse evaluation also needed to be included and asked Dr. Palmer about his expertise in this area. Dr. Palmer stated that in past years he had done many substance abuse evaluations but recently he had been referring those evaluations to others. His employer said that would not be possible but noted that their last evaluator relied on the McAndrews scale on the MMPI–2 and the alcohol and drug dependency scales on the MCMI-III plus some interview questions to "get the job done."

Dr. Palmer realized that he should "beef up" his experience in substance abuse assessment because some collateral interviews were really needed. It would not be sufficient to rely on the original protocol suggested by the employer to provide a valid assessment of the employee (G. Schoener, personal communication, August 13, 2009).

In this situation a psychologist evaluated himself as no longer being competent in a certain area of assessment, even though his employer was willing to cut him some slack and get the job done by simply throwing in a few interview questions and relying on the objective testing subscales. Dr. Palmer knew that he needed additional training to once again be competent in evaluating those with substance abuse as well as to conduct collateral interviews with family members and fellow employees who have observed the candidate's behavior.

Release of Test Data

Since 2002, the Ethics Code has permitted clients and patients to have access to their own test data. These data include raw and scaled scores, their responses to test questions or stimuli, and psychologists' notes and recordings concerning client statements and behavior during an examination. However, psychologists may refuse client access to protect a client or others from significant harm, misuse, or misrepresentation of the data. A client with borderline personality disorder who has only been in treatment for 2 weeks may not be emotionally prepared to view her entire psychological report; she may feel demeaned, criticized, angry, and hopeless if permitted to read it in its entirety at such an early stage of treatment, before diagnosis has even been discussed. Also, in recent years in the legal arena there has been an increase in the use of psychological data, such as in child custody litigation and criminal lawsuits. In these situations the court may order the plaintiff or defendant to have a psychological evaluation to determine his or her mental status, with the psychologist's report then being entered into evidence (e.g., a "not guilty by reason of insanity" defense).

State and federal laws may also have a bearing on clients' rights to their own test data and psychologists' rights of refusal. The Health Insurance Portability and Accountability Act of 1996 privacy rules also address this topic and may preempt the ethical standards under certain conditions.[1]

Assessment by Unqualified Persons

Test publishers normally sell psychological tests only to licensed mental health providers, and psychologists are ethically bound to only purchase and use tests for which they have the competence and training to

---

[1]According to the Health Insurance Portability and Accountability Act, a psychologist may only deny clients or patients access to their own test data if it is reasonably likely to endanger the life or physical safety of the individual or another person or cause equally substantial harm. Those denied access also have the right to have a denial reviewed by a designated licensed health care professional in hopes of reversing the denied access.

administer, score, and interpret. A psychologist may be licensed to practice but rusty in his or her training and current research on, for example, the Rorschach Test. Although technically qualified to administer and score this test, the psychologist would be more compliant with the spirit of the ethical rules concerning competence if the psychologist updated his or her skills and reviewed current research in this area.

Psychologists also have a responsibility to refrain from promoting the use of psychological assessment techniques by those who are not sufficiently trained or proficient. This includes delegating test administration or scoring responsibilities to a clerical helper or receptionist who is obviously not licensed or qualified to practice psychology. It might also include the gray area of predoctoral or postdoctoral psychological assistants whom the psychologist is supervising but who lack sufficient training or basic understanding of the assessment process. Examples are the psychologist who gives supervisees too much independent responsibility for the informed consent of clients at the outset, for administering the test itself, or for scoring as well as the psychologist's failure to properly review a psychological report written by a supervisee before it is filed. Of course, psychologists must limit their own use of assessment procedures, as well, if they lack competence. The following vignette includes issues of competence, multiple roles, and assessment.

> Dr. Brown is a child psychologist in a county hospital who specializes in the diagnosis and treatment of Asperger's syndrome. One day the chief of the psychiatry department, a friend of Dr. Brown's who is involved in a custody battle for his children, mentioned to Dr. Brown that he was worried that his ex-wife is "poisoning" his daughters against him and asked if an evaluation might be able to provide evidence to that effect. Dr. Brown stated that this was possible, although he has never actually performed a custody evaluation before. The chief then asked Dr. Brown to interview the chief's daughters in addition to carrying out psychological testing; the chief then informed Dr. Brown that he would not be able to interview the chief's ex-wife because she was not being cooperative. Dr. Brown decided to perform the assessment to see what would be revealed, believing that he could ethically offer the disclaimer in his psychological report that his findings might have a limitation because only the girls and the father were assessed (but not the mother).
>
> It is significant that although Dr. Brown had never performed a custody evaluation before, he held the misimpression that he could perform a valid assessment in this complicated situation and write an objective and valid report that might be used later by the chief's attorney in pleading his case. It is also significant that Dr. Brown had entered into a multiple-role relationship by agreeing to assess someone with whom he already had several preexisting relationships (friendship and employee–employer

relationship). By so doing, he exposed his psychological work to being challenged by his ex-wife's attorney and possibly undermined the strength of his friend's legal case as well. He would have been wiser just to say *no* to his friend and refer him to a psychologist experienced in these matters.

Test Security

Psychologists must be responsible stewards of the tests that they own and use. This means that they must protect test instruments, protocols, questions or stimuli, and manuals from unauthorized access and use. The reason for this is to protect future clients and patients from learning the actual test questions and items, which would provide them with opportunities to prepare for psychological assessment so that they could influence the outcome, whether in school settings, litigation, employment situations, or anywhere else.

Psychologists must comply with the instructions in the manual concerning test administration, even though they may be tempted at times to gratify a patient's request on the basis of convenience or expediency. Giving an outpatient a copy of the MMPI to take home and complete whenever the patient feels like it not only permits him or her to consult with others while answering but also compromises test security, allowing the person to photocopy test items or even distribute them over the Internet. Discussing and revealing test items to a newspaper or television journalist in the course of a media interview about psychological assessment would also compromise security and could ultimately affect the usefulness of the test in the future.

There are situations in which test data and records may be subject to a subpoena or court order as a consequence of litigation concerning a patient's mental health or competence. This includes such situations as guilt or innocence in a criminal proceeding, a patient's lawsuit against a third party (e.g., a former employer), child custody litigation, a malpractice action against the treating psychologist, or any legal action in which the patient's mental status is at issue. A psychologist must release a copy of the client's test data to him or her if requested to do so. This is consistent with the rights of clients and patients as articulated by federal law (the Health Insurance Portability and Accountability Act). However, the psychologist may usually protect the security of the copyrighted test materials by not releasing them, unless, of course, with certain tests the answer sheets or psychologist's notes that are being requested are combined with the test questions themselves.

Test Construction

Psychologists developing tests, structured clinical interviews, question-naires, or other assessment techniques that they intend to promote for clinical settings, educational settings, management consulting, forensic settings, or other professional settings are obliged to follow certain principles of test construction. These principles include a working knowledge of psychometric procedures and current scientific or professional knowledge for test design, standardization, validation, reduction or elimination of bias, as well as recommendations for use.

It would be unethical for a psychologist to develop and use his or her own inventory or personality questionnaire with his or her psychotherapy clients and patients and falsely promote it as a "standardized instrument" if the psychologist did so without regard for well-established principles of test construction. This might particularly be problematical if a psychologist were to publish his or her unvalidated test in a self-help book, release it to the media, or place it on his or her website for public access and use.

It is useful to consider the psychologist who creates a test to measure whether an individual or his or her spouse has repressed memories about childhood physical abuse but does not adhere to known principles of test construction. As mentioned previously, it is an ethical requirement that any valid assessment instrument, including one purporting to uncover early childhood trauma, adhere to the standard principles of test construction and be administered in a standardized way, not online or in the media. The therapist developing such a test for self-diagnosis or spouse diagnosis exposes the public to the risk of false positives as individuals "discover" that they supposedly have been traumatized in their childhood, when, in fact, this was not the case, and as they conclude that they therefore needed treatment. This area is fraught with misinformation, clinical implications, and ethical and legal risk. For some, merely taking and scoring this test could result in clinical symptoms of anxiety or depression or exacerbate psychological symptoms already present.

From both a clinical and scientific point of view it would be irresponsible, at best, and harmful to the public, at worst, to develop such a test solely on the basis of the therapist's experience treating survivors of childhood abuse. In either case, such a course of action would be contrary to the standard concerning test construction, standards involving competence (requiring psychologists to base their work on established scientific and professional knowledge of the discipline), as well as Principle A: Beneficence and Nonmaleficence.

People who are assessed by psychologists fill a variety of roles—students, clients, patients, candidates for employment, defendants in legal situations, parents in custody evaluations, moribund inpatients for decisional capacity, and many others. It is the psychologist's privilege and duty to honor the trust placed in them by creating and using tests in a fair and competent manner. Sound assessment practices set the stage for better interventions in business settings, schools, court rooms, and therapy offices. Chapter 10 focuses on the treatment setting and the ethical pitfalls and abuses that can spontaneously present themselves as a result of the power differential between therapists and their patients inherent in the setting.

Ethics in Psychotherapy 10

Adam and Britney Miller consulted Dr. Johnson, a psychologist specializing in sex therapy, for Britney's low libido since the birth of their 1-year old daughter. After several sessions Dr. Johnson referred Britney to a psychotherapist for treatment of major depression. The psychotherapist, Dr. Schwartz, began therapy with Britney two times per week. She learned of Britney's private dissatisfactions with the marriage, her husband's lack of affection, his long days at the office, lack of interest in her friendships, and occasional hot temper. She thought it unnecessary to collaborate with Dr. Johnson during this time and saw her professional responsibility exclusively as treating Britney's depression.

By the end of 1 month, Dr. Schwartz had developed a negative bias toward Britney's husband, based on her patient's disclosures; she found herself gently encouraging Britney to withdraw from sex therapy because she judged the marital relationship to be unhealthy, with little potential for salvaging. Dr. Johnson contacted Dr. Schwartz and suggested that Dr. Schwartz might not be aware of some important facts about this couple. Adam had disclosed that his wife was pregnant by another man at the time of their wedding and that this cloud had been hanging over the couple for the past year, a fact that Britney had never revealed to Dr Schwartz.

Dr. Schwartz realized that she had made unwarranted assumptions about Adam without ever meeting him and that by failing to collaborate with Dr. Johnson she was missing important historical information that would have helped in Britney's treatment.

Introduction

Psychotherapy is a collaborative enterprise in which patients and clinicians negotiate ways of working together that are mutually agreeable and likely to lead to positive outcomes (American Psychological Association [APA] Presidential Task Force on Evidence-Based Practice, 2006). It has been defined as a method of working with patients and clients to assist them to modify, change, or reduce factors that interfere with effective living (Corsini & Auerbach, 1998). Other definitions focus on different aspects of the therapy process—what the client experiences, the setting, and the interventions, to name a few. According to Alexander and French (1946), psychotherapy provides corrective emotional experiences, allowing patients to behave in ways that they may have avoided in the past, so as to experience that feared consequences do not occur. Although originally addressing psychoanalysis and psychodynamic-oriented psychotherapy, this concept also has been adapted by learning theorists and other schools of therapy.

Frank (1982) identified four common factors in psychotherapy: (a) an intense confiding relationship with a helper, (b) a healing setting, (c) a rationale, and (d) a set of prescribed treatments or rituals for alleviating the problem. Orlinsky and Howard (1986) conceived of five components common to all psychotherapy: (a) the development of a therapeutic contract in which the patient has an active role (including purpose, format, terms, and limits), (b) therapeutic interventions (e.g., confrontation, immediacy of affective expression), (c) resulting emergence of a therapeutic bond (also termed *therapeutic alliance*), (d) the patient's self-relatedness (lack of defensiveness), and (e) therapeutic realizations and impacts in session.

The outcomes of psychotherapy were described by the APA Presidential Task Force on Evidence-Based Practice as including not only symptom relief and prevention of future symptomatic episodes but also quality of life, adaptive functioning in work and relationships, ability to make satisfying life choices, personality change, and other goals arrived at in the collaboration between patient and clinician (APA Presidential Task Force on Evidence-Based Practice, 2006).

The first Ethics Code (1953a) devoted 32 out of a total of 54 separate paragraphs to psychotherapy (including assessment), nearly 60% of the document. By contrast, the 2002 Ethics Code allotted about 40% of the ethical rules to the topic of psychotherapy and related matters (e.g., assessment, advertising, multiple roles). This change is most likely due to the addition of other topical areas that have become a part of psychological science, teaching, and practice over the years, rather than a diminishing of the importance of ethics in therapy. The sections that follow focus on the subject matter included in the Therapy section of the 2002

Ethics Code, including some topics covered in earlier chapters (e.g., informed consent, definitions of sexual relationships).

Informed Consent in Individual Therapy

Providing informed consent about psychological services is a process that begins at the outset of treatment, often starting with the very first telephone call and continuing throughout the duration of treatment as needed. New clients and patients generally do not know how to inquire about a psychologist's theoretical orientation, nor do they feel confident doing so. They may have little awareness of different interventions and strategies or the benefits and risks of initiating treatment. They likely are able to select an electrician or an auto mechanic with greater confidence than a psychotherapist because the rules of confidentiality prohibit a therapist's referring callers to other "satisfied customers."

Therefore, it is up to the psychologist to anticipate the questions of clients and patients in providing informed consent. This may include discussion and/or handouts on the nature and anticipated course of therapy, fees, health insurance reimbursement, involvement of third parties (e.g., family members, other therapists or health care providers, or the court in the case of legally mandated treatment or evaluation), and confidentiality, including when the therapist is required to report information that is revealed to a government agency (e.g., child abuse or the threat of harm to a third party) and when a psychologist may choose to report information (e.g., reporting a senior who is the victim of emotional abuse).[1] Psychologists must also encourage new and continuing patients to ask questions and allow an opportunity for them to receive answers in language commensurate with their education level and understanding of English.

Sometimes patients are offered innovative treatments that may be lacking generally recognized techniques and established procedures but have been clinically effective nevertheless. In these situations, therapists must inform patients about (a) the developing nature of the treatment, (b) the potential risks and benefits of receiving the treatment, (c) any alternative treatments that are available for the same symptom(s), and (d) the completely voluntary nature of their participation in the treatment. Any claims of success rates, superiority to other theoretical approaches, or uniqueness of the treatment offered must be evidence

---

[1]Please note that these examples pertain to the law in California; reporting rules vary in different states.

based. The psychologist who runs a weight-loss clinic may publicly assert that his or her approach has a high rate of success only if patients following the program lose weight and maintain their progress in follow-up studies.

Patients and clients must be informed whenever their therapist is a trainee, psychological assistant, or psychological technician who is operating under the supervision of a licensed psychologist. They must also be given the name of the supervisor in advance, in part so that they may determine if a multiple role might exist, such as in smaller communities where the frequency of such chance encounters is much higher than in large cities. Mr. Smith, who has begun having panic attacks, may be very pleased with the theoretical approach of Dr. Gray, a psychological assistant, until he discovers that Dr. Gray's supervisor is his neighbor down the street. He may not wish to have a social acquaintance be privy to his psychotherapy, and being informed of this at the outset allows him the option of selecting another therapist.

Informed Consent With Couples and Family Therapy

When more than one person sits in the consulting room of a therapist at a time there may be ambiguity about who actually is the patient and what the treatment goals are. This applies to couples therapy (spouses or significant others) and family therapy (entire biological families, blended families, or any combination of parents or children and extended family members) in which some may be unwilling participants in the process.

It may help the therapeutic process and relieve apprehension to address informed consent matters promptly. Therapists working in these settings must clarify at the outset (a) who of those in the room are considered to be clients or patients and (b) the kind of relationship that the therapist intends to have with each person who is present. This includes describing the role to be played by the therapist (marital therapist, sex therapist, family therapist, court-appointed mediator) and informing clients about the probable uses of the therapy that is being provided. In many cases this would simply be improving the relationship of the couple or family members or addressing the dysfunctional behavior of one or more members. But in some cases the purpose of the meetings might also be to help a dysfunctional couple move efficiently through the process of separation or divorce.

Confidentiality, its exceptions, and the distribution of information are also discussed as a part of the informed consent process, using language that is developmentally appropriate and easily understood by any young children present. Will there be individual meetings with the members who are present? If so, will those disclosures be held in confidence or shared with other family members? And what is the agreement concerning confidentiality with minor children in the family if they have individual meetings with the therapist? And, of course, how does the state law treat confidentiality when children reveal information to therapists in private? If a 15-year-old daughter reveals privately to her family therapist that she is having a sexual relationship with her same-age boyfriend without using contraception, she must know, in advance, what the limits on confidentiality are and whether the therapist will share this information with her parents. Sometimes state laws specifically mandate what a therapist must reveal to a parent when disclosures of a sexual nature are made by a minor son or daughter.

Conflicting roles must also be addressed at the outset as well as later on whenever they arise. It is possible that a therapist treating a husband and wife who eventually decide to separate may be asked to be a supporting witness for one party in the divorce proceedings. However, such a role would have to be authorized by the spouse as well because both parties were present for the marital therapy. The therapist would have to decline such a request or consider withdrawing from initiating couples treatment at the outset if the therapist was being placed in a potentially conflicting role. In reality, therapists are rarely asked to testify in divorce court proceedings, however, and they never render child custody opinions. However, they are frequently asked to consult with child custody evaluators or mediators, which is both helpful and permissible as long as both parents authorize these disclosures (M. Lee, personal communication, August 1, 2009). These situations can sometimes be averted at the outset by consulting with a forensic psychologist or an attorney to learn about conflicting roles that can emerge in the course of treating families and couples.

The *Code of Ethics* of the American Association of Marriage and Family Therapists (2001) is a useful document for psychologists to read, regardless of whether they belong to that association. The document can be accessed online through Pope's website, *Ethics Codes and Practice Guidelines for Assessment, Therapy, Counseling, and Forensic Practice* (http://www.kspope.com/ethcodes/index.php).

Informed Consent
in Group Therapy

Participants in group therapy also receive informed consent at the outset and are instructed about their roles and responsibilities as well as those of the group therapist. Prospective group members are informed about the purpose and goals of the group therapy, meetings, fees, the duration of each meeting, whether the group is open-ended or meets for a fixed number of sessions, confidentiality and its exceptions, how the group generally functions, what one might hope to achieve by participating in it, policies about prohibiting physical interactions between group members (acting out angry feelings or affectionate feelings), and any policies about avoiding multiple roles or refraining from socializing with each other outside of the group meetings.

Confidentiality is particularly important in the group setting, with the same ethical and legal rules and exceptions applying to the psychologist as in any clinical setting. For group members, preserving each other's privacy remains a contractual obligation, not a legal one; each member has a vested interest in protecting each other's privacy as a means of safeguarding the group's functioning. Disclosures about HIV status, marital affairs, religious beliefs, criminal activity of the past, substance abuse, gay or lesbian status, or other private information must remain within the confines of the group. Disclosures that require action on the part of the group therapist, such as child abuse, intent to harm a third party, or serious thoughts of committing suicide (possibly requiring hospitalization by the group therapist) would be discussed at the outset with the group as a part of the informed consent understanding of confidentiality.

Many psychologists belong to the American Group Psychotherapy Association, a multidisciplinary association with a brief ethics code of its own (American Group Psychotherapy Association, 2002). It consists of two sections, Responsibility to Patient/Client and Professional Standards, and is accessible at the association's website (http://www.agpa.org/group/ethicalguide.html).

Sex in the Treatment Setting

Sexual relationships with clients and patients constitute one of the most exploitative and potentially harmful multiple-role relationships that a psychologist could allow to happen, regardless of subjective feelings of love or compassion. Sexual relationships are an explicit betrayal of trust and abuse of power and authority by an individual who has access to a population of naive and vulnerable individuals seeking treatment. There are no exceptions to the rule of avoiding sexual contact with recipients of psychological services.

For over 30 years research has increasingly addressed therapists' sexual attraction to patients and the devastating effects acting on this attraction has on treatment and the patient (Gabbard, 1989; Holroyd & Brodsky, 1977; Pope, 1994, 2000; Pope & Bouhoutsos, 1986; Pope, Sonne, & Holroyd, 1997; Pope & Vasquez, 2007; Schoener, 1990). Kenneth Pope's contributions have substantially advanced the knowledge in the field, and his website summarizes many useful citations (http://kspope.com/sexiss/index.php). For much of this time Gary Schoener's Walk-In Counseling Center in Minneapolis (http://www.walkin.org) has been addressing the needs of clients and patients who were sexually abused by therapists (since the mid 1970s) and the rehabilitative needs of therapists who crossed the line (since the early 1980s).

Pooled data reveal that offending therapists are overwhelmingly male, and exploited clients are overwhelmingly female, with about 7% of male therapists becoming sexually involved with one or more clients and 1.5% of female clients becoming so involved (Pope, 2001). The sequelae of a patient–therapist sexual relationship have been described as akin to the suffering experienced in posttraumatic stress disorder (Pope & Bouhoutsos, 1986). These reactions are described in Pope's (2001) recent research to include the following: (a) ambivalence (including psychological paralysis and the taboo of silence), (b) cognitive dysfunction (attention, memory, and concentration), (c) emotional lability (rapidly shifting feelings), (d) emptiness and isolation (loss of a sense of self), (e) guilt (self-blame, when it is entirely the therapist's responsibility for sexualizing the relationship), (f) impaired ability to trust (irrevocably so in some), (g) increased risk of suicide (about 14% will make one attempt, and 1% succeed), (h) role reversal and boundary confusion (needs and desires of the therapist become all important), (i) sexual confusion (caution and disgust with one's own sexual impulses), and (j) suppressed anger (numbness, self-loathing, and self-destructive behavior including suicide).

The ethical rules forbidding harm and sexual exploitation in the treatment setting are unambiguous. The specific standards in the 2002 Ethics Code prohibit the following: (a) having sex with current therapy clients or patients, (b) having sex with the relatives or significant others of current therapy clients or patients (e.g., spouses, parents, children, close relatives), (c) having sex with former therapy patients within 2 years of formally terminating the professional relationship, and (d) providing therapy to someone with whom the therapist has had a sexual relationship, regardless of how much time has passed.

The proscription against sex with former therapy patients is practically an absolute prohibition against sex with any former patient, ever, in spite of the 2-year posttermination rule, because of the many conditions that must prevail that would allow for such a relationship to avoid exploiting and harming the former patient, as discussed in Chapter 2. In establishing these conditions in 1992, the revision task force, which I chaired, hoped to guide therapists' judgment in a step-by-step process to arrive at an ethical decision that would best protect the welfare of former clients and patients (Canter, Bennett, Jones, & Nagy, 1994). These concepts were retained in the 2002 edition, with the additional prohibition against sexual involvement with relatives or significant others of current therapy patients (APA, 2010). This standard (Standard 10.08, Sexual Intimacies With Former Therapy Clients/Patients) states that a therapist may only engage in sex with a former client or patient even 2 years following the ending of the professional relationship only if he or she can successfully bear the burden of demonstrating that there has been no exploitation in light of certain criteria. They are as follows:

- amount of time that had passed since terminating treatment (2 years minimum),
- nature and duration of therapy (for some people the concept of "once a therapist always a therapist" may prevail because patients sometimes return to treatment years after terminating),
- circumstances of termination (it must not be a hasty or sudden termination in the interest of fostering the new, emerging romantic relationship),
- patient's personal history (e.g., childhood incest, sexual molestation, or other major boundary violations, such as a pattern of sexual acting out with one's professor, personal physician, or boss),
- patient's current mental status (i.e., being able to determine with reasonable certainty that the former patient is not currently clinically depressed, delusional dissociated, psychotic, or otherwise experiencing impaired judgment, diminished insight, or poor mental health),
- likelihood of adverse impact on the patient (i.e., being able to conclusively prove, in advance, that the former patient will not ultimately be harmed by beginning a sexual relationship with the former therapist at the present time), and
- statements or actions made by the therapist during therapy suggesting or inviting the possibility of posttherapy sex (e.g., did the therapist hint, intimate, imply, or frankly state that he or she desired a sexual liaison after treatment ended?).

Although therapists might convince themselves that they met the criteria for beginning such a relationship, if challenged and sued by their former patient months or years later, after the romantic relationship has failed, they may never be able to successfully convince a jury or court that they had complied with this stringent rule.

Interrupting Therapy

Psychologists are responsible for the continuity of treatment once they have initiated therapeutic interventions, including both predictable and unpredictable interruptions. This includes the psychologist permanently leaving the setting for any reason, such as ending a contractual arrangement with their employer (e.g., hospital, clinic, group practice), moving to another part of the country, or retiring. The ethical rule requires psychologists to make reasonable efforts to provide for the orderly and appropriate resolution of responsibility for client and patient care, and this must be anticipated at the outset when entering into the employment setting or contractual arrangement. It may be advisable to create a professional will that helps survivors to deal with patients and clients in the event of the therapist's untimely death or disability (APA Division 42, Psychologists in Independent Practice, has a sample at the following website: http://www. division42.org/MembersArea/PracticePerfect/ProfessionalWill.htm).

A psychologist who joins a group practice is wise to reach an agreement with the owner about such matters as ownership of records and how transitions are handled with patients if the therapist eventually leaves the practice. Paramount consideration should always be the welfare of the client or patient. If the patient experiences a hiatus in treatment because the therapist is leaving the practice but staying in the area to open his or her own practice, the patient must be given the option of continuing with the therapist, and records must be made available for the transition. It should be noted, however, that sometimes employment contracts include noncompete agreements concerning the logistics of leaving the practice and constraints on establishing one's own independent practice within a certain geographical distance of the group practice. A 14-year-old boy with autism who has slowly formed a good working relationship with his therapist may be unwilling to see another therapist if his therapist leaves the practice but may not have the assertiveness or social skills to make his wishes known. This is a situation in which it is the psychologist's responsibility to anticipate the patient's needs and to advocate a specific course of action out of concern for his welfare. The therapist could take the position of formally recommending that the boy continue treatment with him or her, assuming that there is no significant change in fee structure, and take the necessary steps to facilitate the transition. Such an action might not necessarily be welcomed by the owner of the group practice, however, because there may be other therapists also skilled in treating children with autism, and the loss of a patient reduces the income of the group.

At times, unfortunately, financial realities of everyday business can trump consideration of patient welfare in the minds of clinicians–entrepreneurs. When this happens, the professional conduct may fall short of following the spirit of the general principles, particularly Principle A: Beneficence and Nonmaleficence, Principle B: Fidelity and Responsibility, and Principle E: Respect for People's Rights and Dignity. Unfortunately, concerns about managing the practice, paying employees, meeting other expenses, and dealing with day-to-day clinical emergencies and other realities may not leave much time or energy for such matters as anticipating interruptions in treatment. The wise clinician pays attention to these exigencies before a crisis occurs, thereby minimizing additional harm to patients or clients who already are grieving the loss of their therapist.

Terminating Treatment

Psychologists generally terminate treatment when the client or patient (a) no longer needs the services, (b) is not likely to benefit, or (c) is being harmed by continuing. A fourth situation not mentioned in the Ethics Code would be a judgment call by the therapist that the client or patient is no longer benefiting from the services (even though the client or patient may feel that they are necessary). When the goals of treatment have been attained or the patient is unlikely to benefit from continued visits, it is time to discuss ending treatment, exploring new goals that the patient may be interested in, or referring the patient for a different type of intervention. Terminating is a process that may extend over many sessions in which the treatment process and outcome may be reviewed. Unmet goals, details of the therapeutic relationship that may be further explored, and whether additional therapeutic interventions are needed are discussed (e.g., group therapy, couples therapy, a therapist of a different gender or theoretical orientation, mindfulness meditation training, or any other intervention addressing the patient's needs).

There are situations in which a patient's choice to withdraw from treatment may be a wise decision even though treatment goals have not yet been met. The therapist's theoretical orientation may have the temporary effect of intensifying symptoms, yet the patient may not have the psychological resources to endure such an increase in intensity or may require a different sort of treatment. The patient may realize that he or she prefers to work with a therapist of a different gender after treatment has gone on for a while. A therapist might be overly confrontative or too unstructured for the patient's preference. Or it is possible that a therapist may be using an outmoded form of treatment for a particular diagnosis, and the patient may learn of a different intervention offered elsewhere. Sometimes simply participating in psychotherapy can bring strong feelings of sadness, anger, or other negative emotions that may stimulate some patients to consider withdrawing from treatment. Financial exigencies also may force the patient to withdraw from treatment.

Psychologists also have the option of ending treatment if they have received a threat of harm from the patient or someone with whom the patient has a relationship. It is useful to consider the following situation.

> Dr. Altmann, nearing retirement, accepted Laura, a new patient who was alcoholic, depressed, had begun cutting herself, and had attempted suicide on two occasions over the previous 4 years. After

several weeks of receiving treatment that was humanistic and supportive in nature, Laura began sending daily e-mails to her therapist as a means of having more contact with him between sessions. She also discovered where Dr. Altmann lived, began to drive by his house at night, and occasionally parked across the street hoping for a glimpse of him.

Dr. Altmann began to realize that Laura met the criteria for borderline personality disorder and that her mental health was beginning to deteriorate with his treatment. He also began to feel as though he was being stalked by her; attempting to set limits on his patient's behavior, he requested her to stop these intrusive practices at their next session. She became agitated at his request and impulsively accused him of not really caring about his patients after all. In the midst of her angry outburst she said loudly that he would be hearing from her brother, an ex-convict living nearby, and stormed out of the session, slamming the door behind her. For the next week Dr. Altmann continued to receive angry e-mails from the patient, alternately threatening and pleading in tone.

On reflection, Dr. Altmann recognized that he did not possess the expertise to treat someone with borderline personality disorder and that his interventions and attempt to set boundaries only served to rapidly escalate her symptoms. After being repeatedly threatened by her, he exercised his right to end treatment and considered telephoning the police to initiate a restraining order against his former patient.

If possible, a psychologist who is being stalked could make an attempt to offer a referral to a qualified therapist, but if the relationship has deteriorated to the point where the patient is threatening to harm him, this likely is no longer an option. In these situations it is important to consult an experienced clinician and possibly seek the advice of an attorney.

Use of Technology in the Office and Online

The words *information technology, computer,* and *online* are nowhere to be found in the 2002 Ethics Code, and there are few standards that specifically address the use of computer technology in research or therapy settings. Nevertheless, computers have been a common tool of psychologists for many years, as mentioned in Chapter 2.

PRACTICE MANAGEMENT

Rules and regulations regarding record keeping by computer and electronic transmission of patient data (e.g., faxing or e-mailing billing information to third-party payers, patients' clinical records) are described by federal law in the Health Insurance Portability and Accountability Act of

1996 *Notice of Privacy Practices for Protected Health Information* (revised in 2003). State laws also address preserving and maintaining the confidentiality of patient records by requiring psychologists to use computer passwords and backup systems (e.g., external hard drive or some other off-premise secure system), and to train staff and clerical workers who handle sensitive data in procedures for preserving privacy.

CLINICAL SERVICES

Technology has great potential as a means of offering clinical services. Biofeedback training has helped countless patients with migraine and tension headaches, Reynaud's syndrome/disease, chronic pain syndromes, hypertension, irritable bowel disease, and a host of other psychological and physiological symptoms for over 40 years. Clinical research on neurofeedback (also known as electroencephalogram or EEG biofeedback) is now being carried out to help patients with behavioral problems, including learning disorders, attention-deficit/hyperactivity problems, and certain sleep problems.

Computers are being increasingly used in clinical settings, for example, to create virtual reality distractions for treating hospitalized patients with serious burns who are undergoing physical therapy and changes of dressing. These patients experience significant reductions in pain compared with a no-distraction situation, accomplished by simply wearing a virtual reality helmet during the normally painful medical procedure and experiencing pleasant and fanciful images and sounds, much like a computer game (Hoffman, Patterson, & Carrougher, 2000). Virtual reality systems have also been used successfully in treating a variety of anxiety disorders, such as phobias (e.g., fear of flying, fear of enclosed spaces).

RISKS AND BENEFITS OF CYBERSPACE

Other forms of technology—using telephone, e-mail, videoconferencing, or other online means of interacting with consumers of psychological services—are becoming commonplace. This is a convenience for those who live in remote areas, are ill, elderly, disabled, institutionalized (e.g., prisoners), or otherwise unable to have face-to-face therapy and would benefit from technology-assisted psychological services.

An Internet search of *online therapy* results in many millions of websites ready and willing to dispense counseling, therapy, advice and any form of psychological help on a wide variety of topics. Some of these sites offer psychoinformation and can be useful resources that may be roughly equivalent to a well-targeted self-help book. But many sites purport to offer counseling or therapy directly to the public. There are risks to both consumers and psychologists who participate in online psychological services. Such websites seem to enable licensed practitioners to provide services in states and countries where they are not licensed to practice; telephone therapists would encounter the same risks. Although laws and legal precedents involving cyberspace may be scarce, the topic is being explored by the media, and the public is slowly becoming more savvy. An example is a recent article (Lyon, 2009) in *U.S. News & World Report* in which several psychologists, myself included, were interviewed on the topic of online counseling. Unfortunately, online consultation of health care providers is not always advisable, and as of this writing there already has been one tragic outcome to this practice. Christian Hageseth, a psychiatrist from Denver, prescribed Prozac to John McKay, a depressed 19-year-old student at Stanford University, in August 2005, by means of an online medical prescription website, without ever having seen the patient face-to-face (Egelko, 2009). Two months later the student committed suicide by overdosing on the drug, and the psychiatrist, after being extradited to California for trial, was sentenced to 9 months in jail. Ironically, by participating in this unorthodox practice, Dr. Hageseth stated that he felt he was providing a useful service to needy patients, and it is likely true that the patient did appreciate the convenience of being able to order prescriptive medication without ever having to visit a physician's office.

In addition to the issue of practicing without a license, this case raises serious questions of competence and ethical compliance for any psychologist who would offer "psychotherapy" online, in the absence of training or knowledge of the research in this mode of practice (Maheu, Pulier, Wilhelm, McMenamin, & Brown-Connolly, 2005). It also invites psychologists to engage in many activities that may not be evidence based and for which little or no ethical guidance is yet available. Also, knowledge of jurisdictional rules about practicing across state lines is important, and legal issues addressing this are complex and vary from state to state. Although a thorough analysis of this topic is beyond the scope of this book, what follows is an introductory list of issues to consider for the psychologist considering offering services over the Internet:

- Privacy and confidentiality of client information: Who else has access to the client's computer, e-mail, or videoconferencing records?
- Informed consent: Are online clients informed of (a) reasonable expectations for this medium, (b) the limitations of the medium that may affect outcomes, (c) what to do or whom to contact in case of an emergency, (d) confidentiality and its exceptions, (e) parental consent in the case of offering "therapy" to minors online, and (f) all the other customary topics included in authorization of treatment?
- Competence: Is the online therapist trained to take a history, diagnose, offer therapeutic interventions to an unseen client, and deal

with emergency situations such as suicide or wife battering when the interactions are restricted to e-mail exchanges?

■ Public statements: Does the online therapist make honest advertising statements for his or her website or exaggerate what could reasonably be expected?

■ Record keeping: Does the online therapist document the interactions with clients as a therapist would with a patient in the office?

■ Basis for scientific and professional judgments: Does the online therapist follow usual and customary procedures or does the therapist take shortcuts or alter strategy significantly from how the therapist would conduct psychotherapy in the office?

■ Terminating and referring online clients: How does an online therapist handle termination or referral to a local mental health care provider in a distant community, where the competence and specialty areas of local therapists are unknown, and does the online therapist incur liability for making a bad referral?

Careful use of technology has much to offer psychologists when competent training and actively taking steps to avoid harming consumers are primary considerations. At present, unfortunately, few ethical standards directly address incorporating computers or cyberspace into one's clinical practice, although the Health Insurance Portability and Accountability Act of 1996 does include a number of specific requirements concerning the use of computers by health care providers. Undoubtedly the Ethics Code will continue to evolve as computers become increasingly commonplace in the delivery of psychological services, and ethical guidance will be needed in such matters as record keeping, assessment, and the delivery of competent psychological services, both in the office and by electronic means.

Each day many clients and patients place their trust in psychologists, seeking to make changes in their lives by means of individual treatment, marriage counseling, family therapy, and other interventions. What happens in the consulting office behind closed doors cannot be directly monitored by any agency, the "ethics police," or a governmental body. It is ultimately the individual responsibility of all psychologists to learn, understand, and proactively apply ethical principles in the course of their work equally to each client and patient for whom they provide a service. In the next chapter, I examine how ethical awareness applies to investigators dealing with people who take the risk of volunteering to participate in their research.

Ethics in Research and Publication

11

Dr. Bell planned to use telephone interviews to gather data about the health history of older men and women from low socioeconomic positions. His rationale was that the phone typically offers greater privacy than face-to-face interviews, and research participants are likely to be more self-disclosing with the anonymity provided by this medium (Sieber, 1992). He had rejected using the Internet for gathering data because he concluded that this population would be less likely to be familiar with computers and his sampling would therefore be less representative.

He did not know that people from low socioeconomic groups usually do not live alone or have privacy from their families or caretakers when they use the phone (Sieber, 1992). He was also unaware that this population often keeps health secrets from their own family members and, therefore, would be less likely to freely disclose to a researcher information that they would not reveal to a family member who was within earshot. If he had conducted a pilot study or consulted an experienced investigator familiar with the characteristics of this group, he would have known that his methodology was flawed, and he could have made the necessary changes before proceeding.

Introduction

Although the first American Psychological Association (APA) Ethics Code (1953a) devoted many more standards to clinical than research matters, it at least introduced the topic of conducting the science of psychology within an ethical framework. The research section consisted of three parts: (a) Maintaining Standards of Research, (b) Protecting Welfare of Research Subjects, and (c) Reporting Research Results. These parts addressed such topics as preserving privacy, informed consent, harmful aftereffects, suppressing data, and humane treatment of animals—all present in the 2002 Ethics Code.

The first Ethics Code also addressed publication matters, in a section titled Writing and Publishing. This included how to list coauthors when there are multiple investigators, a decision rule for identifying who should be listed as the lead author, and acknowledging published and unpublished material that has influenced the research or writing (i.e., not mentioning plagiarism per se but addressing the topic in a general way).

The current ethical regulations about research and publication incorporate all of these original concepts and more. They have matured into a comprehensive tutorial comprising more ethical standards than any other section in the entire code. In this chapter, I first examine seven ethical areas concerning research, beginning with institutional review boards, and then four areas addressing publication matters.

Institutional Review Boards

When contemplating research, psychologists must obtain approval from institutions where the research is conducted before proceeding (universities, schools, prisons, hospitals, the military, or any other setting). They must also submit their research proposal to the institutional review board (IRB) associated with their place of employment. In reviewing research proposals, the IRB considers institutional commitments and regulations, applicable laws, and standards of professional conduct and practice to safeguard the rights and welfare of people who volunteer to participate in the study.

According to federal rules, the IRB must include at least five members of varying backgrounds and diversity, including race, gender, and cultural matters, who are sensitive to community attitudes (Institutional Review Boards, 1991). Rules of membership are quite clear: include a diversity of professionals (e.g., psychologist, psychiatrist), at least one member whose primary concerns are in the scientific area, at least one member whose primary concerns are in nonscientific areas, at least one member who is not otherwise affiliated with the institution and is not related to a family member of a person affiliated with the institution, and no member who has a conflict of interest with any project under review. If the IRB reviews proposals involving vulnerable subjects, such as children, older people, hospitalized HIV patients, prisoners, pregnant women, or those who are mentally disabled (inpatients or outpatients), then the board must include someone who is knowledgeable about these populations.

Many investigators rely on federal grants for funding, and they must comply with federal rules and regulations, as articulated by the National Institutes of Health's Office of Research Integrity. For the most part these regulatory standards are clear and straightforward, and the investigator can learn which steps to take and what to avoid in protecting the welfare of research participants. These include such topics as minimizing risk to participants, providing thorough informed consent in advance, debriefing, and the like. If investigators are engaged in animal research, they must be well versed in the animal welfare principles as articulated by the federal rules and regulations, such as the Animal Welfare Act (2007), to be discussed in the section that follows.

Planning Research

Investigators are obligated to do research on topics with which they already have some familiarity so as to minimize the likelihood of harm to individuals. No matter how sophisticated investigators may be in their own specialty area, they may be relatively uninformed about a different area of study for a variety of reasons (e.g., type of population, the milieu, research design). If they are completely naive about a topic or a population, they must obtain some training or consult with others who are knowledgeable so as to optimize the research protocol and minimize the possibility of harm.

The psychologist who is researching alcoholism in an American Indian population but who has never directly observed the Indian culture should work with a coinvestigator or consultant who is familiar and skilled with this population. Likewise, an investigator using the Internet as a means of gathering data on patients with major depressive disorder would do well to consult with someone familiar with this medium first to better address informed consent, minimize potential harm to online participants who might be suicidal, and conduct long-term follow-up. By being familiar with the population and milieu, researchers will minimize invasiveness and be able to fine-tune protocols so as to choose procedures that might be more palatable to the research participants without compromising the study.

Informed Consent for Research Participants

Researchers must provide informed consent to individuals considering participating in research, disclosing information sufficient in scope and depth to help them formulate a decision about participating in the study.

VULNERABLE GROUPS

When recruiting minors, investigators must obtain informed consent from parents or legal guardians and must obtain *assent* from the children (i.e., their agreement, regardless of how much the child understands of the research); direct appeals should never be offered directly to a child (Scott-Jones, 2000). An IRB would expect extra measures to be taken when recruiting members of other vulnerable groups, such as American Indians, high school equivalency students, those lacking financial resources (e.g., the homeless), those living in institutions (e.g., prisoners, residents of assisted living settings), those experiencing social stigmas (e.g., due to ethnicity, race, sexual orientation, physical disability), those in poor health (e.g., hospitalized patients), or those with mental limitations (e.g., serious mental illnesses, developmental disabilities, or dementias; Knapp & VandeCreek, 2006).

An example of an extra measure might be assessing a candidate's mental competency to understand informed consent in a study involving experimental treatment by using an instrument such as the MacArthur Competence Assessment Tool for Treatment (Grisso & Appelbaum, 1998). Examples of potential risk to a vulnerable group are examining the ethicality of assigning someone with suicidal ideation to a placebo group or allowing a participant exhibiting the beginning symptoms of mania to continue as a member of the control group. Another example is recruiting someone with dementia for a study involving deception.

Although the rationale and general concepts of informed consent are discussed in Chapter 5, it is useful to examine the specific ethical requirements as they appear in the 2002 Ethics Code. Standard 8.02, Informed Consent to Research, requires psychologists to

inform prospective participants about (1) the purpose of the research, expected duration, and procedures; (2) their right to decline to participate and to withdraw from the research once it has begun; (3) the foreseeable consequences of declining or withdrawing; (4) reasonably foreseeable factors that may be expected to influence their willingness to participate such as potential risks, discomfort, or adverse effects; (5) any prospective research benefits; (6) limits of confidentiality; (7) incentives for participation; and (8) whom to contact for questions about the research and research participants' rights.

They must also provide the opportunity for participants to ask questions and receive answers.

The Stanford Prison Experiment was conducted in 1971 by Phil Zimbardo for the purpose of examining the psychological effects of assuming the role of a prisoner or prison guard (Haney, Banks, & Zimbardo, 1973). It is an excellent example of psychological research going awry and what the investigator ultimately did to protect the participants. The investigators paid 24 college students $15 per day to participate in the research. The students were screened for mental disorders and history of criminal activity and randomized into two groups, prisoners and guards, in a carefully designed "prison" setting in the basement of a building at Stanford University. What was intended to be a 2-week study had to be ended prematurely after 6 days because of the mental deterioration of the participants; the "guards" became sadistic, and the "prisoners" showed signs of extreme stress.

The primary investigator acknowledged that he had become so engaged in his role that he initially failed to appreciate the harm that his experiment could have on the participants. However, to his credit, he subsequently used the experiment for teaching ethical concepts for decades following the research. His website contains interesting video clips of the original study and is narrated by the author himself (http://www.prisonexp.prg/).

Intervention research examines the use of experimental treatments and strategies with those experiencing clinical symptoms (e.g., obsessive–compulsive disorder, chemical dependency, or major depression), and psychologists must always proceed cautiously to protect patients and clients from harm. They must clarify the following to these prospective participants at the outset:

- the experimental nature of the treatment;
- the services that will or will not be available to the control group, if appropriate (i.e., if symptoms become worse during participation and a participant had been randomly assigned to a control group, what can that person expect by way of support or crisis intervention);
- the means by which assignment to treatment and control groups will be made;
- available treatment alternatives if one does not wish to participate in the research or decides to withdraw after the study has begun; and
- compensation for or monetary costs of participating, including whether third-party reimbursement will be sought (e.g., health insurance, Medicare).

An example of how informed consent might apply in intervention research follows.

> A 24-year-old woman had been molested by a priest as a child and had agreed to participate in an experimental treatment for survivors of childhood sexual assault. In addition to being provided with the usual informed consent matters (e.g., description of the study, time involvement, confidentiality, risks and benefits), she was informed that the treatment was experimental in nature, was not evidence based, and had not yet been shown to be effective in reducing symptoms. She was also informed that she would be randomly assigned to a control or experimental group. If assigned to the control group, with no exposure to the experimental treatment, and she experienced a worsening of symptoms, she was told she could opt to consult with a therapist. However, if she chose this option, she would be dropped from the study. She was also informed that she would be compensated $125 for participating in the protocol for (a) completing baseline data and (b) attending 10 group meetings, with this amount to be payable on the last day, whether or not she attended all 10 of the meetings. Finally, she was informed that if she refused to participate or decided to withdraw after the study had begun, she would receive referrals to competent therapists accepting new patients, who were uninvolved with the research.

DISPENSING WITH INFORMED CONSENT

There are situations in which informed consent may be omitted, such as when the research would not be assumed to create distress or harm and confidentiality is protected. The following situations are described in Standard 8.05, Dispensing With Informed Consent for Research, of the 2002 Ethics Code as meeting the criteria for dispensing with informed consent: (a) studying normal educational practices, curricula, or classroom management methods conducted in educational settings; (b) anonymous questionnaires, naturalistic observations, or archival research (e.g., using anonymous patient data in hospitals) for which disclosure of responses would not place participants at risk of criminal or civil liability or damage their financial standing, employability, or reputation; and (c) the study of factors related to job or organization effectiveness conducted in organizational settings for which there is no risk to participants' employability.

The U.S. Department of Health and Human Services discusses the circumstances under which informed consent may be omitted in its *Code of Federal Regulations*, under Title 45, Public Welfare, Part 46, Protection of Human Subjects. It states that an IRB may rule to dispense with informed consent when (a) the research presents no more than minimal risk to participants and involves no procedures for which written consent is normally required outside of the research context and (b) the only record linking the subject and the research is the consent document itself, and the principal risk would be potential harm resulting from a breach of confidentiality (Protection of Human Subjects, 1991, amended 2005). To satisfy the second condition, each subject would be asked whether he or she wants documentation linking him or her with the research, and these wishes would govern. The term *minimal risk* means that the probability and magnitude of harm or discomfort anticipated in the research are not greater in and of themselves than those ordinarily encountered in daily life or during the performance of routine physical or psychological examinations or tests (Protection of Human Subjects, 1991, amended 2005).

Researchers may dispense with informed consent when audio- and videotaping under two conditions: (a) if the research consists solely of naturalistic observations in public places, and it is not anticipated that the recording will be used in a way that could cause personal identification or harm or (b) the research design includes deception, and consent for the use of the recording is obtained during the debriefing stage, after the participant's involvement with the protocol has ended (i.e., the participant may choose to delete the recording at that point).

PROTECTING THE WELFARE OF SUBORDINATE RESEARCH PARTICIPANTS WHO DECLINE OR WITHDRAW

When conducting research with those in a subordinate relationship, such as patients or students, investigators must exercise additional caution to protect the prospective subjects' rights if they decline to participate or withdraw after data gathering has begun. If a patient or student refuses to participate in the study or withdraws after it has begun, he or she is entitled to receive referrals to competent therapists uninvolved with the research protocol who are able to accept new patients. The investigator must be neither coercive regarding participating at the outset nor punitive if the individual withdraws. And if students are required to participate in research as part of a course requirement or for extra credit, they must also be given the option of an equitable alternative if they decline to engage in the investigation.

Offering Inducements for Participating in Research

Investigators commonly offer incentives to prospective participants, such as money, medication, didactic experiences, or therapeutic interventions (e.g., meditation, hypnosis, individual or group therapy). These can be powerful motivating factors for the vulnerable groups mentioned earlier (students, those who lack financial resources, and those who are stigmatized, institutionalized, or physically or mentally ill).

> In an attempt to increase response rate, a researcher planned to offer elementary school children a decorative pencil as a reward for returning a signed parental permission form. The researcher devised this strategy because the school did not give permission to mail forms directly to parents; instead, the school requested that forms be sent home with the children. The researcher emphasized that all children who returned a signed form would receive the pencil, including those children whose parents declined to participate as well as those whose parents agreed. At its initial review, the IRB objected to the pencil as an inducement, asserting that such a reward was coercive. On appeal, however, the IRB reversed its decision, acknowledging that the magnitude of this reward was modest and was unlikely to be coercive. In addition, the reward was given to children for returning the signed permission form, regardless of parents' decision to agree or decline to participate (Scott-Jones, 2000).

If offering clinical services as an inducement, investigators must provide information about the nature of the services, risks and obligations, and limitations. For example, when offering individual psychotherapy to research participants, the investigator must clarify if there is an option to continue in treatment with the same therapist after the protocol has ended. Also, the investigator must clarify if there would be any cost for the treatment, either during the course of data gathering or afterward, and if there is a limit to the number of therapy sessions afterward.

Investigators must avoid taking advantage of prospective participants, exploiting, or coercing them in any way as a means of increasing their sample size. The investigator must carefully consider the value of an inducement with a particular vulnerable group within the local geographical area. Offering too great an inducement diminishes the participant's freedom of choice in weighing risks and benefits (Scott-Jones, 2000). Coercion can occur whenever an individual feels that he or she cannot afford to avoid participating in the investigation because there is so much to gain from the inducement that is offered. A homeless person, prisoner, or someone experiencing panic attacks might feel that the inducements of money, privileges, or clinical intervention would far outweigh any potential adverse experiences that might be inherent in the research. They may give a cursory glance at the risks section of the consent form and make a premature decision to join the study, regardless of personal inconvenience, time required, psychological stress, or other negative factors to be encountered as part of the study. When investigators have questions about the nature of an inducement to offer, they should consult with peers, their IRB overseeing the study, and stakeholders in the study. Even if they are not affiliated with an institution with an IRB, they may seek a review of their protocol with another institution's IRB that is authorized to evaluate external research proposals.

Deception in Research

Deception in research consists of either providing false information to participants about the purpose or goals of an investigation at the outset or deliberately misrepresenting facts or information during the course of the experiment. It remains a controversial topic among psychologists even in this day and age. Questions (Eyde, 2000) to consider are as follows:

- What responsibilities does an investigator have when considering using deception in research?
- How might participants be harmed by the deceptive information about the nature of the experiment?
- Which populations are at the greatest risk of experiencing this harm?
- To what extent are self-reports of no adverse impact by the deception judged to be expected and desirable responses to the experimenter (at the debriefing session)?
- What might researchers do to counteract potential negative consequences of deception?

On deontological grounds it can be argued that it is inherently unethical and undesirable to ever deliberately deceive people. This is consistent with the Principle C: Integrity: "Psychologists seek to promote accuracy, honesty, and truthfulness in the science, teaching, and practice of psychology. In these activities psychologists do not steal, cheat, or engage in fraud, subterfuge, or *intentional misrepresentation of fact*" [italics added]. Principle B: Fidelity and Responsibility reminds psychologists that "psychologists establish relationships of trust with those with whom they work." Lying about the purpose of an experiment or providing erroneous data during its course would seem to violate this principle.

On teleological grounds it can be argued that acts of deception by researchers result in undesirable consequences for the research participant, individual investigator, the public perception of psychologists, and ultimately the science of psychology (Kimmel, 1998; Ortmann & Hertwig, 1997). It undermines individual's trust in psychologists, alters the behavior of future participants in the same experimental protocol (the *spillover effect* whereby future participants are contaminated by learning of past participants' experiences and expect to be deceived), thereby possibly affecting data collection and the ultimate findings of the investigation.

A commonly cited experiment, also mentioned in Chapter 8, was conducted by Stanley Milgram, who published his controversial investigation titled "Behavioral Study of Obedience" in 1963. Milgram studied *destructive obedience* by recruiting 40 participants ("teachers") to administer electric shocks to "learners" (confederates in another room pretending to suffer with each jolt) whenever they made an error. The primary dependent variable was the maximum shock (30 levels of intensity) that the teacher was willing to deliver before refusing to continue. Of the group, 26 participants obeyed all commands, administering the maximum intensity of shock even while hearing screams of anguish from learners; 14 participants broke off the experiment at some point after the victim protested and refused to provide further answers. The procedure created extreme levels of nervous tension in some teachers, including profuse sweating, trembling, stuttering, and nervous laughter. Extensive debriefing followed the experiment, whereby teachers and confederates were allowed to interact with each other, disclose the deception, and process their emotional reaction. Milgram argued that the social benefit of his study outweighed any adverse effects to the participants.

To be sure, Milgram's notorious investigation revealed useful data about the willingness of people to comply with authority, as did Zimbardo's Stanford prison experiment 8 years later. However, neither of these investigations would likely be approved by an IRB by today's standards because the risk of harm to participants would be considered too great, and the use of nondeceptive techniques or lower risk designs might be able to be substituted to attain the same results (e.g., virtual reality settings created on the computer).

There is a fundamental rule against deceiving participants in a research experiment: If the same research can be carried out without deception, then it should be. However, if the prospective value of the research necessitates having some degree of deception in the course of the study, then this is acceptable as long as adequate debriefing occurs so that participants do not feel duped, manipulated, betrayed, or otherwise harmed. Standard 8.07, Deception in Research, of the 2002 Ethics Code sums up the four criteria to be met before an investigator may use deception: (a) Deceptive techniques must be justified by the study's significant prospective scientific, educational, or applied value and only if nondeceptive strategies are not feasible; (b) there must be no deception about the infliction of physical pain or severe emotional distress; (c) the deception must be revealed and participants debriefed as early as feasible—preferably at the end of their participation, but no later than at the end of data collection; and (d) participants must be permitted to withdraw their data after being debriefed. The last three criteria are straightforward and could unambiguously be met by an investigator; however, the first one can be a major hurdle to overcome because it consists of the investigator's personal judgment about the prospective value of the study and is therefore subject to bias.

The *prospective scientific value* of an investigation consists of its significance as a contribution to the knowledge base. The *prospective educational value* of an investigation refers to its benefit to individuals or to society. And the *prospective applied value* refers to industrial and organizational settings, environmental psychology, or direct implications for the ways in which psychologists intervene in the lives of others (Nagy, 2005). Before the investigator proceeds, it is his or her ethical duty to make an objective appraisal of the prospective value of the research using available resources, such as consulting with peers who have addressed similar hypotheses in their research, review of the scientific literature, and seeking advice from the local IRB. The investigator should consider deception to be a last resort, an acceptable choice only after exploring all reasonable options for testing the hypotheses without using deception.

Debriefing

Investigators must provide a prompt opportunity for participants to learn about the nature, results, and conclusions of the research as well as correct any misconceptions that participants may have concerning the investigation. They may delay or withhold this feedback if scientific or humane values justify such a step. For example, as mentioned, it may be important to avoid contaminating the subject pool of future participants by delaying debriefing, and in research with participants with diminished capacity or who are moribund and unable to comprehend the debriefing, it may be more humane to withhold it (Canter et al., 1994).

Debriefing can mollify the effects of research using deception or creating aversive reactions. Certainly the creative measures taken by Milgram, allowing participant and confederate to interact at the conclusion of the study and revealing the true nature of the research, and Zimbardo, ending the experiment after only 6 days and evaluating the participants, helped reverse any long-term negative effects. If investigators discover that being involved in research has harmed a participant, they must take steps to minimize the harm at the end of data collection.

> In a study designed to test the effect of negative emotions on memory, participants were asked to take a psychological test to measure anxiety and depression and then randomized into two groups. One group was given true feedback about test results, and one was given exaggerated false negative feedback results intended to elevate anxiety in the participants. Participants were then asked to memorize a list of paired words, given a distraction cognitive task, and then tested on their memory for the paired-words list.

Immediately following the data collection the experimenter provided an open-ended, extensive debriefing to those who were deceived by having an individual face-to-face meeting. The experimenter explained that participants were given false results and apologized for misleading them. The experimenter asserted a preference for conducting the study without deception but stated that it was essential to create cognitive dissonance in one group by providing falsely elevated anxiety and depression scores and then noting how their performance differed from the other group. The experimenter then showed the participants a bell-shaped curve and explained, in lay terms, what the participants' true scores were on depression and anxiety controlled for age and gender. She monitored the participants' emotional reactions during the debriefing session and encouraged participants to ask questions and seek clarification in an unhurried manner.

The experimenter explained that there still was a possibility that the effects of negative feedback might persist and that people sometimes have a tendency to discount information that is presented during debriefing that is inconsistent with the deceptive negative feedback received during the experiment (Ross, Lepper, & Hubbard, 1975). Simply being aware of this possibility helps dispel the effect. The experimenter assured the participants that pilot testing had been done to ascertain that the deception was believable and that participants were not gullible and should not feel shameful or foolish. The experimenter again apologized for the subterfuge, and on closing the interview, provided a name, telephone number, and e-mail address for any questions or concerns that might surface later. The experimenter asked permission to telephone participants for follow-up after 1 week to check on their frame of mind and make sure that they were feeling all right about the experiment (Eyde, 2000).

The importance of debriefing and removing misconceptions cannot be overemphasized. In a marketing study, participants had been told that a fast-food chain had been rumored to be using red-worm meat in its hamburgers. At the conclusion of the study, one group of participants received a conventional debriefing but continued to hold significantly less positive attitude toward the fast-food chain. The other group received explicit debriefing and did not hold a statistically different attitude toward the chain than the control group, which had not been told of the red-worm rumor (Misra, 1992). Misconceptions can linger for an indefinite period of time, possibly forever, and affect former participants in a variety of ways, even without conscious awareness.

Animal Research

More than 90% of animal research involves the use of rodents (rats and mice) or birds (usually pigeons); use of dogs and cats by experimenters is rare (Knapp & VandeCreek, 2006). Supporters of animal research argue that humans benefit from animal experimentation and that animals do not experience discomfort or restriction of freedom in the same way as humans. Detractors argue that there is limited generalizability from animal research to humans, that animals do experience pain and suffering, that they have rights that should be protected, and that investigators have a duty to protect those rights (Beauchamp, 1997).

Although the first Ethics Code (1953a) contained no specific standards on animal welfare, it referred readers to a separate document, *Rules Regarding Animals,* that was published by the APA Committee on Precautions in Animal Experimentation (1949). The 2002 Ethics Code presents seven standards for the humane care and use of animals: (a) investigators must comply with federal, state, and local laws when acquiring, caring for, maintaining, using, and disposing of animals; (b) investigators must be trained in research methods and supervise all procedures, ensuring comfort, health, and humane treatment; (c) investigators must ensure adequate instruction to those under their supervision in the proper maintenance and handling of the species being used; (d) investigators must minimize discomfort, infection, illness, and pain; (e) investigators must never use a procedure subjecting animals to pain, stress, or privation unless there are no alternative procedures that address the same hypothesis and the goal is justified by its prospective scientific, educational, or applied value (see previous standards); (f) when performing surgical procedures, investigators must always use appropriate anesthesia and follow procedures to avoid infection and minimize pain during and after surgery; and (g) when terminating an animal's life, investigators must proceed rapidly, attempting to minimize pain, in accordance with accepted procedures. The APA Board of Scientific Affairs' Committee on Animal Research and Ethics has also produced videos and other educational materials, among them *Guidelines for Ethical Conduct in the Care and Use of Animals* (1996) (http://www.apa.org/science/leadership/care/guidelines.aspx). Institutions that support animal research have an institutional animal care and use committee that oversees the conduct of all researchers and assistants who maintain, use, and care for the animals.

Federal laws constitute another resource for animal experimenters. Regulations of the U.S. Department of Agriculture were signed into law as The Animal Welfare Act in 1966, with the most recent amendment in 2007, and this law describes specific responsibilities and obligations of researchers for the humane treatment of the animals they use (Animal Welfare Act, 1996, amended 2007). And the Institute of Laboratory Animal Resources, Commission on Life Sciences, and the National Research Council, under the auspices of the National Academy of Sciences, published the *Guide for the Care and Use of Laboratory Animals* (1996). In addition, there is a private nonprofit organization, the American Association for the Accreditation of Laboratory Animal Care, that educates researchers about the minimum legal requirements and provides advice to researchers when needed (http://www.aaalac.org/about/index.cfm).

Reporting Research Results

Fair and accurate reporting of scientific research has been an ethical duty since the very first Ethics Code in 1953, which required psychologists interpreting the science of psychology to do so "fairly and accurately," without "exaggeration, sensationalism, superficiality, and premature reporting of new developments." Since then a number of ethical rules have been developed to guide investigators reporting on their research in individual or collaborative efforts. Original research is generally reported first in professional journals and later released to the media—Internet, radio or television, newspapers, and popular magazines—as journalists become aware of innovative studies.[1] The primary directive in reporting research results is to do so accurately, avoiding deceptive or false statements. Psychologists must never fabricate data—that is, they must never change the reported sample sizes, delete data that did not support the research hypothesis, misrepresent the nature of the independent variables, falsify participants' ratings or reactions, lie about the characteristics of the participants, make false claims about the methodology of the investigation (report on interventions that never occurred, claim that randomized trials occurred when in fact they did not), alter statistical findings (levels of statistical significance, correlation coefficients, analysis of variance findings, chi square results), or misrepresent or distort any aspect of the protocol design or implementation. Also, if they discover significant errors in their published results, they must take reasonable steps to correct them, generally in the form of a printed correction, retraction, erratum, or other means.

One safeguard for preserving the integrity of authors is the peer-monitoring system whereby investigators are obliged to release their research data for verification by others. Researchers must release their data after the results have been published to any competent professional who wishes to verify the substantive claims by reanalyzing the data. However, they may not then use the data for research of their own unless consent is secured from the original investigator.

The Office of Research Integrity (ORI), a branch of the U.S. Department of Health and Human Services (http://ori.hhs.gov), publishes a quarterly newsletter reporting on scientific misconduct at institutions where federally funded research has occurred. Examples from this publication follow; they are taken from the 2006 ORI Annual Report:

> Based on the report of an investigation conducted by the University of Wisconsin-Madison (UWM) and additional analysis conducted

---

[1]Research reports and abstracts of upcoming journal articles may be periodically released to the Internet as a part of publicity for upcoming journals, prior to actual publication of the article (A. Barabasz, personal communication, August 3, 2009).

by the Office of Research Integrity in its oversight review, PHS found that Ms. _____, former graduate student, UWM, engaged in research misconduct by fabricating data in thirty-nine (39) questionnaires of sibling human subjects associated with an autism study. The research was supported by National Institute on Aging (NIA), National Institutes of Health (HIN), grant# _____.

It is particularly sad when a graduate student begins a career in psychology by falsifying research for her doctoral degree, as in the following case.

Based on an investigation conducted by the University of California at Los Angeles (UCLA) and additional analysis conducted by the Office of Research Integrity (ORI) in its oversight review, ORI found that Ms. _____, former graduate student, Department of Psychology, UCLA, engaged in research misconduct by falsifying or fabricating data and statistical results for up to nine pilot studies on the impact of vulnerability on decision-making from the fall 2000 to winter 2002 as a basis for her doctoral thesis research. The falsified or fabricated data were included in a manuscript submitted to *Psychological Science*, in National Institutes of Mental Health (NIMH), National Institutes of Health (NIH), grant application #_____, and in NIMH, NIH, pre-doctoral training grant #_____.

It is noteworthy that even students and researchers carrying out studies at excellent academic institutions still commit research fraud, sometimes falling prey to publication pressures that are a common aspect of academia, as in this excerpt from a 1999 ORI Newsletter.

ORI found that Ms. _____, a former research assistant, Department of Psychiatry at the UIC [University of Illinois at Chicago], engaged in scientific misconduct in clinical research supported by a grant from NIMH by fabricating data in the records of 41 patients, including dates on which she claimed to have conducted interviews in certain clinics, fabricating patient consent forms and questionnaires from patients participating in the project; and submitting false information in "Study Daily Logs" that recorded each day's events. For 3 years beginning December 7, 1998, Ms. _____ is prohibited from serving in any advisory capacity to the PHS, and her participation any PHS-funded research is subject to supervision requirements.

Students are not the only ones who can run afoul of the rules. In 2000, a promising young psychology professor from Harvard University published a research paper in the *Personality and Social Psychology Bulletin* that was based on data that she had fabricated. The fraud was revealed when a colleague asked to see her original data, and she admitted to having used invalid data. The professor's lamentable actions resulted in, among other things, being excluded from U.S. government agency grants, contracts, and cooperative agreements for 5 years (http://grants.nih.gov/grants/guide/notice-files/NOT-OD-02-020.html).

PLAGIARISM AND DUPLICATE PUBLICATION OF DATA

Psychologists must never present portions of another's work or data as their own. Whether using a verbatim quote or paraphrasing another, whether published or unpublished, authors must always acknowledge their sources, including personal communications such as discussions, correspondence, e-mail, or other significant contributing bases for their remarks. Even plagiarizing from oneself is considered unethical. This occurs if an author publishes his original data as seminal research on more than one occasion, such as publishing one's research about using positron emission tomography technology in developing a treatment protocol for those with Tourette's disorder in a psychological journal in 2009 and then again in a psychiatry or neurology journal in 2010 without citing the original publication.

Plagiarism is not restricted to those doing research. Clinicians who do psychological assessment may send a personality test such as the Millon Clinical Multiaxial Inventory-III to a computerized scoring service and receive a narrative report in return. It may be common practice for a psychologist performing an evaluation to include the results of the scoring and even copy complete sentences or paragraphs of the computerized printout for use in the psychological report; however the psychologist must still cite the source, such as Consulting Psychologists Press or Psychological Assessment Resources. These materials are clearly labeled "copyrighted," and plagiarizing them is not only unethical but also illegal under federal law and extending to citizens in most countries of the world.[2]

A relatively recent form of plagiarism involves academic fraud, a student's use of online resources, or "paper mills" for meeting course requirements. Obviously these sources would never be cited, and additional ethical rules beyond avoiding plagiarizing would also be involved.

PUBLICATION CREDIT: A GRAY AREA

Attributing authorship in a joint venture is usually decided in advance and based on the relative scientific or professional contributions of the individuals involved, regardless of their status (e.g., professor, graduate student). Minor contributions to the research or writing are acknowledged in other ways, such as in footnotes or an introductory section.

---

[2]Common answers to copyright questions are available online at http://www.copyright.gov/help/faq/.

Usually a student is listed as the primary author in a multiple-authored article if it is substantially based on the student's doctoral dissertation.

However, ambiguities sometimes present themselves, such as when a friendly, informal discussion between professionals about psychological topics results in one of the parties deciding to proceed with developing a research hypothesis and designing a protocol for examining the question. Should the colleague in the original discussion then be cited, footnoted, or recognized in some other way when the article is published in a professional journal? Remedies for this sort of dilemma can usually be rectified by consulting with the colleague early on and seeking his or her input on resolving it. Problems can also occur when an initial agreement for collaborative work is not honored and disputes for principal authorship result.

> Dr. Banner, the chairman of a psychology department, and Dr. Finnish agreed to principal and junior authorship in collaborating on a study examining the effects of a specific group intervention at a veterans hospital for young women whose husbands had been lost in action in Iraq and Afghanistan. After initially devoting much time to designing the protocol, Dr. Banner became involved in other departmental administrative and teaching tasks and could not contribute to the project in the way he had hoped. Dr. Finnish followed through by training three group facilitators, hiring a clerical worker to help with the logistics, and training raters to evaluate participants' journal entries.
>
> At the end of the data collection, Dr. Banner found time to help with the statistical analysis of the data and to write the review of the literature section also. He still expected that he would be listed as the senior author and was surprised when Dr. Finnish asserted that because he had done far more work on virtually every phase of the project, he felt that he deserved principal authorship. The two had never discussed the change in their respective roles during the previous year, and each held a private assumption that proved to be unshared by the other.

When changes in work responsibilities or functional rules develop in the course of a collaborative effort, which can readily happen, it is important for all parties to be open-minded about reevaluating authorship credit and discuss suitable alternatives before the conclusion of the project is reached.

Confidentiality in Peer Review

Psychologists who review material that is submitted for presentation, publication, grant, or research proposal review must preserve the confidentiality and proprietary rights of the author. They must not only treat as confidential the substance and content of material but also refrain from using it in any way. Discussing or revealing the contents with anyone not specifically involved with the review process is prohibited, as is using or discussing the information with colleagues, students, the media, over the Internet, or in any other personal or professional forum.

It is fair to say that the science of psychology and most of what psychologists do in delivering their services to consumers rests solidly on research that ultimately is published in peer-reviewed professional journals and books. And that very research serves the profession and humanity well when it is carried out in an unhurried, well-planned manner that is consistent with professional, ethical, and legal guidelines for the benefit of all. Students, trainees, and their teachers and mentors depend on the integrity of those doing research in learning and teaching applied psychology. How ethical awareness of teachers and trainers impacts on students of all ages, interns and residents, and even senior clinicians is discussed in Chapter 12.

Ethics in Teaching, Training, and Supervision   12

Dr. Branden agreed to supervise Cheryl as a psychological assistant in his private practice for 1 year prior to her sitting for the Examination for the Professional Practice of Psychology. After 2 months, unfortunately, Dr. Branden developed chronic pain in his back requiring physical therapy. His medical needs and busy clinical schedule demanded so much of his waning energy that he began to reduce the frequency of his clinical supervision with Cheryl. Instead of weekly face-to-face meetings, as required by the state licensing board, he only had time for brief meetings every other week, supplemented by e-mail and telephone conversations.

Although Cheryl was a competent therapist, she was not adequately trained to treat a 16-year-old girl who had begun cutting herself with a razor blade. When the girl presented for a second session with additional cuts on her arm, Cheryl, feeling uneasy about the self-mutilation, ignored the cuts and, instead, focused the session on the girl's learning disability and study skills. Later that day, when her mother discovered the new cuts, she telephoned Cheryl to terminate therapy because she felt that she was not competent to treat her daughter. This was unfortunate because Dr. Branden was skilled at treating adolescents and could have helped Cheryl in treating her if he had only taken the time to provide adequate supervision.

Introduction

Recent editions of the American Psychological Association (APA) Ethics Code have devoted a variety of ethical standards and even entire sections to education and training, and many of these standards were rooted in the original Ethics Code (APA, 1953a, 1981, 1992, 2002, 2010). The 1953 Ethics Code devoted an entire section to Teaching of Psychology, with four long paragraphs: (a) General Responsibilities, (b) Safeguarding Students' Rights, (c) Instructing in Clinical Techniques, and (d) Advising Students. Topics included objectivity in teaching, free expression of criticism and support for various approaches to psychology, students' right to privacy, exploitation of students, competent supervision in assessment, informed consent, multiple relationships, and dealing with the impaired student.

Complaints against teachers and supervisors are relatively rare, ranging from 0% to 5% of all complaints against psychologists, according to the annual reports of the APA Ethics Committee. Examples of typical complaints are absence of timely evaluations and improper termination with a patient while under clinical supervision (APA, Ethics Committee, 2002, 2005). Although a patient may initially bring a complaint against her therapist–trainee, it is ultimately the clinical supervisor who will be the subject of the complaint because the supervisor is the one who is responsible for all professional conduct of the supervisee.

General Principles and Teaching

The general principles provide guidance for teachers at every level, from high school to postgraduate training. The aspirational values described in Principle A: Beneficence and Nonmaleficence guide teachers to safeguard the welfare of their students and trainees and never behave in a way that would harm them. The high school teacher who compels students to publicly participate in discussing sensitive topics, such as their sexual experience or history of physically or emotionally abusive experiences in their family, harms them by exposing them to the judgment of others and also demonstrates poor respect for their right of privacy.

Principle B: Fidelity and Responsibility guides teachers to establish trusting relationships with students and uphold professional standards of conduct. Teachers must also clarify their roles and obligations and manage conflicts of interest. The professor who chairs a graduate student's dissertation committee bears an obligation to protect the student's research from unauthorized use. Plagiarizing the student's work and using it as a part of the professor's own research or publishing it without permission or citation would be exploitative and harmful.

Principle C: Integrity as applied to teaching involves keeping commitments; avoiding unnecessary deception; and promoting accuracy, honesty, and truthfulness in the role of professor or supervisor. Lapses in integrity are demonstrated by the teacher who is careless about accuracy in presenting psychological information to students or the supervisor who abrogates his or her responsibilities for careful monitoring of a student therapist because the supervisor has become too busy with other matters.

Principle E: Respect for People's Rights and Dignity includes educators' respect for the worth of all people and their rights to privacy, confidentiality, and autonomy. Educators respect cultural, individual, and role differences, including those based on age, gender, ethnicity, and other factors that may add to a student's vulnerability. A White male teacher who is openly sarcastic with a Latina student for pursuing a valid culture-based theoretical orientation that differs from his own demonstrates a lack of respect by humiliating her. This is a harmful act that detracts from her self-esteem as well as the learning experience for other students. It also exploits the White male privilege that is bestowed by the construction of gender, race, and ethnicity in society as well as the power bestowed by his role as teacher.

Ethical Standards About Education and Training

It is noteworthy that there are fewer standards concerning teaching activities per se than any other aspect of education and training. Only three topics are examined—designing education and training programs, accuracy in teaching, and assessing academic performance—whereas the remaining four standards pertain to informed consent matters (e.g., describing the curriculum or course requirements in advance) and multiple-role relationships (e.g., prohibiting sex with students, prohibiting engaging in the professor–therapist role concurrently).

DESIGNING EDUCATION AND TRAINING PROGRAMS

Teaching in a secondary school, college, graduate school, or even at the postgraduate level requires careful planning to ensure that course content reflects stated educational goals, as discussed under the sections on competence and informed consent in Chapters 4 and 5. A professor who is teaching an introductory course in theories of psychotherapy must make a good faith effort to broadly represent the variety of treatment approaches, rather than focus predominantly on his personal favorites.

Above and beyond ethical requirements, a psychology department within a university that is regionally accredited (e.g., New England Association of Schools and Colleges) must comply with rigorous standards in providing a learning environment for students.[1] If a training program is accredited by the APA (doctoral programs, predoctoral internships, and postdoctoral residencies), it must meet additional standards of quality developed by this association as well, and graduate students are well advised to seek educational experiences that have this accreditation (http://www.apa.org/ed/accreditation/).

The Ethics Code requires those teaching and supervising advanced graduate or postdoctoral students to include course content and educational experiences that meet requirements for state licensure or certification, consistent with claims made in descriptive materials or brochures. Even psychologists teaching workshops to experienced clinicians must include topics and experiences that qualify for certification or meet continuing education requirements if they are APA-sponsored events.

ACCURACY IN TEACHING

Teachers and supervisors are ethically bound to inform students at the outset about the process of assessing and grading their work and providing timely feedback as needed. And teachers and supervisors must base evaluations of actual performance on program requirements, appraising their students and supervisees on objective criteria, regardless of personal feelings of friendship or animosity. The professor who plays favorites and allows friendly feelings to influence grading of a particular student, regardless of the student's performance, behaves unfairly and conveys the idea that personal friendships can trump knowledge and skills in academia.

Standard 7.03, Accuracy in Teaching, grounded in Principle C: Integrity, requires accuracy of course syllabi regarding the subject matter to be covered, the basis for evaluating progress, and the nature of course experiences. It also requires those engaged in teaching or training at any level to present psychological information accurately. It is useful to consider the psychotherapist who successfully used a clinical intervention with an adolescent who compulsively played computer games 9 hours each day. The psychotherapist may have had good results with this

---

[1]These standards include using research-based knowledge about teaching and learning, using assessment for evaluating student learning, and promoting standards-based curriculum development, to name a few of the requirements (http://www.acswasc.org/).

single patient using a specific therapeutic intervention, but in teaching graduate students, the psychotherapist should present this clinical intervention as experimental rather than evidence based because results attained with one therapist on a single patient would not necessarily qualify as a statistically significant finding.

> Dr. Lernit, a young professor, taught a graduate level course in chemical dependency. She herself was a recovering alcoholic and had been sober for 4 years. Partway into the semester she had the creative idea that an experiential component would be an excellent way for students to understand the nature of addiction and its treatment. She gave the following assignment: Each student was to attend three different 12-step open meetings (e.g., Alcoholics Anonymous, Nar-Anon, Nicotine Anonymous), visit two unfamiliar bars at night to observe those who were intoxicated, and walk or drive during the daytime through a part of town that was notorious for drug dealing.
>
> Some of the students welcomed this nondidactic part of the course and eagerly began to carry out the assignment. However, others voiced objections to it on several grounds. The part of town where drug dealing occurred was also notorious for carjackings and other violent crimes. Even though the daytime drive-through was not considered as dangerous as nighttime excursions, there was still some risk of harm. Other students objected on the grounds that the additional time required to visit the bars and 12-step meetings was excessive and that this was never described in the course catalogue or even the syllabus at the beginning of the semester.
>
> Dr. Lernit listened carefully to her students' objections and began to understand that her last-minute assignment would inflict hardships on most of them even though it may have had merit as a learning experience. She withdrew the requirement and placed it in the course catalogue description for the following semester with suggested modifications.

MANDATORY INDIVIDUAL OR GROUP THERAPY

Some training programs require undergraduate or graduate students to have individual psychotherapy, group therapy, or other therapeutic experience as a part of training. Students must be apprised of this before entering the program and must be given the option of selecting a therapist who is not affiliated with the university or professional school.

Faculty who are or will be responsible for teaching or evaluating students must not, themselves, be the ones who provide the therapy. In this way those in teaching or supervisory positions avoid creating a multiple-role relationship, that of teacher–therapist. The student who is struggling to fulfill course requirements with Dr. Brown or feels that he or she received an unfair evaluation on a project for the class on Monday will likely not feel comfortable confiding in Dr. Brown on Tuesday at the weekly therapy session. And the transparency, self-disclosure, humor, and personal opinions and traits revealed by a teacher in the classroom may well conflict with the somewhat more detached persona of the therapist involved in administering psychotherapy. For example, if the teacher in class expresses a critical view of an antiabortion pro-life political candidate yet is providing psychotherapy to one of the students in the class who holds strongly opposing religious convictions on the subject, the teacher will appear disingenuous in therapy while trying to be accepting of the student's values when the student already knows of the strength of the teacher's beliefs to the contrary. In this example the expectations for the two different roles diverge and conflict, as is often the case in multiple-role relationships.

Supervision

After successfully completing the doctoral degree the therapist–trainee must then complete face-to-face supervision with a licensed psychologist as a postdoctoral intern, fellow, or employee.[2] This is the final hurdle for aspiring psychologists before taking the licensing exam, and it is rapidly becoming a specialty unto itself (Falender & Shafranske, 2004; Haynes, Corey, & Moulton, 2003; Thomas, 2010). Clinical supervision is considered so beneficial that state licensing boards have begun requiring ongoing formal training for supervisors as a prerequisite for accepting their documented supervised clinical hours of trainees.

The process of finding an internship site where trainees will have supervised clinical experience, usually at hospitals and clinics, is facilitated by the Association of Psychology Postdoctoral and Internship Centers (APPIC), which is responsible for matching individuals with internship settings. The APPIC is an educational nonprofit organization that maintains a website for practical use by psychology intern applicants, psychology postdoctoral students, trainers of psychologists, and psychology faculty members (http://www.appic.org/). In recent years there has been an increase in graduate students seeking clinical supervision and a shortage of available internship cites. A total of 3,598 students sought internship positions at 3,051 APA-accredited internship cites for the 2009–2010 academic year (http://www.appic.org/).

---

[2]The APA allows supervision to be acquired before or after completion of the doctorate, but few licensing boards have adopted this change at this writing.

GUIDELINES FOR PRACTICUM EXPERIENCE

Guidelines for the supervision of doctoral, nondoctoral, and uncredentialed individuals who provide psychological services in the United States and Canada have been published by the Association of State and Provincial Psychology Boards (ASPPB, 2003). This organization has also developed other important information, such as guidelines for continuing education for licensed psychologists. Their website can be accessed at http://www.asppb.org/ (ASPPB, 2003).

Although the ASPPB recognizes that there are no explicit criteria for practicum experiences, it has developed seven guidelines for practicum settings that can be used as a basis for developing standards to be used by training programs and possibly incorporated into state licensing board requirements. These guidelines are not currently incorporated into the APA Ethics Code, but it is possible that they might inform future standards concerning training and supervision. The general topics covered are (a) organized sequence of training, (b) breadth and depth of training, (c) hour requirement, (d) supervision, (e) supervisor qualifications, (f) training sequence, and (g) setting. The ASPPB guidelines are available online (http://www.asppb.net/i4a/pages/index.cfm?pageid=3531).

CHARACTERISTICS OF COMPETENT SUPERVISION

The competent supervisor should also be a skilled practitioner in the areas in which that person supervises. This includes having knowledge of clinical matters, current information about ethical and legal issues, and sufficiently robust mental health to endure the daily stresses of carrying out the professional responsibilities involved in supervision and practice.

Rodolfa (2001) summarized the desirable qualities of a supervisor as follows: assumes responsibility for what happens in the clinical and supervisory settings, develops congruent goals with the supervisee, is able to teach the artistry of psychotherapy and also enhance the trainee's creativity, is understanding and nonjudgmental, maintains a suitable balance between support and challenge, encourages disclosure of feelings and thoughts, is self-disclosing, has capacities for intimacy and imagination, respects supervisees' autonomy, and can acknowledge individual differences between supervisor and supervisee. The latter includes tolerance of theoretical differences and awareness, understanding, and valuing of gender differences and multicultural issues. Multicultural factors include a tolerance for (a) variations in definitions of mental health, (b) differing worldviews, (c) relative emphasis on individual versus family, (d) concepts of independence versus dependence as they bear on mental health, and (e) subjective awareness of cultural bias and prejudice that leads to stereotyping clients and patients. Supervisors are ethically obliged to avoid discriminating against supervisees on the basis of other attributes as well, such as religion, disability, age, socioeconomic stratus, national origin, or any basis proscribed by law.

Dr. Handle sent a letter of agreement to her new psychological assistant, Don, explaining how supervision would proceed and gave details about the nature of the patient population to anticipate (largely Latino), the use of one-way mirrors for observation, documentation responsibilities, and other useful information about the upcoming training experience. Don adjusted well to the new setting, and he valued Dr. Handle's weekly supervision, particularly her gentle way of providing feedback about his therapy skills.

Don had one patient who was quite engaging—Carmen, a 26-year-old Mexican woman with anxiety disorder. She seemed friendly and appreciative; it was her habit to stand quite close to him on entering and leaving the office, and after the second session she gave him a kiss on the cheek "out of gratitude" for all the help he had provided. Don felt uncomfortable with her forwardness and hoped that it would not happen again. At the end of the next session Carmen announced that her anxiety was suddenly gone, and she wondered if it would be all right to "treat" her therapist at a nearby Starbucks. This offer took him by surprise, but he agreed to meet her at the end of the day following his last patient.

Don promptly telephoned Dr. Handle to discuss both the kiss on the cheek from several days before and her invitation of today. Dr. Handle explained that Carmen may indeed feel grateful and that the boundaries in the Latin culture are more fluid and allow for more familiarity, even in professional settings. Don had wondered whether Carmen's behavior might suggest a personality disorder or at least poor personal boundaries. Dr. Handle indicated that she saw Carmen's invitation as more likely related to cultural factors. Further, perhaps, her naiveté about the therapist–patient relationship and possible interest in Don as a single male might account for her "flight into health" in feeling anxiety-free and possibly enabling her, now, to explore a personal relationship with him.

Dr. Handle pointed out that the two of them had never processed the kiss at the end of the previous session and that Don's avoidance was likely interpreted as tacit approval by Carmen to initiate the next logical step in the relationship. She also pointed out that Carmen may desire more therapy in the future and that even an innocent cup of coffee at Starbucks, where the discussion would likely be more social and self-disclosing on Don's part, could change the relationship irrevocably. Furthermore, there had been no actual termination session discussing progress, exploring new goals, processing her therapy experience, and making any formal recommendations for the future.

Don admitted to Dr. Handle that he did find Carmen attractive, but he was well aware of the prohibition against developing a relationship with a patient. He welcomed the opportunity to safely explore his feelings with Dr. Handle as he was simultaneously processing the breaking of his engagement to be married several months before he moved to begin his internship.

He decided to refrain from meeting Carmen for coffee and contacted her by cell phone to cancel, while inviting her to return for one more therapy session. At the next session they discussed the kiss, boundaries, their professional relationship, and additional therapeutic goals of Carmen's that surfaced in that session.

PROBLEMS ENCOUNTERED IN SUPERVISION

Some of the problems trainees encounter include supervisors' attitudes and behaviors that result in incompetent supervision. Rodolfa (2001) described the *problem supervisor* as one who may exhibit the following characteristics: lacking knowledge or competence, authoritarian, self-doubting, overly active or passive, poor at listening and communicating (e.g., sarcastic, dismissive, avoidant of important issues), unclear or ambiguous about expectations, focusing only on content (i.e., not process or the therapy relationship), not trusting or engendering trust, tolerating a negative feeling between supervisor and supervisee without addressing it, having personality conflicts or rivalry with the supervisee, or being prone to boundary violations. The latter can contaminate the supervisory relationship if the supervisor is too self-disclosing to the trainee, gives inappropriate gifts, allows for extra supervisory contact to gratify his or her own needs, gives unwanted touches or hugs, or is flirtatious. Other supervisory behaviors that can damage the relationship are being overly inquisitive about the trainee's private life (e.g., family of origin, sexual history) or encouraging the supervision to transcend the normal boundaries and transition into individual psychotherapy (Thomas, 2010).

The lessons learned from teachers, professors, supervisors, and mentors can last a lifetime. The content and knowledge absorbed from classroom, experiential setting, and one-to-one supervision are as important as what the trainee learns by observing the behavior of those who are in teaching positions. The professor or supervisor who manifests poor boundaries by being seductive does not help that trainee toward professional maturation. Rather, the professor or supervisor models a poor example for the trainee to follow when the trainee is in a similar professional relationship. Conversely, the supervisor who openly acknowledges that an interpersonal problem may exist with the trainee or copes with his or her own sexual attraction to the trainee by consulting an experienced colleague or his or her own therapist stands a better chance of modeling ethical and professional adult boundaries and behavior.

Teaching at any level in academia or supervising at any stage of the trainee's professional development can be a gratifying experience for all involved, dispensing a contagion for the love of learning and personal development and growth. The good teacher is aware that there is always more to discover from the science of psychology, and he or she bears a certain humility about the current state of scientific knowledge and curiosity about what may lie ahead. In a larger sense, the quintessential teacher is also aware that there is always more to learn about oneself and that this ultimately may be the origin of the quest as well as the reward provided for entering such a fulfilling, demanding, and richly diverse career as psychology.

References

Adkins, D. C. (1952). Proceedings of the sixtieth annual business meeting of the American Psychological Association, Inc., Washington, DC. *American Psychologist, 7,* 645–670. doi:10.1037/h0053961

Albee, G. W. (1991, August). *A short history of the APA ethics code.* Symposium conducted at the meeting of the American Psychological Association, San Francisco, CA.

Alexander, F., & French, T. (1946). *Psychoanalytic therapy: Principles and application.* New York, NY: Ronald Press.

American Association of Marriage and Family Therapists. (2001). *AAMFT code of ethics.* Retrieved from http://www.aamft.org/resources/lrm_plan/Ethics/ethicscode2001.asp

American Educational Research Association, American Psychological Association, & National Council on Measurement in Education. (1999). *Standards for educational and psychological testing.* Washington, DC: American Educational Research Association.

American Group Psychotherapy Association. (2002). *AGPA and NRCGP guidelines for ethics.* Retrieved from http://www.agpa.org/group/ethicalguide.html

American Psychiatric Association. (2000). *Diagnostic and statistical manual of mental disorders* (4th ed., text revision). Washington, DC: Author.

American Psychological Association. (1953a). *Ethical standards of psychologists.* Washington, DC: Author.

American Psychological Association. (1953b). *Ethical standards of psychologists: A summary of ethical principles.* Washington, DC: Author.

American Psychological Association. (1954). Technical recommendations for psychological tests and diagnostic techniques. *Psychological Bulletin, 51*(2, Pt. 2), 1–38.

American Psychological Association. (1959). Ethical standards of psychologists. *American Psychologist, 14,* 279–282. doi:10.1037/h0048469

American Psychological Association. (1963). Ethical standards of psychologists. *American Psychologist, 18,* 56–60. doi:10.1037/h0041847

American Psychological Association. (1964). Ethical practices in industrial psychology: A review of one committee's deliberations. *American Psychologist, 19,* 174–182.

American Psychological Association. (1966). Automated test scoring and interpretation practices, Minutes of the annual meeting of the Council of Representatives, Item IX, Paragraph F. *American Psychologist, 21,* 1141.

American Psychological Association. (1967). *Casebook on ethical standards of psychologists.* Washington, DC: Author.

American Psychological Association. (1968). Ethical standards of psychologists. *American Psychologist, 23,* 357–361.

American Psychological Association. (1972). *Ethical standards of psychologists.* Washington, DC: Author.

American Psychological Association. (1979). *Ethical standards of psychologists.* Washington, DC: Author.

American Psychological Association. (1981). Ethical standards of psychologists. *American Psychologist, 36,* 633–638. doi:10.1037/0003-066X.36.6.633

American Psychological Association. (1986). *Guidelines for computer-based tests and interpretations.* Washington, DC: Author.

American Psychological Association. (1990). Ethical standards of psychologists (amended June 2, 1989). *American Psychologist, 45,* 390–395. doi:10.1037/h0091617

American Psychological Association. (1992). Ethical principles of psychologists and code of conduct. *American Psychologist, 47,* 1597–1611.

American Psychological Association. (2000). Guidelines for psychotherapy with lesbian, gay, and bisexual clients. *American Psychologist, 55,* 1440–1451. doi:10.1037/0003-066X.55.12.1440

American Psychological Association. (2002). Ethical principles of psychologists and code of conduct. *American Psychologist, 57,* 1060–1073. doi:10.1037/0003-066X.57.12.1060 (Also available from http://www.apa.org/ethics/code/index.aspx)

American Psychological Association. (2003). Guidelines for multicultural education, training, research, practice, and organizational change for psychologists. *American Psychologist, 58,* 377–402. doi: 10.1037/0003-066X.58.5.377

American Psychological Association. (2005). *National standards for high school psychology curricula.* Washington, DC: Author.

American Psychological Association. (2007). *Guidelines for psychological practice with girls and women.* Retrieved from http://www.apa.org/practice/guidelines/girlsandwomen.pdf

American Psychological Association. (2010). *Ethical principles of psychologists and code of conduct* (2002, Amended June 1, 2010). Retrieved from http://www.apa.org/ethics/code/index.aspx

American Psychological Association. (in press). Report of the Ethics Committee, 2009. *American Psychologist.* doi:10.10.1037/a00019515

American Psychological Association, Ad Hoc Committee on Ethical Standards in Psychological Research. (1973). *Ethical principles in the conduct of research with human participants.* Washington, DC: Author.

American Psychological Association, Board of Professional Affairs, Committee on Professional Practice and Standards. (2005). *Determination and documentation of the need for practice guidelines.* Washington: Author.

American Psychological Association, Committee on Ethical Standards of Psychologists. (1958). Standards of ethical behavior for psychologists. Report of the Committee on Ethical Standards of Psychologists. *American Psychologist, 13,* 266–1271. doi:10.1037/h0039809

American Psychological Association, Committee on Precautions in Animal Experimentation. (1949). *Rules regarding animals.* Washington, DC: Author.

American Psychological Association, Committee on Scientific and Professional Ethics. (1947). Report of the Committee on Scientific and Professional Ethics. *American Psychologist, 2,* 488–490.

American Psychological Association, Ethics Committee. (2001). *Rules and procedures.* Retrieved from http://www.apa.org/ethics/code/committee.aspx

American Psychological Association, Ethics Committee. (2002). Report of the Ethics Committee, 2001. *American Psychologist, 57,* 646–653. doi:10.1037/0003-066X.57.8.646

American Psychological Association, Ethics Committee. (2005). Report of the Ethics Committee, 2004. *American Psychologist, 60,* 523–528.

American Psychological Association, Ethics Committee. (2008). Report of the Ethics Committee, 2007. *American Psychologist, 63,* 452–459.

American Psychological Association Presidential Task Force on Evidence-Based Practice. (2006). Evidence-based practice in psychology. *American Psychologist, 61,* 271–285. doi:10.1037/0003-066X.61.4.271

Animal Welfare Act, 7 U.S.C. § 2131-2156. (1966, amended 2007). Retrieved from http://www.nal.usda.gov/awic/legislat/awa.htm

Appelbaum, P. S., & Rosenbaum, A. (1989). Tarasoff and the researcher: Does the duty to protect apply in the research setting? *American Psychologist, 44,* 885–894. doi:10.1037/0003-066X.44.6.885

Association of State and Provincial Psychology Boards. (1998). *Supervision guidelines*. Montgomery, AL: Author.

Association of State and Provincial Psychology Boards. (2003). *Guidelines for supervision of doctoral level candidates for licensure*. Retrieved from http://www.asppb.org

Association of State and Provincial Psychology Boards. (2009). *Guidelines on practicum experience for licensure*. Retrieved from http://www.asppb.org/

Attachment therapy on trial: The torture and death of Candace Newmaker. (2003). Retrieved from http://www.childrenintherapy.org/victims/newmaker.html

Beauchamp, T. (1997). Opposing views of animal experimentation: Do animals have rights? *Ethics & Behavior, 7*, 113–121. doi:10.1207/s15327019eb0702_3

Beauchamp, T., & Childress, J. (1979). *Principles of biomedical ethics*. New York, NY: Oxford University Press.

Beauchamp, T., & Childress, J. (2001). *Principles of biomedical ethics* (5th ed.). New York, NY: Oxford University Press.

Blackburn, S. (2008). *The Oxford dictionary of philosophy* (2nd ed., rev.). New York, NY: Oxford University Press.

Borys, D., & Pope, K. (1989). Dual relationships between therapist and client: A national study of psychologists, psychiatrists, and social workers. *Professional Psychology: Research and Practice, 20*, 283–293. doi:10.1037/0735-7028.20.5.283

Bouhoutsos, J., Holyroyd, J., Lerman, H., Forer, B. R., & Greenberg, M. (1983). Sexual intimacy between psychotherapists and patients. *Professional Psychology: Research and Practice, 14*, 185–196. doi:10.1037/0735-7028.14.2.185

Brabeck, M. M. (2000). *Practicing feminist ethics in psychology*. Washington, DC: American Psychological Association. doi:10.1037/10343-000

Bransford, J., & Stein, B. (1993). *The ideal problem solver: A guide to improving thinking, learning, and creativity*. New York, NY: Freeman.

Brown, D., Scheflin, A., & Hammond, C. (1998). *Memory, trauma, treatment, and the law*. New York, NY: Norton.

Butler, L. Blasey, C., Garlan, R., McCaslin, S., Azarow, J., Chen, X., . . . Spiegel, D. (2005). Posttraumatic growth following the terrorist attacks of September 11, 2001: Cognitive, coping, and trauma symptom predictors in an Internet convenience sample. *Traumatology, 11*, 246–267.

Cal. Business and Professions Code § 2909 (d) (2009).

Cal. Civil Code § 56.10(c)(7) (2009).

California Confidentiality of Medical Information Act, Cal. Civil Code § 56–56.37 (1979).

Cal. Evidence Code § 1011 (2009).

Cal. Evidence Code § 1014 (a)-(c) (2009). Retrieved from http://law. justia.com/california/codes/evid/1010-1027.html

Cal. Evidence Code § 1016 (2009).

Cal. Evidence Code § 1021, 1022 (2009).

Cal. Family Code § 6924 (a) (1 (A, B, C, D) (2009).

Cal. Health and Safety Code § 123115(a)(2) (2009).

Cal. Penal Code §11165.1, §11165.2, §11165.4 (2009).

Cal. Penal Code §15630 (2009).

Callan, J., & Callan, M. (2005). An historical overview of basic approaches and issues in ethical and moral philosophy and principles: A foundation for understanding ethics in psychology. In S. Bucky, J. Callan, & G. Stricker (Eds.), *Ethical and legal issues for mental health professionals* (pp. 11–26). Binghamton, NY: The Haworth Maltreatment & Trauma Press.

Canadian Psychological Association. (2000). *Canadian code of ethics for psychologists* (3rd. ed.). Retrieved from http://www.cpa.ca/cpasite/ userfiles/Documents/Canadian%20Code%20of%20Ethics%20for% 20Psycho.pdf

Canter, M., Bennett, B., Jones, S., & Nagy, T. (1994). *Ethics for psychologists: A commentary on the APA ethics code.* Washington, DC: American Psychological Association. doi:10.1037/10162-000

Cantor, D. (2005). Patients' rights in psychotherapy. In G. Koocher, J. Norcross, & S. Hill (Eds.), *Psychologists' desk reference* (pp. 181–183), Oxford, England: Oxford University Press.

Caudill, O., & Kaplan, A. (2005). Protecting privacy and confidentiality. In S. Bucky, J. Callan, & G. Stricker (Eds.), *Ethical and legal issues for mental health professionals* (pp. 117–134). Binghamton, NY: The Haworth Maltreatment & Trauma Press.

Citizens for Responsibility and Ethics in Washington. (2009). *"I am under a lot of pressure to not diagnose PTSD."* Retrieved from http://www. citizensforethics.org/node/38663

Civil Rights Act of 1964, Pub. L. No. 82-352, 78 Stat. 241 (1964).

Compact Oxford English dictionary. (2009). New York, NY: Oxford University Press.

Conger, J. J. (1978). Proceedings of the incorporated American Psychological Association for the year 1977: Minutes of the annual meeting of the Council of Representatives. *American Psychologist, 33,* 544–572. doi:10.1037/h0078555

Corsini, R., & Auerbach, A. (1998). *Concise encyclopedia of psychology.* New York, NY: Wiley.

Crocker, E. M. (1985). Judicial expansion of the Tarasoff doctrine. Doctors' dilemma. *The Journal of Psychiatry & Law, 13*(1–2), 83–99.

Deontology. (n.d.). Retrieved from http://dictionary.reference.com/ browse/deontology

Egelko, B. (2009, April). *"Telemedicine" doctor gets 9 months in jail.* Retrieved from http://articles.sfgate.com/2009-04-18/bay-area/17193803_1_john-mckay-medical-license-telemedicine

Epstein, R. M., & Hundert, E. M. (2002). Defining and assessing professional competence. *JAMA, 287,* 226–235. doi:10.1001/jama.287.2.226

Ethical standards of psychologists. (1977, March). *APA Monitor,* pp. 22–23.

Ewing, C. P. (2005, July-August). Tarasoff reconsidered. *Monitor on Psychology, 36*(7), 112.

Ewing v. Goldstein, 15 Cal. Rptr. 3d 864 (Cal. Ct. App. 2004).

Eyde, L. (2000). Other responsibilities to participants. In B. Sales & S. Folkman (Eds.), *Ethics in research with human participants* (pp. 61–73). Washington, DC: American Psychological Association.

Falender, C., & Shafranske, E. (2004). *Clinical supervision: A competency-based approach.* Washington, DC: American Psychological Association. doi:10.1037/10806-000

Family Educational Rights and Privacy Act of 1974, 20 U.S.C. § 1232g (2009).

Fernberger, S. (1932) The American Psychological Association: A historic summary, 1892–1930. *Psychological Bulletin, 29,* 1–89. doi:10.1037/h0075733

Foa, E., Keane, T., & Friedman, M. (Eds.). (2000). *Practice guidelines for effective treatments of PTSD.* New York, NY: Guilford Press.

Folkman, S. (2000). Privacy and confidentiality. In B. Sales & S. Folkman (Eds.), *Ethics in research with human participants* (pp. 49–57). Washington, DC: American Psychological Association.

Frank, J. D. (1982). Therapeutic components shared by all psychotherapies. In J. H. Harvey & M. M. Parks (Eds.), *The master lecture series: Vol. 1: Psychotherapy research and behavior change* (pp. 9–7). Washington, DC: American Psychological Association.

FTC consent order is published in its entirety. (1993, March). *APA Monitor,* p. 8.

Gabbard. G. O. (1994). Sexual misconduct. In J. Oldham & M. Riba (Eds.), *Review of psychotherapy* (Vol. 13, pp. 433–456). Washington, DC: American Psychiatric Press.

Goals 2000: Educate America Act, Pub. L. No. 103-227 (1994).

Gottlieb, M. C. (1993). Avoiding exploitative dual relationships: A decision-making model. *Psychotherapy, 30,* 41–48.

Grisso, T., & Appelbaum, P. (1998). *Assessing competence to consent to treatment: A guide for physicians and other health professionals.* New York, NY: Oxford University Press.

Haas, L., & Malouf, J. (1995). *Keeping up the good work; A practitioner's guide to mental health ethics* (2nd ed.). Sarasota, FL: Professional Resource Exchange.

Hagan, J., & Kay, F. (1995). *Gender in practice: A study of lawyers' lives.* New York, NY: Oxford University Press.

Haney, C., Banks, W. C., & Zimbardo, P. G. (1973). Interpersonal dynamics in a simulated prison. *International Journal of Criminology and Penology, 1*, 69–97.

Hare-Mustin, R. (1974). Ethical considerations in the use of sexual contact in psychotherapy. *Psychotherapy: Theory, Research, Practice, Training, 11*, 308–310.

Härtel, C. E., & Härtel, G. F. (1997). SHAPE-assisted intuitive decision making and problem solving: Information-processing-based training for conditions of cognitive busyness. *Group Dynamics: Theory, Research, and Practice, 1*, 187–199.

Haynes, R., Corey, G., & Moulton, P. (2002). *Clinical supervision in the helping professions: A practical guide.* Pacific Grove, CA: Brooks/Cole.

Health Insurance Portability and Accountability Act of 1996, Pub. L. No. 104-191, 110 Stat. 1936 (codified as amended in scattered sections of 42 U.S.C.).

Hobbs, N. (1948). The development of a code of ethical standards for psychology. *American Psychologist, 3*, 80–84. doi:10.1037/h0060281

Hoffman, H. G., Patterson, D. R., & Carrougher, G. J. (2000). Use of virtual reality for adjunctive treatment of adult burn pain during physical therapy: A controlled study. *The Clinical Journal of Pain, 16*, 244–250.

Holtzman, W. H. (1979). The IUPS project on professional ethics and conduct. *International Journal of Psychology, 14*, 107–109. doi:10.1080/00207597908246719

Holyroyd, J., & Brodsky, A. (1977). Psychologists' attitudes and practices regarding erotic and nonerotic physical contact with clients. *American Psychologist, 32*, 843–849. doi:10.1037/0003-066X.32.10.843

Institute of Laboratory Animal Resources, Commission on Life Sciences, & National Research Council. (1996). *Guide for the care and use of laboratory animals.* Retrieved from http://www.nap.edu/openbook.php?record_id=5140

Institute of Medicine. (2001). *Crossing the quality chasm: A new health system for the 21st century.* Washington, DC: National Academies Press.

Institutional Review Boards, Subpart B: Organization and Personnel, 21 C.F.R. 56.107, IRB membership (1991).

Jaffee v. Redmond, 518 U.S. 1 (1966).

Kaplan, A. (2005). Therapist–patient privilege: Who owns the privilege? In S. Bucky, J. Callan, & Stricker, G. (Eds.), *Ethical and legal issues for mental health professionals* (pp. 135–143). Binghamton, NY: The Haworth Maltreatment & Trauma Press.

Keith-Spiegel, P., &Koocher, G. (1985). *Ethics in psychology: Professional standards and cases.* New York, NY: Random House.

Kelman, H. (1972). The rights of the subject in social research: An analysis in terms of relative power and legitimacy. *American Psychologist, 27,* 989–1016. doi:10.1037/h0033995

Kimmel, A. (1998). In defense of deception. *American Psychologist, 53,* 803–804. doi:10.1037/0003-066X.53.7.803

Kitchener, K. (1984). Intuition, critical evaluation and ethical principles: The foundation for ethical decisions in counseling psychology. *Counseling Psychologist, 12,* 43–55. doi:10.1177/0011000084123005

Kitchener, K. (1988). Dual role relationships: What makes them so problematic? *Journal of Counseling and Development, 67,* 217–221.

Knapp, S. J., & VandeCreek, L. D. (2003). An overview of the major changes in the 2002 APA ethics code. *Professional Psychology: Research and Practice, 34,* 301–307. doi:10.1037/0735-7028.34.3.301

Knapp, S. J., & VandeCreek, L. D. (2006). *Practical ethics for psychologists: A positive approach.* Washington, DC: American Psychological Association.

Koocher, G., Norcross, J., & Hill, S. (Eds.). (2005). *Psychologists' desk reference.* Oxford, England: Oxford University Press.

Lifschutz, In Re, 2 Cal. 3d 415, 467 P.2d 557 (1970).

Lyon, L. (2009, September). 7 things to know before logging on for counseling. *U.S. News & World Report.* Retrieved from http://www.usnews.com/health/family-health/articles/2009/09/22/7-things-to-know-before-logging-on-for-counseling.html

Maheu, M. M., Pulier, M. L., Wilhelm, F. H., McMenamin, J. P., & Brown-Connolly, N. E. (2005). *The mental health professional and the new technologies: A handbook for practice today.* Mahwah, NJ: Erlbaum.

Milgram, S. (1963). Behavioral study of obedience. *Journal of Abnormal and Social Psychology, 67,* 371–378. doi:10.1037/h0040525

Milgram, S. (1973). *Obedience to authority.* New York, NY: Harper & Row.

Misra, S. (1992). Is conventional debriefing adequate? An ethical issue in consumer research. *Journal of the Academy of Marketing Science, 20,* 269–273. doi:10.1007/BF02723415

Nagy, T. (1989, August). *Revision of the ethical principles of psychologists: APA Task Force's progress report—Three years later and ready for review.* Paper presented at the 97th Annual Convention of the American Psychological Association, New Orleans, LA.

Nagy, T. (1990, March). *Revision of the ethical principles of psychologists: The final progress report—Four years later.* Paper presented at the meeting of the California State Psychological Association, San Francisco.

Nagy, T. (1992, March). *The new ethical principles of Psychologists: A sword or a shield?* Paper presented at meeting of the California Psychological Association, La Jolla.

Nagy, T. (1995). Incest memories recalled in hypnosis—A case study. *International Journal of Clinical and Experimental Hypnosis, 43,* 118–126.

Nagy, T. (2001, August). *Does the "e" in "e-therapy" also stand for ethics?* Paper presented at the 109th Annual Convention of the American Psychological Association, San Francisco, CA.

Nagy, T. (2005). *Ethics in plain English: An illustrative casebook for psychologists.* Washington, DC: American Psychological Association.

Nash, M. (1994). Memory distortion and sexual trauma: The problem of false negatives and false positives. *International Journal of Clinical and Experimental Hypnosis, 42,* 346–362.

Newman, E. B. (1965). Proceedings of the seventy-third annual business meeting of the American Psychological Association, Inc. *American Psychologist, 20,* 1028–1053. doi:10.1037/h0021092

Norcross, J. C. (2004). Empirically supported treatments: Context, consensus, and controversy. *The Register Report, 30,* 12–14.

Norcross, J. C., & Guy, J. (2007). *Leaving it at the office.* New York, NY: Guilford Press.

Olson, B., Soldz, B., & Davis, M. (2008). *The ethics of interrogation and the American Psychological Association: A critique of policy and process.* Retrieved from http://www.peh-med.com/content/pdf/1747-5341-3-3.pdf

Olson, W. C. (1940). Proceedings of the forty-eighth annual business meeting of the American Psychological Association, Inc. *Psychological Bulletin, 37,* 699–741. doi:10.1037/h0063182

Orlinsky, D .E., & Howard, K. I. (1986). Process and outcome in psychotherapy. In S. L. Garfield & Bergin (Eds.), *Handbook of psychotherapy and behavior change* (3rd ed., pp. 283–330). New York, NY: Wiley.

Ortman, A., & Hertwig, R. (1997). Is deception acceptable? *American Psychologist, 52,* 746–747. doi:10.1037/0003-066X.52.7.746

Pope, K. (1994). *Sexual involvement with therapists: Patient assessment, subsequent therapy, forensics.* Washington, DC: American Psychological Association. doi:10.1037/10154-000

Pope, K. (2000). Therapists' sexual feelings: Research, trends, and quandaries. In L. Szuchman & F. Muscarella (Eds.), *Psychological perspectives on human sexuality* (603–658), New York, NY: Wiley.

Pope, K. (2001). Sex between therapists and clients. In J. Worell (Ed.), *Encyclopedia of women and gender* (Vol. 2, pp. 955–962) New York, NY: Academic Press.

Pope, K., & Bouhoutsos, J. (1986). *Sexual intimacy between therapists and patients.* New York, NY: Praeger.

Pope, K., & Gutheil, T. (2009). Psychologists abandon the Nuremberg ethic: Concerns for detainee interrogations. *International Journal of Law and Psychiatry, 32*(4), 161–166.

Pope, K., Levenson, H., & Schover, L. P. (1979). Sexual intimacy in psychology training: Results and implications of a national survey. *American Psychologist, 34,* 682–689.

Pope, K., Sonne, J., & Holroyd, J. (1997). *Sexual feelings in psychotherapy: Explorations for therapists and therapists-in-training.* Washington, DC: American Psychological Association.

Pope, K., &Vasquez, M. (2007). *Ethics in psychotherapy and counseling: A practical guide.* San Francisco, CA: Jossey-Bass.

Pope, K., & Vetter, V. A. (1991). Prior therapist–patient sexual involvements among patients seen by psychologists. *Psychotherapy, 28,* 429–438. doi:10.1037/0033-3204.28.3.429

Protection of Human Subjects, 45, C.F.R., Pt. 46 § 46.107 (1991, amended 2005).

Rodolfa, E. (2001, September). *Workshop on supervision: Process, issues dilemmas.* Workshop presented at the California School of Professional Psychology, Alameda.

Ross, L., Lepper, M. R., & Hubbard, M. (1975). Perseverance in self-perception and social perception: Biased attributional processes in the debriefing paradigm. *Journal of Personality and Social Psychology, 32,* 880–892. doi:10.1037/0022-3514.32.5.880

Saccuzzo, D. (2003). Liability for the failure to supervise adequately: Let the master beware. *National Register of Health Service Providers in Psychology—The Psychologist's Legal Update, 14,* 1–11.

Sales, B., & Lavin, M. (2000). Identifying conflicts of interest and resolving ethical dilemmas. In B. Sales & S. Folkman (Eds.), *Ethics in research with human participants.* (pp. 109–128) Washington, DC: American Psychological Association.

Schneewind, J. B. (1993). Modern moral philosophy. In P. Singer (Ed.), *A companion to ethics* (pp. 147–157) Cambridge. MA: Blackwell Publishing.

Schoener, G. (1990). *Psychotherapists' sexual involvement with clients: Intervention and prevention.* Minneapolis, MN: Walk-In Counseling Center.

Scott-Jones, D. (2000). Recruitment of research participants. In B. Sales & S. Folkman (Eds.), *Ethics in research with human participants* (pp. 27–34). Washington, DC: American Psychological Association.

Sieber, J. E. (1992). *Planning ethically responsible research.* Newbury Park, CA: Sage.

Sonne, J. L. (2006). *Nonsexual multiple relationships: A practical decision-making model for clinicians.* Retrieved from http://kspope.com/site/multiple-relationships.php

Sutter, E., McPherson, R., & Geeseman, R. (2002). Contracting for supervision. *Professional Psychology: Research and Practice, 33,* 497–498. doi:10.1037/0735-7028.33.5.495

Tarasoff v. Regents of the University of California, 17 Cal.3d 425, 551 P.2d 334, 131 Cal. Rptr. 14 (1976).

Thomas, J. T. (2007). Informed consent through contracting for supervision: Minimizing risks, enhancing benefits. *Professional Psychology: Research and Practice, 38,* 221–231.doi:10.1037/0735-7028 .38.3.221

Thomas, J. T. (2010). *The ethics of supervision and consultation: Practical guidance for mental health professionals.* Washington, DC: American Psychological Association.

Tymchuk, A. J. (1981). Ethical decision making and psychological treatment. *Journal of Psychiatric Treatment and Evaluation, 3,* 507–513.

United States v. Glass, 133 F.3d 1356 (10th Cir. 1998).

United States v. Hayes, 227 F.3d 578 (6th Cir. 2000).

U.S. Copyright Office (2005). *United States Copyright Office: A brief introduction and history.* Retrieved from http://www.copyright.gov/circs/ circ1a.html

U.S. Department of Health and Human Services. (1999, March). *ORI Newsletter, 7*(2).

U.S. Department of Health and Human Services. (2007). *Office of Research Integrity annual report 2006.* Rockville, MD: Office of the Secretary, Office of Research Integrity.

U.S. Department of Health and Human Services, National Institutes of Health. (1996). Informed consent in research involving human participants. *NIH Guide, 25*(32). Retrieved from http://history.nih.gov/ 01docs/historical/2020b.htm

U.S. Department of Health and Human Services, National Institutes of Health, National Institute of Mental Health. (2003). *Internet-based research interventions in mental health: How are they working?* Retrieved from http://www.nimh.nih.gov/research-funding/grants/internet-based-rsch-interventions-chart-may2007.pdf

U.S. Department of Health, Education, and Welfare. (1974). *National research act.* Retrieved from http://history.nih.gov/research/sources_ legislative_chronology.html

U.S. Equal Employment Opportunity Commission. (2002). *Facts about sexual harassment.* Retrieved from http://www.eeoc.gov/facts/fs-sex.html

Uses and Disclosures of Protected Health Information: Personal Representatives, 45 C.F.R. 164.502(g)(5) (2002, revised 2003).

Werth, J., Welfel, E., & Benjamin, G. (2009). *The duty to protect: Ethical, legal, and professional considerations for mental health professionals.* Washington, DC: American Psychological Association. doi:10.1037/11866-000

Younggren, J. N., & Gottlieb, M. C. (2004). Managing risk when contemplating multiple relationships. *Professional Psychology: Research and Practice, 35,* 255–260.

Index

A

Abuse, 62, 120–121, 191

Academic fraud, 214

Academic settings. *See also* Education and training
    competence in, 74–75
    harm and exploitation in, 139–140
    privacy and confidentiality in, 111–112
    public statements in, 137–138

Accessibility, of psychologists, 59–60, 197

Accidental unethical acts, 13

Accreditation, 220, 222

Accuracy
    in diagnosis, 149, 158–159
    in teaching, 220–221

Accuracy in Teaching (standard), 220

Actions, ethical, 15–16

Act step (decision-making model), 165

Adaptive behavior testing, 173

Ad Hoc Committee on Ethical Practices in
    Industrial Psychology, 33

Ad Hoc Committee on Ethical Practices in
    Psychological Research, 35

Administration, of tests, 175, 181

Adolescents, 95, 99–100, 114–115

Advertising, 40–41, 136–137

Advertising (standard), 33

Advocacy, 81

AERA. *See* American Educational Research
    Association

Age, of patients, 82, 202

Alexander, F., 186

Alternative treatments, 99

American Association for the Accreditation of
    Laboratory Animal Care, 211

American Association of Marriage and Family
    Therapists, 114, 189

American Educational Research Association
    (AERA), 78, 172, 174

American Group Psychotherapy Association,
    115, 190

American Psychological Association (APA), 9.
    See also "The Ethical Principles of Psy-
    chologists and Code of Conduct" (APA)
    accreditation, 220
    adjudication of complaints, 25–27
    casebook of, 33–34
    committees of. *See* APA Committee(s)
    on conflicting ethical standards, 22–23
    creation of ethics code, 30
    ethical standards of, 52. *See also* Ethical
        Standards
    membership requirements, 70n2
    practice guidelines, 72–73, 153
    publications of. *See specific publications*
    on sexual relationships, 134
    on sharing research data, 110
    on supervision, 222n2
    task forces of. *See* APA Task Force(s)

Animal Experimentation Committee, 35

Animal research, 33, 35, 210–211

Animal Welfare Act, 211

Anonymity, 13, 101

About the Author

Thomas F. Nagy received his doctorate from the University of Illinois at Champaign–Urbana in 1972. He is currently in independent practice in Palo Alto, California, and is a staff psychologist at the Stanford Center for Integrative Medicine, Stanford, California. He also is an adjunct assistant clinical professor at the Stanford University School of Medicine, Stanford, California, and teaches a seminar on ethical and legal issues for psychology postdoctoral students in the Department of Psychiatry and Behavioral Sciences.

For the past 35 years Dr. Nagy's nonclinical professional activities have focused on ethical issues for psychologists. In addition to giving annual workshops and presentations, he has served as chair of the Illinois Psychological Association Ethics Committee (1982–1986), was a member of the APA Ethics Committee (1985–1987), served on and chaired the APA Ethics Committee Task Force that revised the *Ethical Principles of Psychologists* (1986–1992), was a member of the California Psychological Association Ethics Committee (1988–1993), and is currently a member of the Ethics Committee of Stanford University Hospital and other professional associations. He was an oral examiner for the California Licensing Board for 10 years and has participated in forensic work as an expert witness and consultant to attorneys for many years.

Dr. Nagy provides psychological services and ethical consultation to psychologists, attorneys, educators, and consumers. He is a fellow of the American Psychological Association's Divisions 29 (Psychotherapy) and 42 (Independent Practice) and is also a fellow of the Society for Clinical and Experimental Hypnosis. He is also a recipient of the Illinois Psychological Association's Special Award for Outstanding Contribution to the Profession of Psychology (1986).

Dr. Nagy authored *Ethics in Plain English: An Illustrative Casebook for Psychologists* (two editions) and coauthored *Ethics for Psychologists: A Commentary on the APA Ethics Code* (APA, 1994). He lives in Stanford, California, with his wife, Kären, where he does wood turning, plays the piano and bass guitar, plays squash, studies astronomy, and spends countless wondrous hours learning about the things that really matter from his grandchild Elise.